The Tayloring Shop

The Tayloring Shop

**Essays on the Poetry
of Edward Taylor
in Honor of Thomas M.
and Virginia L. Davis**

Edited by
Michael Schuldiner

DELAWARE

Newark: University of Delaware Press
London: Associated University Presses

Associated University Presses
440 Forsgate Drive
Cranbury, NJ 08512

Associated University Presses
16 Barter Street
London WC1A 2AH, England

Associated University Presses
P.O. Box 338, Port Credit
Mississauga, Ontario
Canada L5G 4L8

The paper used in this publication meets the requirements of the American National Standard for Permanence of Paper for Printed Library Materials Z39.48–1984.

Library of Congress Cataloging-in-Publication Data

The Tayloring shop : essays on the poetry of Edward Taylor in honor of Thomas M. and Virginia L. Davis / edited by Michael Schuldiner.
    p. cm.
Includes bibliographical references and index.
ISBN 0–87413–623–7 (alk. paper)
    1. Taylor, Edward, 1642–1729—Criticism and interpretation. 2. Christian poetry, American—History and criticism. 3. Puritan movements in literature. 4. New England—In literature. 5. Puritans in literature. I. Taylor, Edward, 1642–1729. II. Schuldiner, Michael Joseph. III. Davis, Thomas Marion. IV. Davis, Virginia L. PS850.T2Z83   1997
811'.1--dc20
                                                            96–36754
                                                               CIP

PRINTED IN THE UNITED STATES OF AMERICA

Contents

Prefatory Note

In Satterfield Hall at Kent State University, Professor Davis set aside a room in which he placed at the disposal of his graduate students his collection of Taylor materials, including primary materials such as microfilm copies of titles that Edward Taylor had in his library, as well as secondary sources such as dissertations on Taylor. The sign on the door read, "The Tayloring Shop."

Foreword

Late in 1969, less than two years after receiving his doctorate from the University of Missouri, Professor Thomas M. Davis arrived at Kent State with his wife, Virginia. By that time, Tom had already spent four years at Southern Illinois University teaching English and serving as director of General Studies. He had also begun to establish himself as a publishing scholar. By the end of 1969, he had four books and half a dozen articles to his credit, including a text on reading and writing, two literary anthologies, and a critical collection on fourteen poems by Emily Dickinson; four of the five articles were on the fiction of J. D. Salinger, and one, surprisingly, on a zither factory in Missouri. (Tom has never lost his interest in zithers, and when we catch him in the right mood, he will occasionally take one down from the wall and strum it while quietly humming a tune, more than likely a hymn.)

Tom's early publications gave little indication of the direction he had charted for himself when he selected American Puritan literature as his dissertation field in the early 1960s, but after earning the doctorate, he moved firmly into that area. Nor was it altogether a new one for him in that his initial career choice had been in the church. Like Edward Taylor, to whose poetry and sermons Tom would devote much of his professional life, he was trained as a preacher with an education in theology, thereby acquiring knowledge and experience that would prove invaluable to him in both his research and teaching. Unlike many scholars, however, he remained diverse; if Tom focused on American Puritanism, he also was alert to shifts that were continuously occurring in the popular culture, especially that which attracted his students, and until recently he persistently read all of the new scholarship on Emily Dickinson as it was published—including the dissertations on microfilm.

His rigorous examination of the Puritan writers, however, and of Taylor especially, proved magnetic to graduate students in English at Kent State. Consequently, it did not take Tom long to gain a decided following among them. Known for his meticulous investigations of Puritan documents, Tom awakened their interest in seventeenth-century American literature and generated their enthusiasm over it at the very time that he and Gina were editing the Taylor manuscripts from their own transcriptions made at the Beinecke and Boston Public Libraries, the Westfield Athenaeum, and other institutions holding research collections. Completing this intensely detailed textual editing required many years, not least because of Taylor's crabbed handwriting and the sorry state of the manuscripts. The results began to appear in 1981, when Twayne published the first three volumes of the heretofore *Unpublished Manuscripts of Edward Taylor*; two years later, the remaining writings were brought out in four volumes by Scholars' Facsimiles. The value of these seven volumes cannot be overstated by Taylor scholars.

Within a few years, his students were completing their dissertations in American Puritan literature and history. Not long afterwards, we started finding their names on conference programs, and their publications began to appear in *Early American Literature* and elsewhere. For an excellent example of this remarkable productivity, one had only to attend the 1991 American Literature Association conference in Washington, D.C. The Early American session was organized by one of Tom's former students; of the three presenters, two had written their dissertations under his guidance, and Tom had advised the third on his Master's Degree. Moreover, all four of the participants from that session are represented in the present volume, including its editor. More definitively than anything or anyone else could possibly do, his students and their scholarship testify to the quality of life and mind that Tom Davis brought to Kent State when he arrived here over twenty-five years ago.

Since that time, Tom has served the university well as a distinguished teacher, scholar, and colleague. During the mid-1980s, following two years as a Fulbrighter in Greece, he was instrumental in establishing the exchange program between Kent State and the Aristotle University of Thessaloniki. In addition to faculty exchanges, this program has brought more than a dozen graduate students from northern Greece to study in the English Department at Kent State, as well as a number of others to earn degrees from the School of Library Science. This is another of the ways that Tom's presence as a colleague has added immeasurably to the campus and touched many of the people associated with it.

For a while after the Greek exchange program commenced, Tom's career appeared destined to end prematurely and tragically. In the mid-1980s, he began to suffer from bouts of vertigo and nausea that became more persistent and severe with each passing month. During these years, a series of CAT scans, X-rays, and other examinations, many of them repeated, failed to reveal the cause of his distress until finally the devices were manipulated in such a way that at least five separate aneurysms of varying size and depth were exposed in his brain. Immediately upon discovery of the cause, cranial surgery was scheduled because any of the aneurysms could burst momentarily without warning, and death would follow at once. Two dangerous operations in quick succession were necessary before the aneurysms were all either removed or wrapped if the surgeons considered excision too dangerous to be feasible.

Incredibly, not long after this ordeal—while still in his hospital bed—Tom was reading papers from his graduate students. Moreover, no sooner was he back home on Lynn Road than he initiated a project that had long been simmering in the back of his mind—a critical reading of Edward Taylor's poetry. Tom's courage and Gina's constant support enabled him to complete the project more rapidly than any of his friends and colleagues could have imagined. Early in 1992, *A Reading of Edward Taylor* was published by the University of Delaware Press. It is a highly original study that all Taylor scholars will value for Tom's insights into the poet's artistic development and into the poetry itself. That *A Reading* was written at all under such strain is remarkable, but that it is so estimable a work so rapidly completed amid the heavy circumstances of Tom's recovery almost defies belief.

This Festschrift in Tom's honor carries the blessings as well as the thanks of innumerable students, colleagues, and friends. "My Business is Circumference," Emily Dickinson once wrote, using words that apply nearly as well to Tom Davis. How grateful we are now for having been drawn into his orbit!

SANFORD E. MAROVITZ

The Tayloring Shop

Introduction

MICHAEL SCHULDINER

Some three hundred fifty years after his birth and only sixty years since the modern discovery of his manuscripts, Edward Taylor holds a place in American letters as the first important American poet. One reason for Taylor's prominence, certainly, is the depth of imagery in his poetry. Taylor's sources for his imagery ranged widely, from patristic commentaries to medicinal treatises to tombstone carvings, and, as Thomas M. Davis explains, one of the challenges confronting those who attempt to understand and appreciate such poetry, which is so rich in allusion, is the acquisition of a seventeenth-century knowledge base as large and varied as Taylor's own:

> There is . . . a broad area of Taylor's experience to which we have only limited access, partly because the range of his interests—even for the seventeenth century—is amazingly broad, partly because he seems never to have forgotten anything, and partly because his mind delights in making connections—that are often clear only to him—among all kinds of subjects. (18)

Even when compared with his distinguished contemporaries in England—Herbert, Donne, Crashaw, Vaughn—Taylor's learning is quite remarkable. In America, Taylor's integration of imagery from varied intellectual traditions is unparalleled until well into the twentieth century, when figures such as Pound and Eliot reestablish the place of tradition in the poem, as they attempt to reinvigorate the present with the teachings of the past and to discover an identity for their times and their world that is at once local and universal. Taylor's world, of course, had eternal meaning built into it. Taylor's efforts were devoted to making that meaning present to his audience and himself through his ministry and his poetry.

Taylor used what he regarded as the best of past traditions of interpretation to illuminate for his audience the meaning of Scripture. Exploring, and in several instances endorsing, that same hermeneutic within which Taylor wrote, the writers collected here provide the reader with an understanding of some of the traditions of the past that informed the poetry of Edward Taylor. The objective is to make Taylor's intent more accessible to the present-day reader. For the authoritative review of scholarship about Edward Taylor, the reader should consult Jeffrey A. Hammond's *Edward Taylor: Fifty Years of Scholarship and Criticism*.

Certain critical assumptions hold in these essays—assumptions that only a few years ago would have gone without notice but today require at least brief mention. The first is that it is indeed possible to understand a period from within it. It is sometimes suggested that it is impossible to understand how earlier peoples thought, but such suggestions generally come from individuals who are young to an area of learning and / or who genuinely have difficulty understanding how others might be thinking. Entering a period is similar to learning a new language; in both instances one acquires a new vocabulary with which to participate in the new culture, which opens up to one as one reads more and becomes more familiar with the literature of that period. Not everyone has the same facility for acquisition of languages. Secondly, and as a corollary to the first assumption, the premise is adopted here that cues and signs within a literary work—when combined with a good degree of familiarity with the perspectives, events, and peoples of the period in which the piece of writing was authored—are sufficient to read the intention and motivation behind a piece of writing in the seventeenth or eighteenth centuries.

In this collection of essays, the bodies of tradition discussed range from the Puritan concept of nature to Puritan casuistry. Three of the traditions presented—the nature tradition, the casuistical tradition, and the elegiac tradition—are analyzed primarily for the way in which they help us understand the basic ideas in and development of Taylor's poetry. The other three traditions—the tradition of spiritual elegance, the homiletic tradition, and the psalmic tradition—are analyzed, in large part, for the way in which they help us understand the aesthetic behind the poetry. The focus of all the essays, of course, is Taylor's poetry. Two of the essays focus on Taylor's *Preparatory Meditations,* two on *Gods Determinations,* and two on Taylor's minor poetry, in particular his elegies and valedictory poems.

Jeff Jeske focuses on Taylor's *Preparatory Meditations* in his essay "Edward Taylor and the Traditions of Puritan Nature Philosophy." In this opening essay, the history of seventeenth- and early eighteenth-century New England Puritanism is presented as Jeske charts the development of the image of nature, from nature as wilderness to nature as book to nature as machine. In these contexts, says Jeske, Taylor the poet is a transitional figure whose *Preparatory Meditations* make use of imagery derived from each of these several phases of the development of the image of nature.

According to Jeske, in the beginning, New England thinking emphasizes the spirit over the flesh, and a general distrust of the material and the natural is expressed by an emphasis on the image of nature as wilderness. As secularization takes place in New England and greater emphasis is place upon this world, nature is more often examined as a source of knowledge of God. Nature becomes more important as "book." With the evolution of Puritanism into a more liberal, rational form of belief in the eighteenth century, nature loses its importance as a source of revelation and becomes "an exquisite artifact whose intricate order testifies to the ingenuity of the Artificer." Nature becomes machine.

Taylor's career and intellectual heritage spanned all of these three phases of the Puritan experiment, and his writings made use of the corresponding three images of nature. Taylor's use of the images of nature as wilderness and nature as book complement each other in his *Preparatory Meditations*. The general distrust of nature that informs the image of nature as wilderness is perhaps most evident in the fact that, as Thomas Davis pointed out, almost all the apparently natural imagery in the *Preparatory Meditations* is actually derived from biblical and biblically inspired literature that Taylor was familiar with. It should come as no surprise then to find that the actual image of "wilderness" is employed by Taylor with biblical precedent in mind as he speaks of his need for further regeneration. In his *Meditations,* Taylor asks to be led by Christ through the "wilderness" of this world into the spiritual "garden" of the elect. In fact, it is for the spiritually regenerated individual that the "wilderness" of nature then becomes the "book of nature." It is the spiritually regenerate individual, in Taylor's view, who is able accurately to read in natural phenomena the will of God.

Once one has established nature as a book that can be interpreted and in which one can find edifying and useful information, there easily follows the idea of nature as machine that can be explained scientifically—indeed, a nature that is predictable and can be controlled, as one does a machine. But the concepts of nature as book and nature as machine, explains Jeske, differ significantly in their ability to incorporate the Puritan idea of God. The concept of nature as a machine whose processes are governed by laws and secondary causes over which man might have some control is not easily reconciled with an all-powerful

God who sends men warnings of their fate through His special Providences. In fact, says Jeske, Taylor never tried to reconcile the two. While at the same time looking to the natural world for revelations from God, Taylor employed images in his *Preparatory Meditations* from the contemporary world of science. But the scientific images were crafted by Taylor to serve also the purposes of revelation.

Raymond A. Craig, also focusing on the *Preparatory Meditations*, concerns himself with the aesthetic behind Taylor's verse in "The 'Peculiar Elegance' of Edward Taylor's Poetics." Craig explains that there is a poetics of scriptural allusion operating in Taylor's *Meditations* which, as Craig discovers, has its basis in the concept of "spiritual elegance" found in St. Augustine's *De Doctrina Christiana*. This concept of spiritual elegance is given its New England Puritan formulation in John Cotton's *Singing of Psalmes*. Craig's examination of *Singing of Psalmes* reveals that Cotton viewed spiritual elegance as a product of direct quotation, paraphrase, and allusion to the Bible that might appear in a given piece of writing. In fact, the use of such allusion produces what Cotton called a "new song." Taylor's *Preparatory Meditations* make such extensive use of the allusive elements of what Cotton called spiritual elegance that one can readily identify a complex poetics of scriptural allusion functioning in Taylor's poetry.

According to Craig, Taylor's allusive strategy is directly related to his view of the relationship between grace and Scripture. Focusing on Meditation I.7, Craig shows that the Spirit of Grace and the Word are virtually synonymous for Taylor, and that the graceful Taylor's poetry is resplendent with Scripture quotations and allusions. Meditation I.7, with its headnote from Psalm 45, contains allusions to other Scripture which serve certainly to interpret Psalm 45 christologically. Craig argues, however, that Scripture allusions in the poem also serve to complement the central image in the poem of Christ as still and Taylor as receptacle— an image of the filling of the soul with grace—with other scriptural models of the action of grace. Moreover, these several images of the action of grace, the one available to plain sight and the others understood by way of allusion, serve ultimately to explain to Taylor the dynamic of his own experience of grace.

Examination of Scripture allusions in Taylor's *Meditations* also serves to demonstrate the way in which apparently inconsistent imagery is not inconsistent at all. In Meditation I.39, as Craig shows, the texts to which Taylor alludes through his apparently disparate images—1 John, James, Psalms, Job, etc.—offer explanations that render those images consistent. Further, the entirety of the Legal Unit (Meditations I.38–40), when read with the biblical allusions in mind, make for a single statement about the grounds for Taylor's hope for salvation through Christ. Moreover, even in such poems as the Typological Unit of Series II of the *Meditations,* where allusions to typological manuals clearly dominate as sources for Taylor's patterning of imagery, Craig shows that biblical passages alluded to by Taylor's choice of images are an indispensable source for understanding Taylor's poetry.

Taylor's long poem, *Gods Determinations*, is the focus of Michael Schuldiner's essay "Puritan Casuistry and the Character of the Three Ranks of Soul in Edward Taylor's *Gods Determinations*." In this essay, Schuldiner explains that much of what is obscure in Edward Taylor's *Gods Determinations* is clarified by a familiarity with case divinity, and that the poem can profitably be read as a verse study in Puritan casuistry that is particularly suitable for New England and of special interest because it might very well identify the prominent spiritual concerns of Taylor's parishioners and New Englanders generally.

According to Schuldiner, English Puritans, like their conforming brethren, viewed the study of case divinity as indispensable to those who would minister to the conscience of their parishioners. Like other theologians in England, Puritan casuists dealt with moral "cases"—such questions, for example, as whether it is lawful to wear ornaments of precious stones. As Schuldiner demonstrates, Puritan studies in case divinity such as William Perkins's *The Whole Treatise of the Cases of Conscience* and William Ames's *Conscience with the Power and Cases Thereof* differed from others not only in that these Puritan studies dealt with cases of conscience concerning one's progress in the faith but in that the preferred context in which moral questions, too, were understood was one's progress in faith. Both Perkins and Ames no doubt looked forward to a broad readership. Later Puritan studies in case divinity, such as David Dickson's *Therapeutica Sacra*, differed from earlier Puritan studies in that Dickson, as he explains at the outset, distinguished between "common" cases of conscience and those that concern regeneration. Dickson also chose to discuss exclusively cases of conscience that concern progress in faith.

Gods Determinations made ready use of many of the principles and actual cases that Dickson presented. As Schuldiner demonstrates, Taylor's source for the three ranks of soul in *Gods Determinations* is the *Therapeutica Sacra*, and familiarity with the *Therapeutica Sacra* makes it clear that the three ranks of soul emerge for the first time in "A Dialogue," and not in the later poem "The Frowardness of the Elect in the Work of Conversion," as had previously been supposed. However, familiarity with Dickson's work is most important for our understanding of *Gods Determinations* because it permits the reader to identify, as

Dickson had earlier, not only the psychological identities of the three
ranks of soul but also the various character types that Taylor regards as
noteworthy within those three ranks. As Schuldiner shows, the three
ranks of soul that Taylor presents in "A Dialogue" are those which Dickson had identified as laying impediments in the way of their conversion,
and he had defined these ranks as the "proud," the "distracted," and the
"excessively humble." Within the context of these three ranks, Taylor
made special note of two types of the proud soul, two types of the
distracted soul, and one type of the excessively humble soul.

The excessively humble soul is the one captured by Mercy in "The
Frowardness of the Elect"; when assaulted by Satan a second time, it has
sufficiently strong faith to call upon Christ. The other souls do not have
such strong faith and must be coached by Saint before entering the
church. These include the two types of distracted soul—those who are so
taken up with worldly affairs that they pay no attention to the state of
their souls and those who are simply ignorant of religion and of what
faith entails. These individuals who have only weak faith and must be
coached by Saint also include two types of proud soul—the Arminian
who thinks his works or wealth so great that he need not concern himself
with his salvation and the individual who thinks his sin so small that he
need not concern himself with regeneration. Of all these four types of
soul, Taylor apparently viewed the last—the individual who thinks his
sin small, who extenuates his sin—as the most difficult case of all.
Unlike the other four cases presented, Mercy has no mercy for this type
of soul that extenuates its sin, although it, like all the rest of the souls,
eventually is converted and brought to full church membership.

J. Daniel Patterson, in "The Homiletic Design of Edward Taylor's
Gods Determinations" explains that *Gods Determinations* is informed by
the homiletic tradition. The structure and rhetorical strategies that Taylor
makes use of in the poem are those typically found in the traditional
sermon as well as in the manuals that guided Puritan clergy in the
composition of sermons.

Patterson shows that the form of the Puritan sermon reflected the
psychology of the day, which maintained that the senses were the
gateway to the understanding, and that it was through the understanding
that the will and affections were moved. God's grace acted upon man in
much the same manner, first stirring the understanding and then the
heart. Accordingly, the Puritan sermon was designed, first, to engage the
auditor's sensory memory by the reading of biblical text; secondly, to
engage the understanding by explaining the text and gathering doctrine
from the text; and, lastly, to stir the will and affections in the "uses" or
"applications" portion of the sermon.

The use of rhetorical devices in the sermon was similarly designed to stir the senses and the understanding with a view toward moving the will and the affections. The Scripture allowed for a "plain style" of sermon which all auditors might understand; but by its own example, the Bible also allowed for use of tropes and rhetorical figures, and prescriptions for sermons included the use of various rhetorical figures. Taylor's sermons, Patterson demonstrates, made use of the structure and rhetorical devices of the homiletic tradition. Moreover, argues Patterson, it was because Taylor recognized how suitable sermon structure and rhetoric was for public address that he decided on the homiletic structure and style for his public poem, *Gods Determinations*.

The overall structure of *Gods Determinations* conforms to the general plan of the standard Puritan sermon. It has five divisions. The first division, analogous to the doctrinal section of a sermon, extends from the opening "Preface" to "Gods Selecting Love in the Decree." Here, Taylor's concern is to establish some doctrinal truths: the one on which the poem rests, that God created the world in order that the elect might glorify Him, and the particular doctrinal truth dealt with in this first division, that election is for only some.

The remaining four divisions of the poem are analogous to the "uses" or "applications" portion of a sermon and focus on the doctrine of election. The intention, as in the "applications" portion of a sermon, is to arouse the affections. The second division of the poem, beginning with "The Frowardness of the Elect in the Work of Conversion" and ending with "The Effect of this Reply with a fresh Assault from Satan," presents the general application of the doctrine of election to all of the elect and is addressed to the rational faculty of the reader. In the third and fourth divisions of the poem, Taylor more particularly applies the doctrine of election to two specific groups of saints: members of the first group he refers to as the First Rank; members of the second he identifies as the Second and Third Ranks. Again, the address here is to the rational faculty. The poem's fifth division, Patterson maintains, once again applies election, but this time it presents the joy of the occasion with the intent of stirring the affections of the reader.

Gods Determinations also makes use of a number of rhetorical conventions typical of the Puritan sermon. Among these conventions is the hypothetical objection to the doctrine stated and the minister's confutation of that objection. Taylor regularly employs this device in his sermons and, according to Patterson, in the various dialogues in *Gods Determinations,* such as "A Dialogue between Justice & Mercy." Moreover, Taylor employs a relatively plain style, and his tropes are of the variety sanctioned by the Bible and traditionally found in the sermon.

The reader's attention is next turned to what has been called Taylor's "Minor Poetry," which is really not minor at all, as Jeffrey A. Hammond demonstrates in his essay, "'Diffusing All by Pattern': Edward Taylor as Elegist." Hammond's discussion of Taylor's public elegies reveals that Taylor, in writing public verse such as the elegies, was not hampered by the dictates of Puritan public art, as some might believe, but ably expressed some actual concerns. As is true of his private verse, the *Preparatory Meditations*, which critics generally favor over Taylor's other verse, the elegies, while employing traditional elegiac conventions, are experienced by both Taylor and his community of readers in a manner that stimulates self-definition as a saint and thereby furthers postconversion assurance of salvation.

According to Hammond, the tendency among Taylor critics to slight the elegies in favor of the *Preparatory Meditations* is, in part, due to the type of elegy that Taylor wrote. As Hammond explains, two types of elegies were prominent in Renaissance England: the "literary" or "pastoral" elegy of the "Lycidas" variety that Milton wrote, and what came to be known as the "funeral" elegy.

In Taylor's nine "public" elegies, as well as in such family elegies as the "Funerall Poem" for his first wife, Elizabeth Fitch, one finds the same rigorous self-scrutiny and battle against carnality found in the *Preparatory Meditations*. These actions are those of the redeemed saint, and they must be internalized by both Taylor and his audience in order for their postconversion spiritual development to proceed. In particular, one finds in these elegies (as in the *Meditations*) a mandate to write—in the case of the elegies in order to commemorate the deceased—as well as a feeling of inadequacy to the task produced by a sense of sin on Taylor's part. Yet, through the conventions of the elegy, Taylor is able to universalize this dilemma and link his artistic difficulties with the difficulties associated with grieving. Taylor thus permits the reader to internalize this conflict that is prerequisite to growth in assurance, even as Taylor identifies this dilemma in himself. Similarly, one discerns in the public elegies, as in the *Meditations,* a distance between the holy (in the case of the elegies, the holy departed) and Taylor; but when in the elegiac convention these holy departed are generalized, they become models of sanctity rewarded, imitable in their earthly sanctification by the public readership as well as by Taylor.

In the *Meditations,* it was always Christ's virtues affecting Taylor, and not any skill of Taylor's own, to which the successful poem was to be attributed. Similarly, in the elegy, Taylor resolves the dilemma created by, on the one hand, the mandate to write and, on the other, his feelings of inadequacy because of his sense of sin, by shifting the responsibility for performative success from his skill as a poet to the virtues of the deceased saint. Moreover, the life of the saint in his hopes and fears held balanced and in check—much as Taylor had described them in the *Meditations*—becomes an example to be internalized by the larger community of believers for whom spiritual dilemmas loom as salvific obstacles to spiritual peace. The elegy thus becomes a "neo-gospel" in miniature, in which Taylor speaks as apostle holding up the departed saint's life for imitation.

Further, the *Preparatory Meditations* themselves, according to Hammond, make use of elegiac conventions when death intrudes, as in the meditations written on days that family members died. Taylor's "self-elegies" written toward the end of his life evidence, as Hammond demonstrates, an assurance that Taylor had formerly attributed to others and hence an identification with those saints he had formerly eulogized.

Rosemary Fithian Guruswamy turns the reader's focus to Edward Taylor's "Valedictory Poems" in her essay, "A Farewell to David: Edward Taylor's Valediction and Psalm 19." In that essay, Guruswamy discusses the pervasiveness of psalmody in Puritan life and letters and shows that Edward Taylor used Psalm 19 as the working model for the three drafts of his "Valedictory Poems," thus demonstrating that in Taylor's case the Psalms served as an anchor to his art virtually to the end of his earthly life. In fact, argues Guruswamy, the way in which Taylor adapts the psalmist's imagery and ideas in the "Valedictory Poems" allows him to acknowledge his closeness to glorification in heaven.

Guruswamy explains that use of the Psalms had not varied significantly since the Reformation. In Old England as in the New, Psalms formed a basis for private meditation as well as for public and private singing. In New England, however, the focus was on those Psalms which dealt with the idea of a wilderness wandering, which New Englanders found analogous to their own experience. In fact, Colonial histories and elegies would associate certain of the founding fathers with David. Moreover, in New England, Psalm-singing was elevated to the status of an ordinance, as it came to be viewed as a means of spiritual growth. Of all biblical texts, explains Guruswamy, the Psalms most occupied the attention of New England Puritans.

Taylor, Guruswamy shows, employed the Psalm as a poetic model even to the end of his career and life, when he turned to Psalm 19 as a model for his "Valedictory Poems." As Psalm 19 begins with a declaration that created nature is a testimony to God's work, so too the three versions of "The Valedictory Poems" begin with a consideration of the natural world. However, rather than viewing nature as evidence of God's presence, Taylor denigrates nature at this point. Later, as Taylor says a detailed farewell to nature, he does seem to view natural objects as aids from God to assist spiritual development. This "doubleness," Guruswamy argues, is typical of the poetry Taylor wrote late in life, and it reflects a state of mind central to those who have experienced conversion.

Psalm 19 follows with discussion of the failure of man to listen to Creation's testimony of God. Taylor, however, again assuming the voice of one in the afterlife, alters the message of the Psalmist and suggests that the witnessing of nature on earth is necessarily inferior to that which occurs in heaven. Most striking, however, is Taylor's discussion of the "language" he must use on earth to praise God and the language he will be able to use in heaven—a discussion that the reader found earlier in Taylor's poetry, but never before expressed with such confidence that he will have access to that language of heaven.

In Psalm 19, the Psalmist asks for acquittance from sin. Taylor too asks for acquittance from sin and acknowledges that sin is erased only upon death. However, Taylor also recognizes that he is among the saved, and herein lies his stratagem for employment of Psalm 19, Guruswamy maintains. The Psalmist is earthbound; Taylor uses Psalm 19 to demonstrate, by contrast, that he is not, as he awaits on earth his final glorification in heaven.

The essays here thus span all but the earliest portion of Taylor's life, and they present a good portion of the poetry written in his mature years. Throughout the essays, one witnesses a central concern with the spiritual life of the poet and the way that spiritual life reflects itself in his verse. As the earliest American to display in his poetry so pervasive a concern with the nature of spiritual renewal, Edward Taylor stands at the beginning of a long American tradition. Virtually every great American poet since Taylor has written in a significant way about spiritual change— Whitman, Dickinson, Pound Eliot, Frost; indeed most of America's great authors—prose writers as well as poets—have dealt with the theme. In fact, one might argue that in this regard America's literature has been unique. It is in the sense that virtually all the great American authors have dealt at one point or another in their careers with the nature of spiritual experience that American Literature has distinguished itself from other literature written in English. Edward Taylor's poetry stands at the beginning of that long and very distinguished body of American poetry on the theme of spiritual renewal.

Part 1
The *Preparatory Meditations*

Edward Taylor and the
Traditions of Puritan Nature Philosophy

JEFF JESKE

In *A Reading of Edward Taylor*, Thomas M. Davis notes that he is "primarily interested in the way the poetry—and the poet—changes and develops over the more than half-century when he wrote" (13). Such an interest is not misplaced. As Davis shows us, Taylor's evolving attitudes toward both his art and the state of his soul underwrite "subtle but clear developments in the poetry." Taylor's early and mature poems must not be confused, and Davis's study helps us to understand the differences between them.

Equally important to our understanding of Taylor is the half century itself. The period spanning the late seventeenth and early eighteenth centuries witnessed striking change in the identity of New England Puritanism; by its end, decline and dissolution were well underway. If Taylor is the "typical Puritan" that Norman Grabo terms him, we can expect him to bear that dynamic period's impress both intellectually and theologically. Such is indeed the case.

The story's external elements are well known: increasing worldliness, the secularization of church policies, the loss of the colony's charter, the formation of the Brattle Street church. Davis analyzes, in this regard, the impact on Taylor's ministry and art of Solomon's Stoddard's liberalizing of requirements for admission to the Lord's Supper. Less well charted, however, are corresponding internal shifts within the Puritan intellectual heritage, shifts which proceed from the complexity of that heritage and which move along preestablished fault lines partly in response to the external developments. It is a topographical map of the internal that helps to make sense of both the large-scale evolution of Puritan nature philoso-

phy and the retrograde movement within that evolution of our "typical"
poet, Edward Taylor. Such a map enables us to read the intellectual
coordinates of nature images where they appear in Puritan literature,
whether in sermon, tract, or Taylor's *Preparatory Meditations*.

Among the tangled components of New England Puritanism are
Augustinianism, medieval Scholastic philosophy, humanism, Calvinism,
and seventeenth-century ideology. Each of these systems, moreover,
amalgamates other systems. Augustine, for example, is indebted to the
early church fathers as well as to Plato and Plotinus. Aquinas, who
provides a major alternative to Augustinianism, synthesizes early
Scholasticism and Aristotle. The Reformers utilized both Augustine and
the later Scholasticism of Duns Scotus, while at the same time the
humanist movement renewed the popularity of various Greek and Roman
modes of thought. Add to this the Neostoicism and the developing
scientific naturalism of the seventeenth century, and it is not surprising
that Taylor and his contemporaries express diverse attitudes toward
nature. To speak of a Puritan "idea" of nature is to refer to a complex
hybrid indeed.

Spread over and slightly beyond the time in which Taylor lived and
wrote, the map looks something like this: initially, otherworldly concerns
informed by Christian Platonism dominate the Massachusetts colony,
emphasizing the superiority of spirit to matter and coping with a basic
distrust of nature by advising detachment from it. Perry Miller's phrase
"the Augustinian strain of piety" indicates the direct source of this mode
of thinking, modified as it was by Calvin. When this set of coordinates is
dominant, the crystallizing image of nature is that of *wilderness* set
against the enclosed garden of God's church, the two together
establishing a mythic framework in which the world—and concrete
images of it—have little ontological or epistemological value.

By the mid-seventeenth century, however, a more this-worldly
concept of nature replaces the founders' mythic orientation. This
concept, latent in the intellectual heritage and shaped not by Christian
Platonism but by Scholastic Aristotelianism and humanism, empowers a
new image: nature as *book*. Underlying its use are assumptions different
from those associated with the wilderness, an image which continues to
appear in election sermons and similar documents restating the Puritan
mission and attempting to rekindle piety. The book image assumes that
nature is not to be shunned and that its study enables the constructing of a
natural theology which can support revelation.

As the eighteenth century approaches, yet another configuration
emerges. Nature continues to play an important symbolic function as

wilderness, and the concept of nature's intelligibility as book remains seminal. But a more empirical attitude toward the concrete world generally lessens the use of garden / wilderness symbolism in dealing with sense perceptions, and the new science, evolving theories of natural law, and more positive attitudes toward reason modify the book image significantly and in two stages. First, stabilization and objectification diminish nature's identity as a numinous reflection of God; nature becomes instead a source-book of the Divine Will. Second, and somewhat paradoxically, the same process of despiritualizing causes nature to lose importance as a source of theological knowledge and hence as a source of revelation. A third image of nature becomes dominant— nature as *machine*. This image signals the triumph of secularization and the near-advent of Deism.

Edward Taylor, of course, does not follow this line of development. In fact, as Davis notes, the *Preparatory Meditations* suggest that he moves in the opposite direction. Where Puritanism becomes more secular, Taylor's preoccupations become more sacramental. Where Puritanism becomes more accepting of the natural world and more liberal in its use of nature imagery, Taylor becomes seemingly more detached and distrustful: witness his increasing preference for "nature" images drawn directly from Scripture. Where Puritanism's response to nature becomes more analytic, Taylor's purposes become more meditative and hence more in line with the piety of the founders.

The grand subjects of the *Meditations*, according to Davis, are "God's miracles, the Incarnation, and the perpetual observance of that miracle in the Sacrament of the Lord's Supper" (67), and as Taylor's career proceeds, the Lord's supper becomes more central to his thought, as does Taylor's intent to glorify the risen Christ. Davis notes that Taylor becomes less spontaneous and less individualistic with his imagery. He becomes more "dogmatically and exegetically limited" (139), more restrained by the demands of his texts. In the Series 2 typological poems, he turns from the world's flux to preordained biblical parallels, and in the subsequent poems based on Canticles, he establishes a *hortus conclusus*, a true place of solace and retreat where he can focus on the anticipated union with Christ which he has sought throughout his career. "In this process of withdrawal from the fallen world," Davis observes, Taylor's verse becomes progressively "more removed from the facts of his life" (175).

Nevertheless, Taylor is not as simple as this introductory sketch suggests. He inherits the same tangled traditions as his contemporaries, and his mind moves agilely within them. In his writings, despite their prevailing piety, we find the same multiplicity in the use of nature imagery that appears elsewhere in the age. The same fault lines appear in Taylor that would lead to fracture later.

Nature as Wilderness

It is essentially a Calvinist idea of nature derived from Plato which informs the founders' piety—John Cotton, signal theologian of the first generation, employs it repeatedly to establish a characteristic otherworldly stance—and it is the image of the wilderness, contrasted with the garden of Christ's church, which he uses most often and eloquently to represent nature. Defining his fellow Puritans as latter-day Israelites and New England as the New Canaan, Cotton places nature in a mythic context. As wilderness, nature is either a place of trial like the biblical wilderness in which Moses, the Israelites, Elijah, Elisha, and Christ spent periods of mortification, or an entity to be transformed into a new Eden. In neither situation does nature have intrinsic value except through its participation in the mythic scheme. As testing site, for example, nature is the environment in which God's church must be established. Yet when this occurs, that which is established—the garden / church—is set apart and has a higher ontological value.

As entity to be transformed, nature-as-wilderness is also devalued. The Platonic dualism underlying Calvin's thought stresses that phenomenal nature, and by extension the entire material universe, has no real value, as it is only as it can be. Composed of material substance, nature is inherently flawed, corrupt, and hence "wilderness." Only in becoming spiritualized can nature achieve true merit. If man reorders nature on the basis of spiritual principles, if he transforms wilderness into garden, then he partially accomplishes the promised regeneration of nature and restores its positive, prelapsarian condition. What is produced, however, is a radically altered, mythic, quasi-spiritualized counterpart of the wilderness. Material nature disappears in the process, converted, in mystico-sacramental conversion theory, to the garden planted "eastward in Eden."

Cotton first applies the garden-wilderness motif to the Puritan mission in the sermon delivered to John Winthrop and the four hundred others departing for the New World aboard the *Arbella* and published as *God's Promise to His Plantations*. Preached on 2 Sam. 7:10—"Moreover I will appoint a place for my people Israel, and I will plant them, that they may dwell in a place of their own"—the sermon introduces the main aspects of the motif, especially the concept of being planted in a special place to fulfill a covenanted role under God's direct supervision. This concept, reflected elsewhere in Winthrop's reference to the "citty on the hill," provides the impetus for a dualistic treatment of nature. Underlying the idea of the covenanted community is the Augustinian distinction between the cities of man and God, reformulated in Puritan thought in terms of visible and invisible churches. The church of God's elect is the invisible church; in *A Brief Exposition of the Whole Book of Canticles*, Cotton characterizes it as "a garden enclosed, a fountaine sealed" (110), separated, that is, from the impure world. God Himself, the "Gardiner" and "Husbandman," has decided to uproot and transplant His people, moving them to a place of safety where "the sons of wickedness shall afflict them no more" (2).

Throughout the departure sermon, Cotton uses the organic metaphor to suggest the mystical quality of the relationship between the saint and God. Church members are part of a "choice generation" and are to be called "trees of righteousness, the planting of the Lord" (14). Similarly, in *God's Mercie Mixed with His Justice*, Cotton announces that "we shall carry our roote with us . . . and our fruite wille bee more sweet and savoury" (65).[1] Once in New England, the church is to send out new shoots, resulting in the multiplication of "one garden into many, one Church into above a score" (*Canticles* 166). These gardens, of course, are carved out of nature's wilderness, but what links them is a supranatural mode of being.

Within the garden, a special people lives the mystico-sacramental religious experience which God's nearness makes possible. Outside, according to Cotton, all the world is "as a wildernesse, or at best a wilde field where all manner of unclean, and wilde beasts live and feed" (*Canticles* 104).[2] Here live the devil, enemies of the church, and sinners in general: symbolically, the wilderness is a place of reprobacy.[3] To protect the garden's inhabitants from these external threats, Cotton asks God to "restraine (the foxes, the little foxes) the enemies of the Church, of greater or lesser power. . . . These spoiled the vines, hindered the proceeding of the building of the Temple, and the peace of the Church" (Canticles 139). Fortunately for New England, God has separated garden from wilderness by means of the hedges of grace, such that "neither Dragons, nor wild Bores, nor Foxes shall herafter root it up" (*Canticles* 139). Nature is contaminated, the source of the carnal allurements which provoke men to "actual" sin. In Anne Bradstreet's traditional Platonic dialogue, "The Flesh and the Spirit," the soul insists, "my ambition Lyes above" (383); Michael Wigglesworth advises the Christian in "A Song of Emptiness" to "Learn what deceitful Toyes, and empty things, / This

World, and all its best Enjoyments be: / Out of the Earth no true
Contentment springs, / But all things here are vexing Vanities" (*The Day
of Doom* 87).[4] John Cotton declares that "the universality of all creatures
is vanity" and concludes that "all . . . creatures are under the Sun, but our
happiness is above it . . . neither can things below the Sun carry us up to
a condition above the Sun" (*Ecclesiastes* 262,11).

Nor does nature offer epistemological benefits. The "light of nature"
which processes sense perceptions is weak and consists of "vain
imaginings."[5] Even after regeneration, man's ability to evaluate natural
phenomena is limited and even dangerous. Repeating the familiar
Platonic view that nature is an unstable object of knowledge, Cotton
asks, "How should that which is restlesse . . . procure us setled rest and
tranquillity, which accompanieth true happiness?" The saint seeking
intellectual stability had better avoid nature, for "the mind of man . . . is
somewhat assimilated into the nature of the object which it studieth"
(*Ecclesiastes* 13). Cotton admits occasionally that secular study of the
creatures is a duty imposed by God, but he also points out that too much
of such study "drieth up the sweetest moysture of the body" and, more
dangerously, may bring "fastidious loathing of Scriptures" (*Ecclesiastes*
271). If anything, contact with nature should drive man toward more
substantial, supranatural concerns and perusal of Scripture. The most that
material things can teach, as Calvin had noted, is man's inexcusableness.
Beyond this, nature offers little to the saint.

Nature as Book

As long as the facts of the Puritan experience supported the concept of
a special, covenanted community set apart from an impure world, the
garden-wilderness motif viably expressed the Puritan relationship to
nature, with an otherworldly attitude resulting. At first the concept did
reflect the actual situation. The Puritans clustered in small communities
which were separated by dangerous tracts of genuine wilderness. Within
these communities, the theocratic New England society instituted
rigorous admission requirements to insure the purity of the churches. The
founders assumed that the church stock would be replenished by the
children of the regenerate, to whom a covenant relationship was
transmitted at birth, thereby providing the colonists with a mystical
cohesion analogous to the racial relatedness of the Israelites, that other
group sojourning in an inhospitable wilderness.

Changes soon fragmented and secularized God's special garden, however. Most immediately, a new generation that did not share the intense zeal of the founders and that was unable to testify to its conversion began to press for church membership. Acknowledging that some provision had to be made to bring these visibly godly under control of the church, such ministers as Thomas Hooker began early to modify the stringent admission requirements, for example by substituting a system of questions and answers for a public relation of saving faith. This more liberal attitude toward church membership became tentatively incorporated in the credal platforms of the 1640s. The result of the changed admission requirements, according to Williston Walker, was that the church became a "half-way house between the world and full Christian discipleship" (250). Meanwhile, Thomas Shephard and others established a definition of regeneracy which restored the Adamic Covenant of Works, with moral actions becoming necessary testimony to Christ's grace. This modification, as well as Hooker's interpretation of conversion as a long, slow process in time, was incorporated in the Cambridge Platform of 1648, initiating movement away from the Pauline concern with immediate participation in Christ and toward moral conduct. Nature was no longer merely a wilderness to be shunned by the elect, but the important site of the working out of one's salvation.

At the same time, sheer familiarity with the wilderness made the Puritans less likely to invest it with the demonic, despite pulpit rhetoric to the contrary. In the beginning, the wilderness was an actual place outside the hedge. Migrations to Connecticut in the mid-1630s, however, breached the enclosure, transforming the wilderness from mysterious territory into land one had to traverse in order to visit friends. Economic survival required that one know the wilderness in order to extract necessary stuffs from it. And did not Scripture itself command that the wilderness be subdued and conquered for human benefit?[6] In his letters, John Winthrop expresses confidence that "whatsoever we stand in need of is treasured up in the earthe by the Creator, and is to be fetched thence by the sweatt of our browes" (II.136). Such "fetching," praised by John Norton as a way of converting the wilderness into "a place of Merchandize" (58), was to help bring about a secularized worldview stripped of the religious preoccupations underlying Winthrop's own asceticism. His son, John Winthrop Jr., who learned well of the abundant buried treasures (e.g., iron, lead) that God had placed in the New England hills, became one of the foremost entrepreneurs of his generation.[7] In 1652, the year of John Cotton's death, "worldly-mindedness" appears for the first time as the reason for a fast ordered by the general court. In the late 1650s and 1660s, the cries against worldliness, and particularly against preoccupation with trade, steadily increase. And when the "Reforming Synod" was convened in 1679—the same year that Edward Taylor was elected pastor in Westfield—its analysis of New England's provoking sins revealed that, in general, wordliness was among the chief sins and that mystico-sacramentalism had continued to decrease. The devout had succumbed to the worldly spirit, specifically identified as an "inordinate affection to the world"; the things of religion had been "made subservient unto worldly interests" and "all seeke their own, not the things that are Jesus Christ's" (Walker 431, 432).

Preachers continue to employ the garden-wilderness imagery motif as a point of reference well into the eighteenth century, especially in the election sermons, whose purpose was to remind the New Englanders, in Jonathan Mitchel's words in *Nehemiah on the Wall in Troublesom Times*, that "it is our Errand into the Wilderness to study and practice true Scripture Reformation," not primarily to achieve material prosperity (28). The same John Norton who approves of the wilderness as a "place of Merchandize" invokes the concept of the garden in the election sermon for 1659 to declare that "it concerneth N. E. alwayes to remember that Originally they are a plantation religious, not a plantation of trade" (17). However, the motif of the church as community detached from nature appears progressively less frequently; beginning in the last quarter of the seventeenth century, sermons reveal a major change in emphasis. The garden appears sadly deteriorated and under constant assault by external enemies. Moreover, it is no longer easy to distinguish clearly between garden and wilderness, mystico-sacramental community and nature. In *A Brief Recognition of New England's Errand into the Wilderness*, the election sermon for 1670, Samuel Danforth cites a text that must have later seemed prophetic: "The vineyard is all overgrown with thorns, and nettles cover the face thereof, and the stone wall thereof is broken down"(33). Danforth asserts that God is punishing Puritan worldliness by dismantling the hedges which separate the community from the world at large. By removing the founders through death, He has taken "the principal stakes out of our hedges; the cornerstones out of our walls" (74). When King Philip's War erupts in the mid-1670s, Increase Mather interprets this most threatening of all intrusions into the garden as a direct result of God's having removed Himself as protector (*The Day of Trouble is Near* 6). The natural and political catastrophes which mounted in the decades that followed caused the garden to refer less to the visible church and more, as in the case of Edward Taylor, to the individual.

As the wilderness image became less accurate in describing the actual relationship of the Puritans to nature, and as the garden image became interiorized, a different image became prominent: that of the "book of nature." Its presuppositions, most notably that one must actively search nature for knowledge of God, better suited the intellectual temperament of the later seventeenth century and differed radically from the presuppositions informing the concept of wilderness. Christian Platonism views the epistemological relationship between man and nature as blasted even after regeneration; Scholasticism, the major source of the book image, asserts that even natural man can—and should—learn much of God and His attributes by investigating nature. In this view, natural theology is not a dangerous distraction but a divinely imposed responsibility.

The image of nature as book actually appears frequently in the writings of early Puritanism, even in Calvinist works. The popular poet Guillaume du Bartas, for example, characterizes nature as a "folio, printed all With God's great Works in Letters Capitall" (7). In so doing, he echoes Calvin himself, who, in an uncharacteristic passage, had admonished his followers to "let the world become our school if we desire rightly to know God" (60). The more representative early Puritan position, of course, is displayed in Richard Mather's remark that those who have none but the book of the creatures are in a perishing condition. Similarly, James Fitch, an orthodox New England Calvinist, insists that "none can learn religion by the book of nature . . . for the book of nature is blurred by man's sin, the curse is fallen upon the works of Creation, and thus this book is darkened" (1). Nevertheless, for other important shapers of the New England mind, the book was not significantly darkened at all. Johann Alsted, for example, whose compendious *Encyclopaedia Scientiarum Omnium* provided a "North-West Passage" to the Puritan sciences, concludes from his researches that "a genuine reading of the book of nature is an ascenscion to the mind of God, both theoretical and practical" (Miller 209). Besides, explicit even in such early works of piety as Winthrop's *Journal* is the pervasive Puritan confidence that the will of God can be read in His Providences. When He preserved a saint in a storm, or caused a blaspheming sailor to drown in public view, it was customary to charge these natural phenomena with transcendent meanings.

Several factors encouraged the substitution of "book" for "wilderness." Chief among these were elements in the Puritan intellectual heritage which had trusted in nature's knowableness: most notably, Scholasticism, Ramistic logic, and science. Despite the Augustinian orientation of the founders, for example, Scholasticism provided the New England Puritans a systematic mode of understanding the universe. As early as 1653, fifteen years before Taylor's arrival, Harvard theses such as "Quantity is derived from matter and quality chiefly from form" indicated that both physical and metaphysical theories regarding matter's constitution were based not on the Platonic dualism upon which Augustine relied, but on Aristotelian hylomorphism. The Aristotelian principle that entities are indissoluble combinations of matter and form is assumed by such orthodox New England theologians as James Fitch in his widely praised *First Principles of the Doctrine of Christ* (see Walsh). It is possible, of course, to adapt Scholastic means to Augustinian ends, and Fitch's acceptance of Scholastic views does not prevent his *First Principles* from being a thoroughly Calvinist work. Nevertheless, Scholastic assumptions chiefly support Scholastic conclusions. When the tenor of Puritan thought became less otherworldly as the seventeenth century progressed, certain important Scholastic conclusions related to nature's intelligibility became more prominent, carrying intellectual consequences which the founders seem not to have anticipated when they brought to New England the Scholastic texts they had studied at Cambridge.

One such consequence was an enhanced attitude toward reason. The Thomist belief that natural reason is an important tool encourages the use of material phenomena in the pursuit of knowledge, thereby confirming a principle which is at least implicit in Calvin.[8] In adapting this belief, the Puritans gradually modified their Calvin-inspired distrust of reason and established the foundation for an epistemological rapport with nature. Meanwhile, and of more direct significance, the Scholastic, non-Calvinist conviction emerged that nature itself is stable and thus intelligible. The wilderness image assumes that nature is a shifting—and thus dangerous—object to the mind seeking the transcendent and stable unity of divine wisdom. In the Scholastic view, on the other hand, nature does not house the unstable shadows of divine exemplars but is a concrete piece of divine artisanry, one established on regular, immutable principles analogous to the Stoic *lex naturae*, which Thomism incorporates. Throughout the seventeenth century, sermons display a lively sense of God's direct and enigmatic participation in human affairs. But again thanks to Thomism, which postulates that God bestows self-sufficiency on nature via secondary causation, the underlying theology becomes progressively more rationalist and God's unpredictability in nature less a factor.

A second important tradition informing the book of nature image was humanism, inasmuch as the classical authors' views on the observable order in—and readability of—nature often reinforced those of Scholasticism and its this-worldly natural theology. Throughout the seventeenth and eighteenth centuries, such authors as Cicero, Virgil, Ovid, and Horace were widely studied in New England grammar schools and universities.[9] Cicero's Stoic view of man, nature, and the *lex naturae* became particularly influential, and his writings were cited progressively more often in Puritan sermons, especially as the eighteenth century approached. As at Cambridge in England, Harvard, even before Edward Taylor arrived, also made available the other Stoics, Epicureanism, and atomistic theories of the universe. That natural philosophy served as handmaiden to theology in the this-worldly view clearly justified the allotting of a portion of the academic day to what John Cotton would have regarded as "vain strivings." Charles Chauncy, early Harvard president and widely respected educator of New England ministers, declared that "whatsoever is contained in the scriptures of the works of God [i.e., nature], and as farr as it concerns a minister to preach all profitable and Scripture trueths, the knowledge of Arts & Sciences is usefull and expedient to him to hold them forth to his hearers" (Miller 85). By designating the works of God as "scriptures" and suggesting to ministerial candidates that they use materials from that source in their sermons, he anticipates the eighteenth-century belief that the book of nature is not only coextensive with, but actually more authoritative than, the book of revelation.

Humanism's most direct effect on Puritan New England's concept of nature came, however, via Ramistic logic. By means of it, Puritanism significantly modified Scholastic this-worldliness and insured future secularizing developments. Ramus's works were widely used throughout New England and studied by Taylor; his *Dialectics* and *Institutiones Logicae* were Harvard textbooks. Ramus's method inspired substantial confidence in logic and supported the faith in natural intellect which was already present in Puritan thinking through the Scholastic heritage.[10] More directly important for the book-of-nature image, Ramistic logic underlay the influential theories of Puritan theologians Alexander Richardson and William Ames. Richardson regarded nature as *encylopaidia*, a compendium of divine arts and laws forming a comprehensive system of knowledge about God. Ames extended the same concept: his *technometria* assumes that the divine attributes are systematically expressed and systematically discoverable in nature. The physical universe is a kind of handbook containing the rules of human activity. Like Aristotle in the *Nicomachean Ethics*, Ames argues that the goal of all education is *eupraxia*. Man's entire active life is subject to the technological rules and arts, and these arts, all of which have a divine source, can be derived immediately from the book of nature.

Where Ames differs most from Scholasticism is in reversing Thomistic teleology. Aquinas maintained (as did Aristotle), that the Deity potently causes creatures to strain upward and imitate God as much as possible—most notably His unity. The goal of all creation, then, is a state of final rest, and the aim of knowledge is a tying together of the forms inherent in creatures. In other words, the searching intellect likewise attempts to come to rest in unity. In the Amesian mode of thinking, however, the emphasis is upon God's wish to express Himself in multiplicity. Ames's substitution of physics for metaphysics is prophetic. In 1653, *theses technologicae* begin to replace *theses metaphysicae* on the Harvard sheet and continued to appear at both Harvard and Yale until almost the end of the eighteenth century. The pragmatic Amesian emphasis appears in such titles as "True welfare [*eupraxia*] is the object and end of arts" and "Art is a method of various precepts useful for life." Such titles reflect the growing moralism in contemporary religious practice and reveal why the book of nature is an indispensable part of the program, even more so than in Scholasticism. In the Thomistic system, with its goal of upward striving, it is possible to exclude nature by relying solely on revelation. In the Amesian scheme, man must consult the book of nature constantly and in detail to further God's purpose, the realization of the arts in all activity. Ames observes that not only do the creatures that constitute the book's pages "declare God's glory," they "give occasion to us to know, and seeke God" (8, 21).

Nature as Machine

First-generation Puritans generally displayed only a minor interest in natural science, partly because of the Platonic base of Augustinian piety, partly because of their situation: the early years offered little stimulus for scientific study. In *Harvard College in the Seventeenth Century*, Samuel Eliot Morison notes that when the college was established in 1636, the curriculum provided by President Dunster, modeled as it was on the Cantabrigian counterpart, exposed students to little about the natural world that Dante did not know, even though courses were provided in astronomy, botany, and physics (I. 215). Despite instruction in geometry, the actual cultivating of a systematic mathematics—the basic language of empirical investigation—did not begin until the second half of the seventeenth century.

Still, there existed in Puritanism a latent interest in natural science, and like the Puritan technological bent, it may well have been in advance of the society at large in terms of secularization, thereby helping to bring forward a climate uncongenial to the founders' piety. A glance at the combination of Puritans and science in contemporary England reveals a telling and prophetic statistic. When the Royal Society was founded in

1663, forty-two of the sixty-eight members were nominal Puritans. The ideals of this organization, which was highly regarded by New Englanders, were at the beginning religious and certainly consonant with Puritan orthodoxy as the latter was expressed in Aristotelian themes (e.g., a God operating in the universe via secondary causes, man as controller).[11] The research of the Society's Puritan members became thoroughly secular, however, and their motives increasingly nontheological.

As early as the 1660s, members of the second New England generation began corresponding with Royal Society fellows and reading its *Transactions*.[12] At Harvard, the previous decade had witnessed, along with a new president in Charles Chauncy (1654), the appearance of the new astronomy and physics; both sciences were well established in the curriculum by the year that Zechariah Brigden's *New England Almanac for 1659* incorporated a complete exposition of the Copernican system.[13] Even before 1672, when John Winthrop Jr. presented the college with a telescope, Harvard students were well aware of contemporary theories of the heavens. Similarly, Newtonian physics won easy acceptance, if not as quickly, and by 1700 had completely replaced its Scholastic predecessor. The Platonic and Aristotelian strains in Puritan thought underlying the images of wilderness and book actually facilitated the process. The Platonic, presupposing the superiority of spirit to matter, made the question of *which* physics a matter of little importance. The Aristotelian, encouraging human understanding of God's creation, approved any scientific progress that enabled better explication of the divine law published in the universe.

The impact of the converging traditions of Puritan nature philosophy in the late seventeenth century is evident in Edward Taylor's friend, Increase Mather, who combines commitment to the mystico-sacramentalism of the founders with a Scholastic intellectual frame and deep interest in modern developments. On the one hand, he elaborates in such works as *A Briefe History of the War with the Indians* (1676) the Platonic mythology of garden and wilderness. On the other, his deep indebtedness to Aristotle results in important roles for nature and reason—and for the image of nature as book. In allowing for a natural theology akin to that practiced in England, he does not rely solely upon Scholastic method either. Like the humanists, he can turn against the "pagan master" Aristotle and champion Ramus, Richardson, and Ames. His own humanism plunges him into contemporary empirical science, especially geology, medicine, and astronomy. When in London, he visited Gresham College, an important center of scientific investigation, and in 1684 he helped to found the Philosophical Society, a colonial equivalent of the Royal Society. Throughout his career, he stayed abreast of the Royal Society's *Transactions* and composed works which reveal technical understanding of the scientific revolution then taking place. [14]

Mather brings his various attitudes toward nature into precarious balance in the *Kometographia*. In this work, whose title literally suggests the readability of at least one aspect of nature, he uses a traditional agent of portent, the comet, to argue for nature's general intelligibility. Ostensibly, the work operates in the Calvinist / Platonic mode. Mather opens with the image of an omnipotent God flashing His anger through dread signs and proceeds to develop a traditional major premise, namely, that comets carry specific, ad hoc divine messages. This development takes a familiar tack, witnessed in other works of both Mather and his son, Cotton: namely, the recording of God's special Providences. In the course of exhaustively accounting for all recorded comets from creation through the year 1682, Mather emphasizes God's active, unpredictable role in history. He also notes that God has been more active recently, reflecting the orthodox Puritan belief that God exercises a higher degree of Providence in His covenant. Comets, Mather suggests, are portents having both signal and causal significance. When such ensigns "appear amidst the Heavenly host," what man observes is the hand of God "writing its Mene, Mene" (n.p.). John Sherman, in the book's preface, asserts in a similar vein that comets are "Red Letters, Asterisms" which have been placed "in the Margent" of nature, the "great and glorious volume of his [God's] Works" (n.p.). Their general purpose, according to Sherman, is "to awaken unto a more heedful attention and serious consideration, the dead hearted sleeping and secure World of Mankind" (n.p.).

Despite the traditional rhetoric, Mather does not ground his book-of-nature image in Augustinian faith, as he does in *Essay on Illustrious Providences*, published the following year. Rather than accepting his sources' authenticity without investigation, as in the *Essay* (thus deemphasizing the factual observation of nature), he documents the *Kometographia* using a purely Scholastic formula, the marshalling of authorities, here comprising "all the wise Men who lived in all former Ages" (131). Moreover, he begins the book with a chapter which approvingly analyzes contemporary scientific research on the subject. Although he occasionally refers to Scripture in this chapter, he mainly seems to want to bring his own statements into line with the theories of Royal Society scientists and their European counterparts. He appeals to relevant contemporary theory (discussing parallaxes, for example) and to contemporary authorities like Kepler and Hooke. In short, he tries to synthesize his theological piety with the new science, and the result is a necessary stabilizing of the phenomenon whose mystery he is attempting to maintain. By recognizing the authority of science and its empirical perspective on nature, Mather concludes that the "great and glorious volume" of God's works can be interpreted by the secular mind because the book is characterized by an observable rational order—the same conclusion supported by Scholastic and Ramist strains in the intellectual heritage. The concept of nature as book, more suited to the interests of the late seventeenth century than was the wilderness, still functions here as theological symbol. But this is a symbolism which does not necessarily make intelligibility solely the province of faith, Scripture, and a saint's regenerated reason.

The obvious conflict between the new science and the traditional orthodoxy that Mather is supporting becomes clear in the *Kometographia*, boding change for the future. By aligning his work with contemporary scientific theories, he confuses his defense. Such theories tend to repudiate empirically the very argument that he wishes to prove, namely, that comets cannot be predicted because they are the agents of a God whose will man cannot know in advance. Mather easily discredits the occasional chance prediction of astrology, noting that "if an Astrologer (as the blind man hits the mark) chance to praedict right once, more notice is taken of that, than of his mistaking an hundred times over" (17). However, he deals less successfully with the then-current observation that the conjunctions of planets seem to produce comets. Not wishing to contradict his scientific Puritan colleagues, he forces himself into an uncharacteristic admission: "Yet I will not deny, but that a probable conjecture, as to the year of a Comets appearance, may be made from the conjunction of the superiour Planets" (16). If successful conjectures regarding comets *can* be made by observing natural phenomena, even God's special Providences may indeed be bound by natural law. His Will can then be scrutinized, analyzed, and even predicted—and from a solely secular standpoint. Instead of facing the implications of this concession to mechanism, Mather moves quickly to the safer rejection of astrology noted above. Later in the chapter, when he discusses the empirical observation that comets are not always followed by evils, he manages to work out a solution that tentatively satisfies both his science and his theology: "God may in his merciful providence, cause such sights to be observed that so he might awaken Mortals to Repentance. He sometimes threateneth because he would not strike" (22). Nevertheless, in his zeal to accommodate the new science developed by his fellow Puritans in England, Mather demonstrates a frame of thinking about nature which would eventually help to void the Puritan universe of the numinosity that the latter-quoted statement affirms.

Meanwhile, even the nonscientific-minded of the period generally regard nature intellectually in the this-worldly terms of the Scholastic and humanist traditions. The consensus view is that nature is thoroughly pervaded by reason, so much so that the more Calvinistic orientation of earlier Puritans like John Cotton seems forgotten. In 1700, Mather's son—and John Cotton's grandson—Cotton awards nature virtually unrestricted praise in *Reasonable Religion*, declaring, "Let Reason look upon the World, the Various Parts of it, the curious Ends of it, the incomparable order of it; it will see a World of Reason" (15).

As the "World of Reason" became an increasingly descriptive phrase, nature became further secularized and objectified. In this context of change, empirical investigation revealed nature to be less a theophany of Divine Will and Wisdom than an exquisite artifact whose intricate order testifies to the ingenuity of the Artificer. An affinity developed for mechanistic theory to explain natural phenomena and the laws which govern their actions. Nature began to be regarded less as a book of revelation than as a handbook of physics and, perhaps secondarily, a digest of practical ethics. Not inappropriately, an important new image emerged: nature as machine. The foundation for such a view already existed, product of developments in continental mathematics and astronomy, and the view itself is implicit in the Puritan intellectual past, specifically in the Scholastic and Ramist belief in the inherent, objective order of the universe. Obviously, once one defines nature as a stable and regular subject of observation, the image of nature as a self-regulating machine, product of a distant Creator, requires only the abandonment of Aristotelian physics. The New England Puritans did not hesitate to follow their English contemporaries in taking that step.

Despite the early predominance of wilderness and book images, nature-as-machine (especially imaged as the clock) occasionally appears even in pre-emigration Puritan writings. John Preston, for example, argues for the evident workmanship in nature by declaring, "When you see the wheeles of a Watch fitted one to another . . . you say this is done by some Art, this is not by accident; Even so it is in nature"; Richard Sibbes uses the same image in describing how "by a continued kind of creation he [God] preserves all things in their being and working, . . . If God moves not, the clock of the creature stands" (Miller 225, 234). Numerous American Puritans follow their example in referring to the "wheels of providence," such that when a contemporary of Cotton Mather's, Ebeneezer Pemberton, describes in *The Divine Original and Dignity of Government* how "God has in all Ages so turned the Wheels of Providence as might suit the End of Government," or notes how according to God's direction "the Wheels and Loving Creatures move below," he recapitulates a long tradition (30, 53).

Cotton Mather uses a traditional conjunction of wheels and watch imagery to argue for nature's intelligibility in *Reasonable Religion*: "Were Ten Thousand Wheels Casually thrown together, would they fall so, that Seven or Eight of them, would form a well contriv'd Watch?" (15–16). His image does not indicate, of course, that he actually thinks of nature as a self-operating machine that is totally separate from God; the connections which Scholasticism assumes between God and man are too intimate and immediate for Mather's use of the machine image to be more than rhetorical strategy. In the subsequent *Christian Philosopher* (1721), however, the predominating frame is no longer Scholastic. Throughout this work, Mather displays great admiration for the "harmonious Regularity in the Motion of Bodies" (36). He applies the term "machine" to nature as a whole (87) and to its constituent parts. "Brutes" are "simple Machines" (209); man, a more complex organism, is "a Machine of a most astonishing Workmanship and Contrivance" (222), "a Machine composed of so many Parts, to the right Form, and Order, and Motion whereof there are such infinite number of Intentions required" (232). Such anatomical elements as the "motory Muscles," he declares, "we find in the Wheels of our Clocks" (271). Mather may deny that a mechanical agency conducts natural phenomena, yet he nevertheless describes the actual working of those phenomena in mechanical terms. In doing so, and by suggesting that a clock-like stability and precision are the properties of all nature, he comes to conclusions regarding Providence similar to those of the mechanists (see Jeske).

In the following decades, the incidence of machine imagery increases and evolves, revealing progressive Puritan acceptance of contemporary science's contention that nature *is* a machine rather than simply *like* one in an inductive proof of God's existence. Writings of the late 1720s and 1730s reveal extensive use of science and natural philosophy as occasions for piety, further securing a mechanistic outlook. Benjamin Colman, for example, refers to gravity, magnetism, electricity, and Newtonianism in general; his sermons are orthodox in context, but his use of scientific materials indicates a more modern, less directly theological world-picture than Calvin's. Meanwhile, a general negative attitude develops toward the traditional Puritan learning underlying the nature-as-book concept. Thus, Thomas Prince and Joseph Sewall, in their preface to the 1726 edition of Samuel Willard's *Compleat Body of Divinity*, apologize for their author's intellectual attachments, noting that "some Readers indeed may find the Author less exact in his Philosophical Schemes & Principles, which happen to be of a more ancient Date. . . . [O]ur Author chiefly flourish's when we were just emerging out of those Obscurities" (n.p.). What replaces the "Obscurities," however, are empirical assumptions at odds with the whole structure of Willard's belief, based as it was on Calvin and Ames.

A year after Mather's *The Christian Philosopher* and Willard's *A Compleat Body of Divinity*, and two years before Edward Taylor's death, a work appears which best illustrates the new mechanized concepts of Providence and hence of nature: James Allin's *The Wheels of the World Govern'd by a Wise Providence*. In an otherwise orthodox context, Allin paradigmatically transforms the traditional Puritan "wheels" image into the basis for a non-Puritan, quasi-scientific view of nature. He contends that, despite man's "short and contracted sight," God's Providence in nature is completely regular, on the model of a machine with a complex system of interlocking gears; even "those motions of the wheels that seem most confused are all regular, and there is nothing casual in them." Moreover, God is the consummate technician: He "always acts the geometrician, that is in all his works he keeps an exact proportion and harmony" (32). Even special Providences—if there are such—are actually part of nature's regular order, not interruptions of it. Only man's imperfect understanding prevents him from contemplating the machine-like precision of the whole: "There is a wheel in the midst of a wheel. As the lines of circles on a globe intersect one another, so the wheels of the world seem perplexed, and to our view and conception move without any regularity, and run one upon another" (28).

Allin uses Scholastic elements which qualify the secularizing tendencies suggested by the machine, but they still support a deist pattern. By insisting, for example, that the "wheels are moved by some external cause, and have no inherent vital principle of motion" (9), Allin preserves God's active role as "First Mover" whose constant attention maintains nature's order, i.e., "all the wheels of the affairs in the world." However, by deputing the actual management of nature to angels, Allin removes God from direct participation. In other words, Allin interposes mediate operators who increase the impersonality of God's role of Creator in His creation and whose agency contradicts the more characteristic position, expressed by Cotton Mather, that God "can easily govern the Machine He could create, by more direct Methods than employing such subservient Divinities" (*Christian Philosopher* 87). Allin's mechanistic interpretation denies both resemblance and the immediate connection of nature and the supernatural. Nature appears instead as a completed and separate monument to God's glory.

The machine image reflects Puritanism appropriately in its final stage. As orthodoxy became more rational, it also became more fixed and rule-bound, more legalistic. When acceptance of science increased, as did confidence in God's commitment to order and design, Puritanism lost the essential spirituality which the nonrational, quasi-mystical Calvinist core had formerly invested in both man and nature. In this new, nonaffective context, Puritanism ceased to be a dynamic entity; the second third of the eighteenth century, in which the final evolution of Puritanism takes place, reveals in effect the mechanization of what had been a vital religious form. In the 1730s, the expanding influence of literal, rational doctrines created relative dislike and suspicion of traditional Calvinist orthodoxy, the basic source of the emotional fervor of the founders. The Great Awakening of the early 1740s, partially a renewal of mystico-sacramentalism, actually brought an opposite effect by stimulating a counterreaction which opposed "enthusiasm" by making right reason the arbiter in religious experience. The Puritan schools remained basically orthodox for another decade, but with a greater admixture of rationalism and moralism. When such representative ministerial spokesmen as Ebeneezer Gay and Lemuel Briant began to enunciate opinions which resembled those of the Deists more than they did Calvin's, Puritanism—as a distinct mode of belief—disappeared altogether, though the sad apologetics of fundamentalism remained.

Taylor and the Traditions

Edward Taylor's poetry expresses most visibly the ontological and epistemological assumptions of Christian Platonism. Norman Grabo's phrase "mystical introversion" (173) well describes the poet's primary orientation. In a world where, as Taylor declares in his *Preparatory Meditations*, "The Creatures field no food for Souls e're gave" (I.1.14), the goal becomes transcendence; the fuel for upward flight is the passionate desire for union with Christ, who is pure being. Hence the prolific images of the wedding feast and the often baroque representation of the wished-for access to the mystical body.

The relationship between Taylor's sermons and poems in the process of mystic ascension has been well charted, the two together exemplifying a classical meditative pattern whose goal is heavenly mindedness and whose driving force is hunger for consummation of the intimacy that the poem prefigures. First comes the sermon, which awakens the mind and its rational desires and sets forth Christ's qualities in a rigid intellectual analysis. Then, when the limits of the world-bound mind have been reached, occurs the liberating "O Altitudo," the flight into colloquy with

the object of desire, the flight into song. "Meditating in poetic form,"
suggests Karen Rowe, "becomes his [Taylor's] personal process for
imprinting spiritual images within his soul in a repeated act . . . that
reminds him constantly of his need for the Savior and reassures him of
his status as an elect saint" (249). In both the *Preparatory Meditations*
and *Gods Determinations*—also primarily a meditation—the movement
is away from nature and toward union with Christ.

Taylor establishes nature's lack of epistemological value in his
Christographia: "All the Wealth, and Wisdom of this World is not
comparable to the Treasures of Wisdom in Christ. . . . He is altogether
the best" (128). Taylor expresses the same principle poetically in the
Preparatory Meditations:

> The Suns bright Glory's but a smoky thing
> Though it oft 'chants man's fancy with its flashes.
> All other glories, that from Creatures spring
> Are less than that. . . .

(2.100.31–34)

Given that one's meditative goal is to reflect on divine wisdom and
glory, Taylor asks, "Where should the Hongry man goe for good but to
the Cooks Shop? Where should the Thirsty go for water but to the
Fountain? No man will let his bucket down into an empty Well if he be
aware of it. No man will Seek Riches in a beggers Cottage"
(*Christographia* 134).

Not only is the image of grace comparatively indistinct in the "beggers
Cottage" of nature, but nature's very position in the Platonist cosmology
requires the seeker after the image-in-nature to look away from Christ,
who occupies a place either in heaven or, as in "The Reflexion," "'Tween
Heaven and Earth." To tarry in nature while ransacking it for metaphors
is to risk becoming further enmeshed and thus less able to transcend, for
"Flesh and Blood, are Elementall things / That sink me down, dulling my
Spirits fruit. / Life Animall a Spirituall Sparke ne'er springs" (II.82.8–
10). Taylor warns, in sermon 8 of the *Christographia,* that the physical
world is "So ready to inchant the Carnall Eyes of men with her poisonous
trinkets" (255).

It is not surprising, then, that Taylor's nature images are so often
derived not from direct observation but from the Bible and from
exegetical, typological, and emblem traditions: Christ has irradiated the
first directly; the latter three provide time-tested metaphorical systems.
The fact that Taylor is classed with the metaphysicals provides an
appropriate commentary, given that the word itself—"metaphysical"—

literally means "beyond the physical." Further, Norman Grabo notes, unlike the other metaphysical poets, Taylor chooses images which suggest that his poetry is "rooted as firmly in the Middle Ages as it is in his own century" (172).

As Alan Howard points out in "The World as Emblem: Language and Vision in the Poetry of Edward Taylor," the wild metaphysical juxtaposition of images often demonstrates that Taylor "has moved with rather traditional decorum between two related allegorical comparisons already drawn for him by the church fathers" (362). The emblem tradition existed, according to Howard, as a preexisting "metaphorical landscape" (363), and thus it is within the hearts, candles, trees, and lanterns of that conventional body of images that Taylor's poetry must be read. The insect motif in "Upon a Spider Catching a Fly," for example, comes directly from two medieval Latin exempla. "Huswifery" derives entirely from the emblem tradition. Grabo argues that "*all* of Taylor's symbols are conventional in devotional literature" (emphasis mine) and says, "Only his [Taylor's] strange eye for peculiar details, his going one step beyond the convention, and his domesticating his symbols with kitchen details give his symbolism a quaint, sometimes grotesque, individual quality" (154). Specific usages, such as "Heaven's sugar cake" and "Zion's pastry," may be inventive, but the allegorical subject—the feast—is commonplace.

Given Taylor's theological and artistic preoccupations, it is entirely appropriate that, besides the wedding feast, it should be the garden / wilderness relationship which provides the most predominating imagistic theme in both of the *Preparatory Meditations*, notably in the series of Canticles poems which depend entirely upon the *hortus conclusus* motif. For one thing, the opposition of garden and wilderness graphically expresses the fundamental dualism at Christian Platonism's core. There is the perfect, spiritual world of the garden and the corrupted, rank, and inferior world of the wilderness. Nature, Taylor tells us in I.43.7–8, is "Corrupt, a nest of Passion, Pride, / Lust, Worldliness, and such like bubs." Finding oneself in the latter, the goal of the seeker after grace is to somehow translate oneself, as suggested by Taylor's alchemical imagery, into the former.

Moreover, the garden / wilderness theme accords well with the Puritan's defining errand, permitting direct typological correspondences with the Israelites' exodus from slavery in Egypt to a new covenant in Canaan. Taylor explores these relationships directly in the *Preparatory Meditations* (e.g., II.58–61), finding both social and personal resonance in the imagery. On the one hand, "This Garden, Lord" is "thy Church, this Paradise" (II.83.19); the new Canaan is the Puritan community, established as Winthrop's "Citty upon a Hill." On the other, the garden is also the wished-for destination and identity of the individual soul. In the drama of salvation, each individual must pursue a course through the wilderness of sin to reach the union with Christ that Taylor's wedding imagery expresses. Hence Taylor's plea,

> Then lead me, Lord, through all this Wilderness
> By this Choice shining Pillar Cloud and Fire.
> By Day, and Night I shall not then digress.
> If thou wilt lead, I shall not lag nor tire
> But as to Cana'n I am journeying
> I shall thy praise under this Shadow sing.

(II.59.31–36)

The poet, himself a part of the "transplanting" from England, asks, "Hast made mee, Lord, one of thy Garden Beds?" (II.84.1). He beseeches, "Open thy garden doore: mee entrance give / And in thy Nut tree garden make me live" (II.63.53–54). This is the "sweet Rosy Bower" set apart from the "gawdy world" in I.4.; it is the site of "The fairest Rose that Grows in Paradise," in whose leaves Taylor seeks to lodge (I.4.16). Within the garden, he will thrive beneath Christ's sunshine (II.54) and showers (II.31), suck in "Aromatick aire of blesst perfume" (II.63.52), blossom like a lily (II.69), feast on "bitter Myrrh" and "Sweet Spices" (II.84.7, 22).

As a garden bed set with "True Love. Herb of Grace with Rosie Sheds" (II.86.33), Taylor expects to enjoy a special ontological relationship with Christ, suggested by his question in "The Reflexion," "Shall not thy Rose my Garden fresh perfume?" (37). In fact, Christ is not only the gardener but, as suggested in poems imaging Christ as either Rose of Sharon or lily of the valley, a flower planted in Taylor's bed. Thus, in I.5:

> My Blessed Lord, art thou a Lilly Flower?
>   Oh! that my Soul thy Garden were, that so
> Thy bowing Head root in my Heart, and poure
>   Might of its Seeds, that they therein might grow.
>   Be thou my Lilly, make thou me thy knot:
>   Be thou my Flowers, I'le be thy Flower Pot.

(ll. 1–6)

Taylor also uses the "knot" image in "Upon Wedlock, and Death of Children," where he envisions himself being planted in "A Curious Knot God made in Paradise" (l. 1) and then himself knotting out in his children. In this poem, Christ is depicted as external to the garden: His is the hand which comes "from glory," guarded by angels, to crop his children / flowers and bring them to heaven. However, in II.40, which Taylor composed upon the death of his "primrose" son, James, the poet suggests that Christ's indwelling in the garden can heal his acute sorrow. Taylor asks,

> Yet let the Rose of Sharon spring up cleare,
>   Out of my James his ashes unto mee,
> In radient sweet and shining Beames to cheer
>   My sorrowfull Soule, and light my way to thee

(ll. 13–16)

The recurrent negative note sounds when, in assessing his relationship to the heavenly gardener, the poet looks within optimistically only to "finde my Garden over grown with weeds" (II.4.2; cf. the "throng of Stinking Weeds" in II.131). This discovery leads logically to fear of abandonment, for, if the Lord *has* established Taylor as one of his garden beds, Taylor expects that He will have "Stub'd up the Brush, toore up the Turfy head," "Combt it with thy Harrow teeth likewise," and "set therein thy Myrrhy Trees that so / Sweet Spice might in this Garden bed forth flow" (II.84.3, 4, 5–6). The inevitable discovery of the wilderness element, partly a contamination from outside the hedge, reinforces his orthodox desire to flee the things of this world. It is from without that comes the "inkefac'd sin" that destroys paradise in "The Reflexion," from without that blows the "Hellish breath" that singes the plumes of Taylor's children in "Upon Wedlock, and Death of Children." In a turn on the knot image that demonstrates the danger to the soul / garden of the external world's intrusion, Taylor notes in I.24.29 how "Earth's Toyes ware Knots of my Affections": the budding, in other words, may no longer serve the Lord.

Before the Fall, nature's situation was wholly different:

> That Bowre, my Lord, which thou at first didst build
> Was pollished most gay, and every ranck
> Of Creatures in't shone bright, each of them filld
> With dimpling Glory . . .

(2.28.1–4)

But now it is a scene of "Beauty blasted" and "Bliss befrighted," and Taylor occupies "This lowest pit more dark than night" (II.77.18). The New Jerusalem exists elsewhere, not in this world, which Taylor, like John Cotton before him, characterizes as a "Wilderness of Sin." He as

well as his congregation must turn away, seek purification, bid farewell
to "My Old-New Cloaths my Wildernesses Ware" (II.10.21).

It is true that Taylor specifies that his wilderness is "the unplanted
wilderness of New England's frostbitten clime." As Grabo notes,
Taylor's gardens are "curiously removed to New England, where grains
as well as flowers abound" (152). Nevertheless, one can argue that the
particularization of images in *Preparatory Meditations*, the linking of his
theme to a specific physical place, signifies not a lapse from the
prevailing Platonism but the poet's deliberate extending of allegory to
fuel further his flight *from* place. As Alan Howard notes of *Gods
Determinations*, the individual image often exists "only at the point at
which it touches the idea of God. . . . Each image is . . . shorn of any
associations with the context from which it was drawn, cleansed of the
penumbra of connotations which belong to the world of accidental
appearances rather than of essences" (382). Where the images of the
lower world are concerned, the poet asks appropriately, "Should Stars
Wooe Lobster Claws?"

Given Taylor's use of garden / wilderness imagery, especially to
define allegorically his relationship with Christ, given his specific
interdictions of the natural world, and given his stated hesitancy to look
at it, much less seek traces of the divine glory there, one must tentatively
classify Taylor as far less of a "nature poet" than Anne Bradstreet, far
less a prefigurer than Jonathan Edwards of the Puritan—and
Transcendental—nature philosophy that was to come.

A keen student of Ramistic logic, Taylor validates nature's positive
ontological and epistemological status despite his Platonism. For
example, in *Preparatory Meditations*, he characterizes nature as:

> Thy Lower House, this World well garnished
>   With richest Furniture of Ev'ry kinde
> Of Creatures of each Colours varnished
>   Most glorious . . .

(II.93.13–16)

The poet suggests that, after the Fall, nature still expresses the divine
prerogative and the divine glory. Christ continues to sustain nature
directly: it is the site of "Love Divine," "Love" which "doth swim /
Through veans, through Arteries, Heart Flesh" (II.34.27–28).

Even had Taylor not known the Scholastic texts, he would have found
this other, more positive, perspective in Scripture. The predominating
atmosphere in both Testaments is this-worldly. As a record of temporal
history, the Old Testament shows no bias for detachment but rather

savors of earthly experience and high esteem for God's works. Likewise, the Synoptic Gospels and non-Pauline Epistles display respect, if not affection, for the things of the world. Matthew's Gospel, in contrast to John's, floods a mystic twilight with the common light of day. The ennobling of material existence by Christ's Incarnation, an afterthought in Paul and John, is continually highlighted in the convincing Synoptic presentation of Jesus as a living person.

Neither does the Synoptic Jesus recommend detachment. Passages advising the surrender of personal property and the severing of familial relationships, and statements such as "Whosoever will lose his life for my sake shall find it" (Matt. 16.25), only seem to support a world-denyingness as far-reaching as Paul's. The difference is that the Synoptic Jesus does not recommend denying earthly things because they have innate defects. The more immediate reason is that, because the Kingdom of God is at hand, bringing with it total dissolution of the status quo, whoever wishes to participate in the Kingdom must see to the immediate spiritual preparations God requires. The Synoptic Jesus does not devalue nature intrinsically; He approves of the rain, the sunshine, and the lilies of the field (Matt. 5.45, 6.28–29).

The Synoptic Jesus preaches conversion but not absorption into a mystic body which is at odds with nature. In declaring "Except ye be converted, and become as little children, ye shall not enter into the kingdom of heaven" (Matt. 18.3), Jesus advises man to seek *metanoia*, the change of heart which brings about a changed manner of living. Synoptic conversion does not consist in ontological transformation, and individual salvation in the Synoptics does not depend upon separation from the world but upon obedience to God's will in it (Matt. 7.21).

In the Preface to *Gods Determinations*, Taylor declares that God "Gave All to nothing Man indeed, whereby / Through nothing man all might him Glorify" (ll. 37–38). In doing so, he specifies another type of conversion that man can accomplish: the conversion of nature into an expression of the divine glory which it already implicitly embodies. In the *Christographia*, Taylor reminds us that the "whole Creation doth bring all its Shining Glory, as a Sacrifice to be offered up to God from, and upon the Altar of the Rationall Creature in Sparkling Songs of praise to God" (312). Ironically, nature is superior in this enterprise to the human product, for "Nature doth better work than Art" (II.56.43). Art is but "Nature's Ape." Nevertheless, man is enjoined by God—and by Richardson and Ames—to use his art to celebrate and perhaps explicate the divine glory found in the world.

It is not surprising, then, that Taylor's poetry provides a digest of images drawn from nature. Moreover, even though these images often do come secondhand through Scripture, the poetry remains grounded in the concrete circumstances of Taylor's life so much so that, as William Scheick has demonstrated in "'The Inward Tacles and the Outward Traces': Edward Taylor's Transitions," a coherent interpretation of some of the *Meditations* depends upon thorough knowledge of seventeenth-century lore. In general, Taylor's multiple roles as minister, physician, and cultivator yield a rich fabric of specific, sensory images which contribute a kinesthetic quality to his poetry. Karen Rowe observes that the poems "abound with tropes of disease, putrefactions, scatology, of rivers, gardens, farming, wine casking, weaving, games, cookery, birds, beasts, insects, journeys" (246). We find references to cockerils, tennis balls, tobacco, oaten straw, the "linsy-wolsy loom," inoculation, candied apples, and marigolds used to treat trembling of the heart. This "Earthy Globe" is a "Cocoe Nut" (II.34.1). We find "Canoes" which are "Paddling with joyes along Christ's bloodstream" (II.78.32). Where the soul is the womb, "Christ is the Spermadote" (II.80).

Nature also has great epistemological value for the poet. In imitating Christ, one may not ignore that the Savior's life was a teaching life, that He used parables to bridge the spiritual and the temporal, dignifying nature in the process. For the poet eager to share in both the hidden knowledge and the living Covenant of Grace, nature offers a bridge via metaphor. Though blasted by the Fall, nature remains a repository of divine wisdom, and this wisdom is implicitly available to human understanding. "Oh the wisdom of the Works of the Creation!" declares Taylor in the *Christographia*:

> Cast an eye upon the Elementary Bodies from the Stars to the Centre of the earth, the Various Sorts of Birds, fowls the various Sorts, and Kinds of Beasts, Dragons, Scorpions, Worms, Insects, Fishes, etc. So the variety of Herbs, Flowers, Bushes, Shrubs, plants, Seeds, Fruits, trees: and all these made exactly according to the Draught of the Decree, in Nature, Matter, Form, Shape, Size, Properties, Qualities, Vertues, Spirits, Tempers, Springings, growing, Durations, Decayings, to keep their Natures, Seasons, etc., and so successfully on to go by the hand of Providence to the end of the World. I say, the Wisdom that hath done all this, and chiefly that hath made Man, and put Wisdom into the inward parts, is Wonderfull. Here is Wisdom indeed. (114–15)

In acknowledging that nature displays divine wisdom, Taylor draws upon the rich Renaissance concept of the "book of nature," a concept central to the emblem tradition that Taylor found so influential in his art and whose assumptions are reflected in such Taylor statements as "There stands *imprinted* upon the nature of the creation a declaration of the will of God in semblences of one part unto another; and one thing unto another. So also in the disposal and management of the whole, and of each part" (Grabo 89–90; emphasis mine). Finding that this view of nature's epistemological usefulness conflicts with his more otherworldly orientation, Taylor reconciles it by claiming it for only the elect. Like Jonathan Edwards, who posits a "new sense of things" as a condition of regeneracy, a new sense that enables one to comprehend divine revelation not only in Scripture but in nature, Taylor identifies a new "discerning," one that is specific to the spiritualized person and unavailable to the unconverted (see North). In the context of the Lord's Supper, this discerning enables the communicant to perceive the body of Christ in the sacrament. In the context of the physical world, it enables the perception of God's wisdom in nature by allowing one to see beneath the defilement which the Fall has spread over creation, a defilement that Taylor repeatedly depicts in the *Preparatory Meditations:* the state of sin is a state of blindness; Christ provides the "Eye Salve" to correct the "Sin blind Eye" (2.147). The infusion of grace is a shower of beams of glorious light that dispatches darkness and permits true vision. [15]

If divine wisdom is manifest in nature and available to the regenerated sense of the saint, and if the highest goal is union with the Savior, it is not surprising that yearning for nature should arise. Granted, unlike Edwards, Taylor does not reach out with feeling to nature for the divine essence—there is no hint of pantheism—but he does reach out with his regenerated reason to explore the creaturely field of vision and claim it for poetic use. It is worth noting that Taylor shares with his contemporaries great confidence in regenerated reason's efficacy. His faith—and his sermons—are extensively based in the intellect. Noting his prodigious output, Karen Rowe calls him a "defiant intellectual" (25), and Norman Grabo suggests that he emphasized reason "even more than most of his colleagues, and they are startling for their rationality" (45). The result, when Taylor applies reason to nature for poetic purposes, is the formation of types and tropes. The legitimacy of both depends on a commitment to nature's intelligibility as a book.

Taylor understands the nature of divine illumination to mean that typological relationships inhere in nature: the light of divine glory shines through natural phenomena (the types) to fall directly on the antitype, Christ himself, who reflects it back outward in turn. Thus Taylor's phrase "The glory of the world slickt up in types" (II.1.13) and his suggestion of specific typical relationships (e.g., sun / Son) which the regenerated eye can perceive. On this basis, Karl Keller claims kinship for Taylor with Jonathan Edwards and beyond with the Transcendentalists ("The World

Slickt Up in Types"). Edwards, of course, for whom the traditional concept of the book of nature is also integral, moves much farther than Taylor, actually defining a system of specific typological correspondences in *Images or Shadows of Divine Things*. In doing so, he integrates Lockeian empiricist epistemology and fundamentally alters the essence of the typological scheme. Exegetical typology is linear and historical; for Edwards, "type and antitype [are] present together in the eternal mystical moment that transcend[s] all time in a 'sweet' and beautiful experience of union" (Lowance 243). Taylor does not pursue such nature-bound mystical possibilities. Nor does he believe that nature offers an equally weighted alternative to scriptural revelation. Nevertheless, by establishing that typological relationships do exist in nature, he lays an epistemological foundation for the developments that Edwards embodies.[16]

Perhaps realizing the dangerous implications of natural types, Taylor is much more comfortable with tropes, i.e., fanciful, individually fashioned correspondences between observed phenomena and spiritual truth. Tropology takes two chief forms in Taylor. One, a distinguishing feature of the *Preparatory Meditations*, is the often "metaphysical" use of images from nature in metaphor and analogy, as in Meditation I.4, where Taylor establishes a correspondence between the use of syrup of roses as purgative with Christ's role of "chymist" and the use of his blood as purgative. The second is Taylor's "spiritualizing" of nature's events. Orthodox Puritan tract writers and sermonizers ardently sought moral meanings and lessons in Providence's events and used these to "improve" readers and listeners. Taylor, characterizing the world as "big belli'd with all Wonders rare" (II.89.6), follows their lead.

Where Taylor's metaphors and analogies pay tribute to the creating wisdom expressed statically by "The Works of Creation," spiritualizing often takes as its province the kinetic "Managing Wisdom" expressed in "The Works of Providence": "Creation having brought all things into being, doth forthwith deliver them up into the hande of Providence to mannage and Conduct them thro' the various Successions of the world unto the uttmost period of time . . . in all their Actions, Passions, Motions, Mutations, Uses, Influences, Complections" (*Christographia* 115). Taylor acknowledges in the same passage that "such knowledge is too wonderful for me," but this limitation does not prevent him from speculating on the meaning of events.

The seventeenth century, in David Hall's words, presented a "world of wonders," a universe full of events which demonstrated the presence of the supernatural, both divine and demonic. Miracles demonstrated not only God's power to suspend natural order but also His wish to communicate His will, however veiled this might be from men's minds. Karl Keller documents how Taylor collected "remarkable Providences" throughout his career, as early as his Harvard notebooks. His common-place books reveal him "hunting constantly for evidence of the divine in the phenomenal, bizarre, and exotic" (*Example* 61). He furnished exam-ples of such Providences to Increase Mather for Mather's use in his *Essay for the Recording of Illustrious Providences*, published in 1684.

Demonstrating again the usefulness of the book image, this fascination with collecting Providences, along with the corresponding tendency to moralize them, occasionally appears directly in the poetry, as in "Upon the Sweeping Flood August: 13.14, 1683," where Taylor allegorizes the significance of the overflowing of the Connecticut and Woronoco rivers:

> Oh! that Id had a tear to've quencht that flame
>> Which did dissolve the Heavens above
>> Into those liquid drops that Came
>>> To drown our Carnall love.
> Our cheeks were dry and eyes refusde to weep.
> Tears bursting out ran down the skies darke Cheek.
>
> Were th'Heavens sick? must wee their Doctors bee
>> And physick them with pills, our sin?
>> To make them purg and Vomit, see,
>>> And Excrements out fling?
> We've griev'd them by such Physick that they shed
> Their Excrements upon our lofty heads.

(1–12)

Such spiritualizing, unlike his flirtation with natural types, reaffirms orthodoxy. Based on the conviction of Providence's fundamental unknowability, expressed in miracles that transcend common sense, spiritualizing keeps human reason within limits and supports Taylor's keen preference for more certain knowledge of the resurrected Christ found in Scripture and for a life pitched in the world of spirit rather than the world of nature. Addressing Christ, Taylor declares, "Life Naturall indeed is in the Bill / Thou with thy Father drest up, it to buy. / Life Spirituall much more; which ever Will / As Heaven doth Earth, all Naturall Life out Vie" (II.89.31–34).

Still, Taylor is also willing to approve of the empirical investigations that in his time were charting the harmonious regularity of God's "Managing Wisdom," wisdom that, in being better known and under-stood, could no longer be "too wonderful" for poetic use. Ironically, the same minister / poet who had fought with Solomon Stoddard to preserve

the garden helps to secure—and, given future developments, simultaneously undermine—the image of nature as book.

Edward Taylor, grandson Ezra Stiles later observed, "was . . . Very
curious in Botany, Minerals, and nat. History." Among the volumes of
his large library were numerous texts related to science and medicine.
The diary he kept aboard ship on his passage to America, with its
detailed observation of fish and birds, was only the prelude to the
recording which occupied him throughout his active life as a minister,
cultivator, and physician. Following studies in natural history at Harvard,
he set himself at Westfield to copying extracts from other authors and
combining them with his own observations in two large compendia, one
dealing with metallurgy and the other, his *Dispensatory,* with plants and
their medical applications. Karl Keller notes the "scientifically sensitive
eye" demonstrated in observations regarding natural phenomena which
Taylor sent to Increase Mather in 1681 (*Example* 61).

Keller goes on, however, to emphasize Taylor's limitations as a
scientist. He states that, unlike Cotton Mather,

> who worked with smallpox inoculation, ornithological nidification, plant
> hybridization, psychiatry, and theories of disease—Taylor was little more
> than a conventional religious consoler, bloodletter, and herb-healer. He did
> not have the open and encyclopedic mind of Mather; he was neither erudite
> nor original. (67)

Taylor's world was chiefly Ptolemaic and his interest in it theological.
He distrusted his senses and regarded the universe as shot through with
special Providences that carried the direct voice of an inscrutable creator.
Scientific observations served only to strengthen faith, and they remained
subordinate to it—thus the absence in Taylor's writings of inductive
reasoning, the keystone of the modern scientific method.

Taylor's subordination of scientific learning is clearly evident in his
poetry. Even the special Providences that he observed in nature tend not
to appear, and when they do it is to serve a meditative end. Though the
phenomenon is noted, the poet's attention does not tarry there; the goal is
transcendence, not empirical analysis. William Scheik observes that
Taylor does employ contemporary scientific knowledge when, in
Meditation II.10, he compares Joshua to a comet and suggests the same
relationship between Joshua and Christ that current theory posited as
existing between comets and the sun ("That Blazing Star" 10–11). But
whereas Increase Mather had acknowledged a damaging kinship with his
science-minded colleagues in acknowledging that "a probable

conjecture" could be made about comets by observing the planets, and Cotton had gone even further, citing Seneca's prediction "that a time should come, when our Mysteries of Comets should be unfolded" and declaring that such time "seems almost accomplished," especially given Halley's calculations for predicting a comet's return (*Christian Philosopher* 43–44), Taylor focuses squarely on the comet's signal role and on the typological relationship between Joshua and Christ:

> Our Joshua doth draw his Troops out to
>   The Lunar coast, this Jericho the world
> And rounds it while the Gospell Levites blow
>   Their Gospell Rams Horn Trumpets till down hurld
>   Its walls lie flat, and it his sacrifice
>   Doth burn in Zeale, whose Flame doth sindge the Skies.
>
> As Joshuah doth fight Haile Stones smite down
>   The Can'anites: so Christ with Haile Stones shall
> Destroy his Enemies, and breake their Crown.

(II.10.31–39)

Appropriately, given Taylor's concurrent role of physician, it is medical imagery that appears most frequently of the "scientific" images. It is here, if anywhere, that we see Taylor moving—if only preliminarily—along the path leading to modern, secular science. In "'This Brazen Serpent is a Doctors Shop': Edward Taylor's Medical Vision," Catherine Rainwater demonstrates that, although Taylor's medical references often depend upon the more traditional Galenic philosophy, he is clearly attracted to the "new medicine" of Paracelsus, which attributes disease to the invasion of the body by foreign substances and looks to the natural world for curative agents. Taylor is able to synthesize Paracelsus with Augustinian theology through a significant common element, namely, the interpretation of physical disease as an outward sign of spiritual affliction. The Paracelsan healing act necessarily includes a spiritual dimension. Plants, herbs, and chemicals are "ordained channels for spiritual healing" (Rainwater, "Brazen Serpent," 60). Given the close correspondence between natural and spiritual phenomena, the Paracelsans regard nature as a book that, along with the Bible, can lead to God's truth. It is not surprising that, as both a minister and a physician treating with herbs, Taylor would find Paracelsan medicine interesting. The system also accords well with his willingness to see nature as an instructive book: because of the close correspondence they posit between material and spiritual phenomena, the Paracelsans logically also regard nature as a book, a book that along with the Bible can lead to God's truth. The framework takes on an added numinous character for the christocentric Taylor, who regards nature then as the conduit for Christ's immanent healing influence.

Examples of poems containing Paracelsan-related medical references appear in both series of *Preparatory Meditations*. In "The Reflexion," Taylor identifies Christ not only as "Meat" but "Med'cine"; the poet seeks to be infused inwardly with the healing agent of grace: "let thy spirit raise my sighings till / These Pipes my soule do with thy sweetness fill" (ll. 17–18). Corresponding to the supernatural agent, though, is the physical agent, that can treat the physical ill that follows from and mirrors its spiritual counterpart.

Taylor provides a catalogue of such physical agents—Catholicons, Palma Christi, Gilliad's Balm, Unguent, Apostolorum—in Meditation I.4, agents whose healing action resembles "The Reflexion's" "Golden Spade" of grace, which can "cleare this filth away." Just as the heavenly "Chymist," God, distils "Oyle, Syrup, Sugar and Rose Water" from the Rose of Sharon / Christ into a "Cordiall" which can ease "Heart burns Causd by sin" (ll. 43–47), so can the human chemist "make a Physick sweet, sure, safe." Of this poem, Davis comments that Taylor is "perhaps too insistent on bringing into the poem all the medicinal plants he can think of in contrast to Sharon's Rose . . . too insistent on running the range of ailments" (56). Ironically, it is this intrusion of sheer physicality that threatens the poem's complex thematic texture, this in a poem that opens with establishing the poet's preference for Christ / the rose of Sharon over the allurements of the "gawdy World."

Poems influenced by Paracelsan thinking also occur in Series II, where Taylor is otherwise retreating from the affairs of the world and toward union with Christ. Meditation II.61, for example, links the physician's caduceus with the serpent that Moses lifted on a wooden pole to heal the spirits of the querulous Israelites (a type of Christ on the cross) and lays out the Paracelsan notion that like heals like:

> This Brazen Serpent is a Doctors Shop,
>   On ev'ry Shelfe's a Sovereign remedy.
> The Serpents Flesh the Sovereign Salve is got
>   Against the Serpents bite, gaind by the eye.
>   The Eyebeames agents are that forth do bring
>   The Sovereign Counter poison, and let't in.

(ll. 31–36)

Underlying such poems is Taylor's acceptance of a system in which (1) a fixed book (nature) can be read and interpreted by a fixed body of knowledge, and (2) man can use the results of this reading empirically and concretely to bring positive benefit to the world in a process that not only images but may be the actual vehicle of Christ's healing activity. For Taylor, this system is itself sacramental and thus conservative. Nevertheless, Rainwater argues convincingly that Taylor's eclecticism in grafting a Paracelsan vision onto his orthodox poetry demonstrates how he "resembles many of the great innovators of his age in his progressive attitudes toward change and uncertainty" ("Brazen Serpent" 53).[17]

Though referring to current theories of comets or optics, Taylor displays no inclination, as Cotton Mather does in the *Biblia Americana*, to reconcile the new learning with Scripture directly. He is content to let the new material stand as just one more source of knowledge to be used in support of his poetic aims. Given his predominating piety, Taylor appears unaware even of the potential for conflict that the assimilation of empirical science brings. After all, his own fixation on the eternal guarantees that the distance between the world and the craftsman God portrayed in *Gods Determinations* does not secularize the former. Nevertheless, in legitimizing empirical science as a touchstone for understanding, however indirectly, Taylor makes it possible for others who are less spiritually focused to study nature for its own secular merits and in a larger sense to dichotomize theology and science.

Taylor displays this tendency himself in the unfinished poem titled "The Great Bones of Clavarack." The occasion for the poem was the discovery, in July 1705, of giant bones and teeth in New York. As in earlier instances where Taylor recorded unusual events, he copied the account of this discovery into his diary. After more bones and teeth were found in 1706 and Taylor himself was able to witness one of the teeth, he recorded his observations and began writing the poem. What is striking about the observations, notes Lawrence L. Sluder, is that they are "notably objective and lack any Biblical references, whereas both Governor Dudley and Cotton Mather, the latter reporting the curiosity to the Royal Society, make references to Biblical types" (267).

The poem consists of a prologue and two subsequent sections (apparently of an intended three), for a total of 190 lines. What is remarkable—for Taylor—is that, like his recorded observations of the discoveries, the poem features empirical observation free of theological "improvements." In the Prologue, God scarcely appears. Sluder notes that this section of the poem contains imagery that can profitably be compared with that in Meditation II.47, a poem based on the same theme of "Originall Spring or rise of [nature]," but that

in his poem on the bones Taylor has taken a personal relationship and abstracted it to the natural world, from the Tree of Life to the Tree of Nature.

In the *Meditations*, Taylor talks of himself and he cannot talk of himself without in the same breath mentioning God; but when he perceives Nature in this poem, he perceives nature's wonders as predominant, while God the Prime Mover is in the background. (269)

Recalling the mediate operators of the "natural theology" tradition, which was peaking in England in the late seventeenth and early eighteenth centuries, Taylor delegates supervision of the earthly realm to "Nature." Thus, in the Prologue, it is "kinde nature that raised up these monstrous Bulks of Humane kinde." No mention is made of the sustaining influence of Christ or the Holy Spirit. The secular emphasis also appears in the poem's two following sections, "The Gyant described" and "The Description thus Proved," where it is human reason, rather than piety, which engages directly with the wonders both to measure and to verify. What is verified is not God's but "Natures glory." The "sweet musicke" of the earthly sphere, Taylor declares in the Prologue, is produced not by the heavenly host but by nature herself—"By all her Bagpipes, Virginalls and Harps."

Never in his extant poems does Taylor employ the image of nature directly as "machine." However, the *Preparatory Meditations* are laced with the images of clocks, comets, magnets, and current theories of optics, all of which, as his contemporaries demonstrate, can be used to support the nature-as-machine concept—once the assumptions underlying a poem such as "The Great Bones of Claverack" are developed and expanded.

Conclusion

Karen Rowe has observed that, partly because he is "at the nexus of so many traditions," Edward Taylor "has continued to defy ready assimilation into single categories" and that he "raises issues as fascinating as they are problematic" (xi). A survey of his poetry suggests that, in terms of Taylor's views of nature and use of nature imagery, Rowe is correct. Platonic, Scholastic, and, to a much lesser extent, contemporary scientific thought intermingle in his poetry, helping account both for its richness and, ultimately, for the contradictions which in a larger view characterize Puritanism itself in his period.

What holds together and dominates the various strands in Taylor's thinking is his Augustinian piety. Poetry and sermons alike are Christocentric. Types, emblems, and images from nature all unify ultimately in the Savior, and the poet's trajectory is upward, away from the world even as he celebrates it. Norman Grabo suggests that only once in the *Meditations*, in II.99, does Taylor "describe a natural phenomenon as if he wished to capture its nature rather than to apply it to some other use," and that "even in this description of the moon, the focus immediately shifts upward as the moon's illumination appropriately disappears in the light of the Sun of Righteousness" (151). Generally, Taylor finds even the "Excellency in Created Shells" insufficient, for "Choise things" are "a Shaddow," and types merely dull shades compared with the Lord's dazzling glory (II.1.8, 14, 16).

Nevertheless, "Choise things" do exist, and there is an "excellency" in the lower world. Nature is not only a wilderness but a book in which can be read God's wisdom. Rainwater suggests in this regard that "over the years, Taylor more and more confidently interprets the new and strange phenomena of a revised Book of Nature as signifiers in a system circumscribed by a constant book of God" ("Brazen Serpent" 57). In this view, nature exhibits an independent positive value which can be maintained even if the spiritual and temporal split, as happens progressively in the eighteenth century. Unlike Jonathan Edwards, Taylor does not show pantheistic tendencies in his works, such that when the split begins to occur, a dangerous chasm opens: God remains transcendent, detached; nature, as in "The Great Bones of Claverack," becomes independent and partly the source of its own glory. For Taylor himself, this division is not consequential. For others, though, and for Puritanism generally after Taylor, nature loses its spiritual charge, and when it does, mystical flight using nature as a springboard becomes more difficult.

It is not easy to reconcile empirical science and a sacramental universe. Moreover, the implications of the view that God has established everything with the original act of Creation, and that events unfold without His active intervention, are obvious. Without special Providences, the image of nature as wilderness, at least as it was defined by the Puritan fathers, has little meaning. Even the image of nature as book loses its descriptiveness once it is agreed that causality in the creatures does not *immediately* reflect divine principles but demonstrates the activity of a secondary agent—nature itself. As secularization increases, nature inevitably becomes little more than a physics text detailing the formulae with which an immaterial Creator works when setting material nature in motion. Increase Mather, who posits the concept of nature-as-book as well as embraces the new science, recognized this difficulty and after the *Kometographia* did not deal with the issue directly again. In *Illustrious Providences*, he retreated to an atomistic version of divine control, attempting to reinvigorate the

otherworldly belief in special, supernatural dispensations by focusing
almost exclusively on Providences, many of them fantastic, which
occurred in New England. Later, he solaced himself with chiliasm.
Cotton Mather demonstrated a similar retreat after *The Christian
Philosopher*. Having contributed to a more empirical view of nature, he
backtracked from natural theology to regard nature more conservatively
as chiefly an occasion for pious spiritualizing.

Edward Taylor did not approach this juncture. Davis notes his "total
commitment to a crumbled system of values" (204) and charts his progressive withdrawal from current events, a withdrawal into what in *Gods
Determinations* he had called "God's Curious Garden fenced in / With
Solid Walls of Discipline." This withdrawal would have lessened his
awareness that the grand intellectual drama spanning his period was
reaching its climax. What had been taking place within Puritanism was
no less than the most comprehensive reformulation of nature philosophy
in the history of Christianity, a reformulation proceeding from the joining
together of two previously irreconcileable points of view represented
respectively by "otherworldly" Augustinianism and "thisworldly"
Thomism. Of greater importance with regard to the intellectual traditions
of the past, this was to be the last such reformulation and the final time
the major Christian proto-ideas of nature would together play a central
role in the life of a culture.

Ultimately, each idea—one leading to the image of wilderness, the
other to the image of book—failed to describe the reality of the colonists'
experience. Each was then slowly discarded in a shift made possible by
the distinctive flexibility of Puritan thought, a flexibility enabling New
England Puritanism to be the site of a dynamic coming-to-terms of early
American philosophy with its historical European traditions. The
collective Puritan "idea" of nature that evolved, its multiplicity reflected
in Edward Taylor's imagery, was thus neither failure nor aberration but a
necessary first step, a prelude to American Deism, to Emersonian
Transcendentalism, and to the major philosophical redefinitions of nature
to come. We do not see the final transition actually occur in Taylor, but
in studying the uses of nature in his poetry we can see why it was to
happen shortly thereafter.

Notes

Quotations from Edward Taylor's Preparatory Meditations cite the Series number, Meditation number, and line number(s), if any. Taylor's poetry is taken from *The Poems of Edward Taylor*, edited by Donald E. Stanford. The poem entitled "The Great Bones Dug Up at Clavarack" appears in *Edward Taylor's Minor Poetry*, edited by Thomas M. and Virginia L. Davis.

1. For another use of similar imagery, see Johnson 81.

2. On this point, Cotton and his most insistent opponent, Roger Williams, agree. In *The Bloody Tenent yet More Bloody*, Williams declares how "the world lies in wickedness, is like a wilderness or a sea of wild beasts innumerable, fornicators, covetous, idolaters, &c. with whom God's people may lawfully converse and cohabit in cities, towns, &c., else must not live in the world but go out of it" (44).

3. Thus Thomas Shephard declares in *Parable of the Ten Virgins* that the wilderness is where the man who neglects prayer should live (2:58).

4. Elsewhere, Wigglesworth uses the same Platonic terms to describe man's present relationship with nature, calling him a "pilgrim," the body "an useless wight," and the earth "a prison" (*Meat Out of the Eater* 19).

5. For Cotton's negative attitude toward human reason, see *Some Treasures Fetched out of Rubbish* (9, 28–29).

6. Thus Leo Marx observes, "To describe America as a hideous wilderness . . . is to envisage it as another field for the exercise of power" (43). For a general discussion of Puritan "improvement" of the wilderness, see Carroll 181–97.

7. In contrasting John Winthrop with his son, Richard S. Dunn portrays the "secularization of the New England conscience." He describes John Winthrop, Jr., who launched New England's first industrial projects, as "a man of the Restoration, cosmopolitan, tolerant, and worldly, charming and wily, an entrepreneur who practiced the new science and technology" (vi).

8. In fact, this development was in part an organic outgrowth of the garden motif. George Williams, speaking in *Wilderness and Paradise in Christian Thought* of the development of that motif in early New England, refers to a "Paradisic theme" in the community of learning: "Though reason had been impaired by the Fall, the dedicated community of scholars might still hope, through self-discipline and the integration of faith and reason, to rectify the error of primal man and safeguard knowledge, human and divine, from distortion and fragmentation." (157).

9. See Middlekauf. Samuel Eliot Morison concludes in *The Intellectual Life of Colonial New England* that "Puritanism in New England preserved far more of the humanist tradition than did non-Puritanism in the other English colonies" (17).

10. One secularizing by-product of the Ramist confidence in reason was modification of the early Puritan doctrine of mystico-sacramental conversion. Thomas Hooker and Thomas Shephard, whose descriptions of preparation were "tailored in several specific ways to requirements deriving ultimately from the Ramist dialectic," contributed to an interpretation of the process of conversion quite different from Cotton's. For them, conversion was "less of an enigma, and more a recognizable sequence of events than it was for Calvin" (Parker 159).

11. As Claude Lloyd notes in "The Literary Relations of the Royal Society in the Seventeenth Century," clergy dominated the Royal Society throughout the first ten years of its existence (271). He also suggests that the reason so many Puritan divines took part in this enterprise was not purely scientific; rather, natural philosophy "offered refuge from political as well as theological disputes"—and Charles II was a staunch advocate of its practice (65). See also Purver.

An early prototype of the Royal Society described by John Evelyn in a 1659 letter to Robert Boyle—though never actualized—postulated a semimonastic society organized as a college and dedicated as much to prayer as to scientific examination (Lloyd 59–60).

In defending the Royal Society in "Some considerations touching the usefulness of Experimental Natural Philosophy" against attacks by clerical opponents of natural science, the Puritan Boyle states two Scholastic principles succinctly in declaring that "two of God's principal ends were the manifestation of his own glory and the good of men." He argues that "those, who labor to deter men from sedulous inquiries in to nature, do take a course which tends to defeat God of both those mentioned ends" (Klemm 190).

12. A fitting example is John Winthrop, Jr., who, besides being a technologist and entrepreneur, was also an avid scientist. Chosen a fellow of the Royal Society at its first regular election in 1663, he maintained contact with important Society members—notably, Boyle, Hooke, and Newton. He brought at least two telescopes to America, and his scientific library was the largest and most influential in the colonies until near the end of the seventeenth century.

13. Morison notes the irony in the fact that while the church fought the new astronomy in other countries, the New England clergy actually propagated it, chiefly through the almanacs: "The clerical Harvard Corporation, with a clerical President, watched over by clerical overseers, sponsored these almanacs, which for the most part were composed by candidates for the ministry" (*Harvard College* 217).

14. In fact, Mather actually abets the revolution. In his preface to *An Essay for the Recording of Illustrious Providences*, he calls for a "Natural History of New-England" according to "the Rules and Method described by that Learned and excellent person Robert Boyle Esq" (n.p.). Boyle's method was a contributing factor in the rise of empiricism in England. See also Lowance, *Increase Mather*, 80–92.

15. William Scheik, in "Edward Taylor's Optics," explains the "mysterious transition [in Taylor's poetry] between the postlapsarian spiritual eye as an Aristotelian reflector and the regenerated spiritual eye as a Platonic emitter of light."

16. Taylor's more conservative typological practice is evident in Series II of the *Preparatory Meditations*, where he devotes himself to explicating biblical rather than natural types. It is worth noting that in this practice, Taylor is "tracing the hand of God in his providential intrusions into history" (Davis 140) and thereby assuming that events in the world can yield knowledge of God, even if here in secondhand terms.

17. See also "Edward Taylor's Reluctant Revolution: The 'New Astronomy' in the *Preparatory Meditations*," in which Rainwater explores Taylor's awareness of and use of Copernican scientific data in "theological, aesthetic, and intellectual accommodation to the new astronomy." She concludes that, though Taylor's poetry "reveals aesthetic nostalgia for the pleasant order of the crystal spheres," the poet "responded to cosmological revision without the overt mental anguish suffered by many of his English Metaphysical counterparts" (4–5).

Works Cited

Allin, James. *The Wheels of the World Govern'd by a Wise Providence*. Boston, 1727.

Ames, William. *The Marrow of Sacred Divinity*. London, 1642.

Bartas, Guillaume du. *Bartas: His Devine Weekes and Works*. 1605. Translated by Joshua Sylvester. Gainesville, Fl.: Scholars' Facsimiles & Reprints, 1965.

Bradstreet, Anne. *The Works of Anne Bradstreet*. Edited by John Harvard Ellis. New York: Peter Smith, 1932.

Calvin, John. *A Commentary on Genesis*, 2 vols. Translated by John King. London: Banner of Truth Trust, 1965.

Carroll, Peter. *Puritanism and the Wilderness*. New York: Columbia University Press, 1969.

Cotton, John. *A Brief Exposition of the Whole Book of Canticles*. London, 1642, 1655.

―――. *A Brief Exposition with Practicall Observations upon the Whole Book of Ecclesiastes*. London, 1654.

―――. *God's Mercie Mixed with His Justice*. London, 1641.

―――. *God's Promise to His Plantation*. Boston, 1686.

―――. *Some Treasure Fetched out of Rubbish*. London, 1660.

Danforth, Samuel. *A Brief Recognition of New England's Errand into the Wilderness*. Cambridge, 1671.

Davis, Thomas M. *A Reading of Edward Taylor*. Newark: University of Delaware Press, 1992.

―――. *Edward Taylor's Minor Poetry*. Edited by Thomas M. and Virginia L. Davis. Boston: Twayne, 1981.

Dunn, Richard. *Puritans and Yankees: The Winthrop Dynasty of New England, 1630-1717*. Princeton, N.J.: Princeton University Press, 1962.

Fitch, James. *The First Principles of the Doctrines of Christ*. Boston, 1679.

Grabo, Norman S. *Edward Taylor*. New York: Twayne, 1961.

Hall, David D. *Worlds of Wonder, Days of Judgment: Popular Religious Belief in Early New England*. New York: Knopf, 1989.

Howard, Alan B. "The World as Emblem: Language and Vision in the Poetry of Edward Taylor." *American Literature* 44 (1972): 359-84.

Jeske, Jeff. "Cotton Mather: Physico-Theologian." *Journal of the History of Ideas* 47 (1986): 583-94.

Johnson, Edward. *Wonder-working Providence of Sions Saviour in New-England . . .* 1654. Reprint. Delmar, N.Y.: Scholars' Facsimiles & Reprints, 1974.

Keller, Karl. *The Example of Edward Taylor*. Amherst: University of Massachusetts Press, 1975.

―――. "'The World Slickt Up in Types': Edward Taylor as a Version of Emerson." In *Typology and Early American Literature*, edited by Sacvan Bercovitch, 175-90. Cambridge: University of Massachusetts Press, 1972.

Klemm, Friedrich. *A History of Western Technology*. Translated by Dorothea Waley Singer. New York: Scribners, 1959.

Lloyd, Claude. "The Literary Relations of the Royal Society in the Seventeenth Century." Diss., Yale, 1925.

Lowance, Mason I., Jr. "'Images or Shadows of Divine Things' in the Thought of Jonathan Edwards." In *Typology and Early American Literature*. Amherst: University of Massachusetts Press, 1972.

―――. *Increase Mather*. New York: Twayne, 1974.

Marx, Leo. *The Machine in the Garden: Technology and the Pastoral Ideal in America.* New York: Oxford University Press, 1964.

Mather, Cotton. *The Christian Philosopher: A Collection of the Best Discoveries in Nature, With Religious Improvements.* 1721. Edited by Josephine K. Piercy. Reprint. Gainesville, Fl.: Scholars' Facsimiles & Reprints, 1968.

———. *Reasonable Religion.* Boston, 1700.

Mather, Increase. *The Day of Trouble is Near.* Cambridge, 1674.

———. *An Essay for the Recording of Illustrious Providences.* Boston, 1684.

———. *Kometographia. Or a Discourse Concerning Comets . . .* Boston, 1683.

Middlekauf, Robert. "A Persistent Tradition: The Classical Curriculum in Eighteenth-Century New England." *William and Mary Quarterly* 18 (1961): 54-67.

Miller, Perry. *The New England Mind: The Seventeenth Century.* New York: Macmillan, 1939.

Mitchel, Jonathan. *Nehemiah on the Wall in Troublesom Times.* Cambridge, 1671.

Morison, Samuel Eliot. *Harvard College in the Seventeenth Century.* 2 vols. Cambridge: Harvard University Press, 1936.

———. *The Intellectual Life of Colonial New England.* Ithaca, New York: Great Seal Books, 1956.

North, Michael. "Edward Taylor's Metaphors of Promise." *American Literature* 51 (1979): 1-16.

Norton, John. *The Heart of N-England rent at the Blasphemies of the present Generation.* Cambridge, 1659.

Parker, David L. "Petrus Ramus and the Puritans: The 'Logic' of Preparationist Conversion Doctrine." *Early American Literature* 8 (1973): 140-62.

Pemberton, Ebeneezer. *The Divine Original and Dignity of Government.* Boston, 1710.

Purver, Margery. *The Royal Society: Concept and Creation.* Cambridge: M.I.T. Press, 1967.

Rainwater, Catherine. "Edward Taylor's Reluctant Revolution: The 'New Astronomy' and the *Preparatory Meditations.*" *American Poetry* 1 (Winter 1984): 4–17.

———. "'This Brazen Serpent is a Doctor's Shop': Edward Taylor's Medical Vision." *Studies in Puritan American Spirituality* 2 (1992): 51–75.

Rowe, Karen E. *Saint and Singer: Edward Taylor's Typology and the Poetics of Meditation.* Cambridge: Cambridge University Press, 1986.

Scheik, William J. "Edward Taylor's Optics." *American Literature* 55 (1983): 234-40.

———. "'The Inward Tacles and the Outward Traces': Edward Taylor's Transitions." *Early American Literature* 12 (1977): 163-76.

———. "Tending the Lord in All Admiring Style: Edward Taylor's *Preparatory Meditations.*" *Language and Style* 4 (1971): 163-87.

———. "'That Blazing Star in Joshua': Edward Taylor's 'Meditation 2.10' and Increase Mather's *Kometographia.*" *Seventeenth Century News* 34 (1976): 36-37.

Shephard, Thomas. *The Works of Thomas Shephard.* 3 vols. Edited by John Allbro. New York: AMS Press, 1967.

Sluder, Lawrence L. "God in the Background: Edward Taylor as Naturalist." *Early American Literature* 7 (1973): 265-71.

Taylor, Edward. *Edward Taylor's 'Christographia.'* Edited by Norman S. Grabo. New Haven: Yale University Press, 1962.

———. *The Poems of Edward Taylor.* Edited by Donald E. Stanford. New Haven: Yale University Press, 1960.

Walker, Williston. *The Creeds and Platforms of Congregationalism.* Boston: Pilgrim Press, 1960.

Walsh, James J. "Scholasticism in the Colonial College." *New England Quarterly* 5 (1932): 483-532.

Wigglesworth, Michael. *The Day of Doom: or, a Description of the Great and Last Judgment*. Boston, 1662.

———. *Meat Out of the Eater: or Meditations concerning the necessity, end, and usefulness of Afflictions unto God's children* . . . Boston, 1670.

Willard, Samuel. *A Compleat Body of Divinity in Two Hundred and Fifty Expository Lectures on the Assembly's Shorter Catechism* . . . Boston, 1726.

Williams, George. *Wilderness and Paradise in Christian Thought*. New York: Harper, 1962.

Williams, Roger. *The Bloody Tenent yet More Bloody* . . . London, 1652.

Winthrop, John. *Winthrop Papers*. 2 vols. New York: Russell & Russell, 1968.

The "Peculiar Elegance"
of Edward Taylor's Poetics

RAYMOND A. CRAIG

*Coll. III Let the word of God dwell plenteously in you, in all
wisdome, teaching and exhorting one another in Psalmes,
Hymnes, and spirituall Songs, singing to the Lord with grace
in your hearts.*

—Bay Psalm Book

Several times each week, Edward Taylor would open a psalter, as would
Puritans and Pilgrims all over New England. Greeting these readers,
nearly regardless of the psalter or edition, were the same few epigraphs,
such as the Pauline injunction above from Col. 3:16 or the following,
similar injunction from Ephesians, partially quoted on the New England
Psalm Book title page and quoted in full on the title page to Henry
Ainsworth's *Book of Psalmes*:

Ephe. 5.18.19. Be ye filled with the Spirit: speaking to your selves in Psalms,
and hymnes, and spiritual Songs: singing & making melodie in your hart to
the Lord.

Another popular choice was the injunction from James 5:13: "Is any
among you afflicted? let him pray. Is any merry? let him sing psalms."
When one of the passages did not appear, the editor would refer or allude
to the passage elsewhere—as in the opening of Ainsworth's preface:

I have enterprised (Christian reader) this work, with regard of Gods honour, & comfort of his people; that his word might dwel in us richly, in al wisdom; and that we might teach and admonish our selves, in psalmes & hymnes and songs spiritual. (Sig. **2)

Sing psalms, sing hymns, sing spiritual songs—this is the lesson of the New England psalters. In most literary histories, however, the psalters represent a different lesson: these garbled psalms are the poems of an unpoetic people, restrained or damaged by a scowling aesthetic. This different lesson is supposedly presented to us by no less an authority than John Cotton, whose admonition at the end of his preface to the Bay Psalm Book, "Gods Altar needs not our pollishings," is said to belie a literary sensibility in the production of the translation and, by extension, in Puritanism itself.[1] To ignore the emphasis that all the psalters place on the right use of psalms, hymns, and spiritual songs is to ignore both an explicit concern for art and the foundation of Puritan poetics—and, of course, Edward Taylor's poetics. The concern in both the psalters and Cotton's preface should be recognized as a legitimate interest in the attractions of poetry or song, which conflicts, to some extent, with the desire for "great plainness of speech" that Paul advocates in other epistles.[2] In this essay, I delineate the Puritan poetics that is explicit in the work of Cotton, Ainsworth, and other exegetes, one that derives from Paul and Augustine and that defines for us the poetics at work in Edward Taylor—a poetics that moves beyond that suggested by most readers of Taylor's poetry, especially those who see the poems as verse merely informed by familiarity with the Scripture. I argue for a poetics, "a peculiar elegance," in Taylor's work that derives from but also extends biblical intertextuality into poetry.

When, in 1612, Ainsworth published his psalter, which was used later by Pilgrims in New England, he attempted to resolve the conflicting demands of accuracy (he felt his translation should be "agreable to the original Hebrue" and "retain the grace of the Hebrue tongue" [Sig. **2]) and aesthetics in the outward features of poetry and song—diction, meter or measure, and tune—by providing annotations to clarify and change them whenever necessary to make the verse appealing.[3] Cotton's awareness of the problematic qualities of psalm and song is quite clear in both his preface to and important treatise on the Bay Psalm Book, *Singing of Psalmes, a Gospel Ordinance*.[4] In both texts, but especially in the treatise, Cotton demonstrates a sophisticated literary sensibility through a series of dichotomous distinctions—distinctions between "Spiritual elegancies" and "artificial elegancies," spiritual gifts and God-given gifts of

"Nature and Art," the right use of these gifts to produce spiritual songs and the implied incorrect use of God-given gifts in the production of "drunken songs" and "wanton sonnets," and "psalms, hymns, and spiritual songs" fit for public performance and spiritual songs fit for private devotion. Before Cotton, Ainsworth had described a similar distinction, suggesting a broader acceptance of poetry:

> The scripture sheweth us two sorts of psalmes. First such as were written by the Prophets, (and specially David,) to be left unto the church as a part of the Canonical word of God, Luk. 24.44. Secondly such as were uttered by voice in the assemblies, and now written, but served for the present use of the church, as other gifts of doctrine, interpretation &c, I Cor. 14.26. (A Preface, declaring the reason and use of this Book, n.p.)

Cotton, of course, elaborates significantly on the types of songs permissible, and his explanations in *Singing of Psalmes* make clear the tension between poetic and "plain" language. Moreover, Cotton's explanations make an explicit statement on Puritan poetics that justifies the psalters and may in turn be applied to the production of various kinds of poems in New England. Unlike the condemnation of poetry implicit in his prefatory admonition, Cotton's defense of English psalms presents us with the model for a new taxonomy of Puritan poetry.

Despite the modern insistence that Cotton and other translators ignored literary concerns altogether, Cotton's admonition in the preface clearly presupposes a literary sensibility and a sophisticated understanding of biblical poetics. Cotton bases much of his argument for singing psalms in English and English meter on his recognition of poetic qualities that differentiate Psalms from other books of the Bible: "The psalmes are penned in such verses as are su[i]table to the poetry of the hebrew language, and not in the common style of such other bookes of the old Testament as are not poeticall" (Sig. **2). From this premise, Cotton argues that translating the Psalms into English meter follows the Lord's prescription:

> The Lord hath hid from us the hebrew tunes, lest wee should think ourselves bound to imitate them; soe also the course and form . . . of their hebrew poetry, that wee might not think of ourselves to imitate that, but that every nation without scruple might follow as the graver sort of tunes of their owne country songs, soe the graver sort of verses of their owne country poetry. (Sig. **2)

Of course, on the heels of this argument follow the more cautious remarks for which Cotton is famous and that lead to the final warning not to polish God's altar:

> Neither let any think, that for the meetre sake wee have taken liberty or poeticall licence to depart from the true and proper sence of Davids words in the hebrew verses, noe; but it hath beene one part of our religious care and faithfull indeavour, to keepe close to the originall text. (Sig. **2)

However, it needs to be seen that the admonition itself is made necessary not by an *absence* of literary sensibility, or even a rejection of it, but by Cotton's anticipation of the literary expectations of his audience:

> If therefore the verses are not alwayes so smooth and elegant as some may desire or expect; let them consider that Gods Altar needs not our pollishings: Ex. 20.1. (Sig. [**4]).

Why else was the meter supposed to be "smooth," the phrasing "elegant"? We need not rely on a reassessment of Cotton's language, however, to illustrate Cotton's literary sensibility; in *Singing of Psalmes,* he fully develops both his spiritual and literary concerns. While he is most concerned with defending the Bay Psalm Book and the public singing of psalms, he draws on a received aesthetic of scriptural language that is in harmony with both Pauline injunctions—to "sing psalms, hymns, and spiritual songs" and to use "great plainness of speech."

Cotton's admonition is grounded in the belief that the Word "bee so full and so perfect" that the spirit of the Word need not be altered, that altering "the stamp of the Word of God" would be blasphemous, and, most importantly, that, as "Gods Altar," the Scriptures have their own "peculiar elegance."[5] The highly nuanced notion of "full and perfect" and "peculiar elegance" of the Scriptures was commonplace for the Puritans and other Protestants. The translators of the King James Bible, for example, observed the fullness and perfection of the Scriptures and, despite considerable license in their translations, felt that the Word was not altered (although considerable discussion of the problems of phrasing and style appears in the prefatory remarks).[6] Rather, the Bible has either "peculiar eloquence" or, as exegete Benjamin Keach states in the preface to *Tropologia*, "peculiar elegance." For Keach, this is due to the "royal descent, or divinity of the Scriptures," which comprises both the "Spirit of God speaking in them" and "that extraordinary and inimitable style wherein they are written":

The style of the sacred Scripture is singular, and has peculiar properties, not elsewhere to be found; its simplicity is joined with majesty, commanding the veneration of all serious men. (ix, xv)

Keach traces the concept of special elegance, or eloquence, of the Scripture not to Paul but to Augustine in the *Confessions:*

Augustine says, That the Scriptures seemed rude and unpolished to him, in comparison of Cicero's adorned style, because he did not then understand its *interiora,* or inward beauty; but when he was converted to Christianity, declared, That when he understood them, no writing appeared more wise or eloquent. (xv)

In *De Doctrina Christiana,* and in language that Keach and Cotton also use, Augustine elaborates on scriptural style that he finds so striking:

It is not the qualities which [sacred] writers have in common with the heathen orators and poets that give me such unspeakable delight in their eloquence; I am more struck with admiration at the way in which, by an eloquence peculiarly their own, they so use this eloquence of ours that it is not conspicuous either by its presence or its absence. (127)

Throughout books 1 and 2 of *De Doctrina Christiana*, Augustine argues that the right use of knowledge is in understanding the eloquence of the Scriptures, in understanding the "unknown and ambiguous signs" there. The "peculiar eloquence" is crucial to meaning and provides "unspeakable delight" through, in part, its simplicity or plainness of speech. In effect, Augustine and the later Puritans were recognizing a distinction between adorned style and the "plain style" of the Scriptures, the latter's inward beauty exceeding that of outward ornament. The tension evident in Paul's Epistles is resolved in Augustine, in which it is seen as "paradox." Later commentators, Ainsworth, Cotton, and Keach among them, do not seem to view this as tension or paradox; it is instead a quality of the Word, and potentially of most language acts. Cotton expresses this fundamental concept explicitly in *Singing of Psalmes,* arguing that because the Psalms are "the divine Meditations, and spiritual expressions of holy men of God in Scripture, which God hath prepared for the setting forth of his own glory," the translation must "expresse lively every elegancy of the Holy Ghost" (29, 56).[7] In both his preface and treatise, Cotton is concerned with the edification imparted by singing and reading the Word—both of which, in Cotton's view, share the same status of ordinance as hearing the Word opened through the preacher's sermon. Thus, Cotton's admonition has much to do with the possible marring of the Word by an inept translator of the spiritual elegancy. However, if the spiritual elegance is maintained, then the Word may be used in other applications—for which Cotton finds scriptural justification. That is, the Word may be used for new songs.

Cotton devotes an extensive passage in the treatise to demonstrating how the spiritual elegance of the Word makes new spiritual songs possible, and he provides some insight into what spiritual elegance might be. Citing the "Song of the Lambe" in Rev. 15:3, which "point[s] at sundry songs of David," Cotton lists the "Song of the Lambe" on the left side of the page and the passages from the Psalms on the right side to demonstrate how spiritual songs are composed (28):

Rev. 15.3	Psal.86.10.
Great and marvellous are thy works, Lord God Almightie.	*Thou are great, and doest wondrous things, thou art God alone.*
	Ver. 8. *Among the Gods, there is none like unto thee, nor any works like thy works.*
	Psal.111.2. *The works of the Lord are great.*
	Ver. 4. *And Wonderfull.*
	Ver. 7. *The works of his hand are truth*
Just and true are thy wayes, Thou King of Saints.	*and judgement.*
	Psal.71.22. *O thou Holy One of Israel.*
And ver. 4. *Thou onely are Holy. Who shall not feare thee, O Lord, and glorifie thy Name? For all Nations shall come and worship before thee.*	Psal.86.9. *All Nations whom thou hast made, shall come and worship before thee, O Lord, and glorifie thy Name.*
	Psal.9.16. *The Lord is knowne by the Judgement which he executeth.*
For thy Judgements are made manifest.	Psal.64.9. *All men shall feare and shall declare the worke of God; For they shall wisely consider of his doings.*

He cites Psalms 86 and 111 as containing "those special sentences, which were fetched from thence, though with some finall variation" (28). In citing these passages, Cotton demonstrates his belief in the Scripture as a "single composite whole." The "pointing" he finds here is a way of establishing a continuity between two ideas and two texts; he perceives

them as already absorbed into the same "whole." In fact, the Old
Testament source could be said to have undergone a change in meaning
as a result of the "pointing" in Revelation, although Cotton is not
creating the meaning—he is merely "opening" the Scriptures—the "finall
variation" is certainly greater than we might expect.

Cotton's treatment of the new song is instructive on spiritual elegance
in one other way as well. Cotton introduces the new song with a passage
that suggests an awareness of intertextual patterns between the Psalms
and the poem in Revelation; he identifies the spiritual significance of
these special sentences in a new context while he simultaneously calls on
the spiritual significance of the Psalms to which the new song alludes:

> The Song of the 144000. followers of the Lambe, it is not expresly said to be
> a *New Song*, but as it were a *New Song,* Rev. 14.3, *New* to them who had
> been wont to heare the worshippers of the Beast to *sing* and rejoyce in their
> own merits, and superstitious devotions: And new also in respect of the
> renewed affections, wherewith they sang it: But yet the same ancient Song
> which the sheepe and Saints of Christ, were wont to *sing,* even in *Davids*
> time, of the righteousnesse of Christ, even of his onely, and of their owne
> blessednesse in his not imputing their sinnes to them. Thus *Davids Psalmes* in
> the spirituall use and sence of them are new Songs, or as it were *New Songs,*
> to this day, unto all that are renewed by grace. (26–27)

Here, Cotton argues a scriptural precedent for direct quotation,
paraphrase, and more tacit forms of allusion to the Word as a strategy for
creating new songs and poems. Some critics have pointed to the
overriding concern for accuracy in "the stamp of the Word" as the
underlying cause of the bad poetry in translations of the Bay Psalm Book
as well as in other Puritan poetry that depends on and alludes heavily to
the Scriptures. Cotton's remarks in the treatise suggest, however, that the
special elegancy of the Word produces strategies that enrich the poetry
primarily through extensive forms of paraphrase and allusion to the
Bible, beyond the use of biblical tropes as a kind of shorthand, as
described by Barbara Lewalski (86–104). If we are to believe Cotton,
respect for the Word does not deny a Puritan poetics; it is the very
foundation of that poetics.

In chapter 10 of *Singing of Psalmes,* Cotton also acknowledges the
sense and use of "artificial elegancies" in the translation of Hebrew
psalms into English verses. After having established the lawfulness of
singing psalms, Cotton's defense of the translation rests on the distinction between spiritual gifts (with the power of grace) and "Nature and
Art," or gifts for "outward work":

It might as well be said, the translating of the Hebrew Scriptures into English, is not a spirituall gift, but a Grammaticall, or Rhetoricall gift. Whatsoever the art or skill be, Grammaticall, Rhetoricall, Poeticall, they are all of them gifts of God (though common) and given chiefly for the service and edification of the Church of God. (57)

In this chapter, Cotton is arguing primarily for the use of meter and for the arrangement of lines, or sentences, into English verses, and clearly this passage calls for much more art and skill to be employed in the service of spiritual song. His argument proceeds out of a recognition of the artificial elegancies of the original Hebrew psalms:

... for it is an artificiall elegancy which the holy Pen-men of Scripture used that they penned the *Psalmes,* and such like Poeticall books of Scriptures not in prose, (which men use in common speech) but in verse, which observe a certain number and measure of syllables, and some of them run in meeter also, as those know that know the Hebrew. (56)

Cotton knows that the Hebrew tunes are hidden, are unknown to translators, but in a subsequent passage he finds it appropriate "to expresse all the artificiall elegancies of the Hebrew Text, so farre as we are able to imitate the same in a translation" (56). Ainsworth before him made a similar (if briefer) argument, wishing to "retain the grace of the Hebrue tongue" (Sig. **2).

While neither Ainsworth nor Cotton saw the use of artificial elegancies as essential to the spiritual value of the Psalms, both argue for their use. Moreover, as part of the activity of exegesis, Cotton also recognizes a discursive activity or intertextual patterning that occurs between texts (or within the "single, composite whole") as a result of allusion. Cotton does not use allusion as a "literary device," a "Poeticall gift"; it is nonetheless a principal device of exegesis and, in the production of spiritual songs or translations of Hebrew psalms, an aspect of spiritual elegance. In *Singing of Psalmes,* Cotton's defense of psalm translation and psalm singing is a poetics that combines the essential spiritual elegancies of the Word with the artificial elegancies of nature and art.

Cotton's argument extends beyond a defense of the psalters, however, because he provides a scriptural precedent for the use of nature and art in the production of new spiritual songs. While Cotton argues in his preface that there is no precedent for ministers composing their own psalms, in *Singing of Psalmes* he encourages "any private Christian" to compose spiritual songs and further argues that Christians could "compile a *spiritual Song* out of Davids words of praise dispersed in several Psalmes of David, and other Psalmists in Scripture, and to sing them, composed together as a Psalme of praise unto the Lord" (28–29).[8] Moreover, he also defines the occasions of spiritual songs:

> 2. Wee grant also, that any private Christian, who hath a gift to frame a spirituall Song, may both frame it, and sing it privately, for his own private comfort, and remembrance of some Speciall benefit, or deliverance. . . . Neither doe we deny, but that in the publique thanksgivings of the Church, if the Lord should furnish any of the members of the Church with a Spiritual gift to compose a *Psalme* upon any speciall occasion, hee may lawfully be allowed to sing it before the Church, and the rest hearing it, and approving it may goe along with him in Spirit, and say Amen to it. (15)

This earlier passage does not focus on the use of David's Psalms. Instead, Cotton describes several types of spiritual songs, which in turn we find among the Puritan poets: paraphrastic poems or translations of poems, spiritual songs composed entirely of "Davids words of praise," and now new spiritual songs of praise or thanksgiving. To all these private poems, Cotton adds public psalms—the only apparent restriction is that they must be devotional.[9]

Not all Puritan poems are devotional, but the vast majority do conform to Cotton's prescription for spiritual song. Taylor, of course, is best known for the devotional *Preparatory Meditations*—which, as Rosemary Fithian Guruswamy has demonstrated, owe much to the psalm tradition—but he also paraphrased Job, Psalms, and David's Lamentation for Saul and Jonathan as well as the Songs of Moses, Deborah and Barak, and Hannah. He wrote songs of deliverance ("Upon my recovery"), songs of thanksgiving, and a number of elegies—all poems falling within Cotton's definitions of psalms, hymns, and spiritual songs and thus within the Pauline tradition. Moreover, Taylor, of all Puritan poets, seems most aware of the poetic application of special elegance, evidenced by his use of quotation and extensive and complicated use of scriptural allusion.

Edward Taylor's poetry has received much more praise than blame from modern critics, but a survey of the criticism makes clear the confusion his poetics engenders. Alan Shucard describes the principal complaint: Taylor's imagery is inconsistent and excessive. Shucard attributes "Taylor's roughness" to a point of doctrine turned rhetorical strategy; Taylor's language is intentionally imperfect to reflect his own imperfection when compared to the divine (29–31). Albert Gelpi also puzzles over the poetics despite his favorable assessment that Taylor is "foreshadowing an indigenous American poetic tradition" (15). Gelpi attributes Taylor's idiosyncratic language to the deprivation of the wilderness:

> Why should Taylor's fancy turn so frequently to gold, gems, perfumes, liquors, brocades, incense—things which were clearly not part of his life at Westfield? The question implies the answer: exactly because his rich and convoluted imagination dwelt in a wilderness. . . . The insufficiencies of nature and society drove him into the privacy of his imagination where his passionate nature could articulate the Puritan vision of the city on the hill which John Winthrop had voiced to the first shipload of Puritans in the misery and anxiety of their earthly condition. (42–43)

These two arguments accurately describe two critical approaches to the "flaws" in Taylor's poetics, critical approaches that are neither necessary nor accurate. Taylor's imagination did not dwell in the wilderness, nor was it convoluted; Taylor's imagination dwelt in the Bible and was no more convoluted than Christian and Puritan exegesis of the period.

Taylor's poetry has been vigorously and successfully defended against these and similar charges by a number of critics.[10] William Scheick argues, for example, that there is "an adept poet behind the mask of the Lisping Child" and that while Taylor's "unity of expression" is unusual (129–30), it is unified either through his Puritan epistemology or through some native human desire to exercise the imagination—exercise purportedly denied by the Puritan view of the world. The key to the adept poet, as Scheick and Michael Clark argue in "The Subject of Text," is in understanding the dependence of Taylor's poetry on his view of language, specifically the Word.[11]

This critical examination of Taylor's use of scriptural materials has been underway for some time. Barbara Lewalski successfully articulates the importance of the emblem book and meditation tradition to Series 1 of *Preparatory Meditations* but finds Taylor unable to adopt biblical tropes "as his own" (108). Karen Rowe's work on Taylor's typological sermons and Series 2 of the *Meditations* impressively documents the importance of Scholastic typology to these poems. Thomas M. Davis, Rosemary Fithian-Guruswamy, and Jeffrey Hammond have also defined Taylor's cosmology and poetics in relation to the scriptures and exegetical texts with which Taylor was familiar. Davis demonstrates persuasively that "Taylor's sole model was the Bible" (203), while Fithian sets out the specifics of the Davidic influence in Taylor's

Meditations. In *Sinful Self, Saintly Self,* his recent work on the Puritan reader's experience of poetry, Hammond defines the Puritan aesthetic as always grounded in theology, in exegetical traditions, and, significantly, in "biblical patterns." Hammond goes somewhat further in articulating the nature and uses of biblical patterning to explore the intertextual relation between Taylor's poems and the "biblical metatext" in the Puritan imagination.

I extend these arguments by suggesting that Taylor's use of the Scripture's "peculiar eloquence" extends to the nonhistorical, tropological use of the Word. The study of biblical poetics as understood by Cotton and others demonstrates that Taylor's inconsistent imagery and "roughness" may be understood as a coherence of spiritual significance—revealed not through reference to a textually bound biblical object or event but instead through the spiritual meaning of scriptural word and phrase in the new context.[12]

Clearly, Taylor's allusive strategies suggest a fierce faith in the potency of the Word and words. Moreover, the poems suggest that Taylor's use of exegesis and his general conception of language produce a poetics that, if not unique to Taylor, at least approaches a definition of Taylor's poetry as poetry. So, while an understanding, however belated or nostalgic, may be derived from examining Taylor's exegetical sources (and indeed, I rely significantly on that method of reading Taylor's poetry) or his "subjectivity," we must explore more carefully those moments when the language of the exegetical commentary becomes poetic product.

Taylor's poetics does not seem to develop as a process per se. However, for the purpose of defining the poetics, various "levels of poeticity" may be located in the poems, particularly as they are indicated by Taylor's allusive strategies. At one level, Taylor employs the poetics of the revealed Word, the intertextual play suggested by the notion that the Bible is a single, composite whole, a notion that is also strictly within the exegetical tradition. Taylor's poems, insofar as they employ this biblical poetics, rely on the "peculiar eloquence" of the Word for meaning and coherence. Taylor expands this basic element of Puritan poetics by employing this same intertextual play between select images across the *Preparatory Meditations.* This results, finally, in full intertextual play across a broad range of meditations—a sophistication we suspect but have not located precisely and that demonstrates how Taylor modifies the "peculiar eloquence" of the Word into his own poetics.

Taylor's allusive strategies center on his understanding of the relationship between grace and the Word. Taylor repeatedly tells us how his poems work, as in this early meditation:

7. Meditation. Ps. 45.2 Grace in thy lips is poured out.

Thy Humane Frame, my Glorious Lord, I spy,
  A Golden Still with Heavenly Choice drugs filld;
Thy Holy Love, the Glowing heate whereby,
  The Spirit of Grace is graciously distilld,
  Thy Mouth the Neck through which these spirits still.
  My Soul thy Violl make, and therewith fill.

Thy Speech the Liquour in thy Vessell stands,
  Well ting'd with Grace a blessed Tincture, Loe,
Thy Words distilld, Grace in thy Lips pourd, and,
  Give Graces Tinctur in them where they go.
  Thy words in graces tincture stilld, Lord, may
  The Tincture of thy Grace in me Convay.

That Golden Mint of Words, thy Mouth Divine,
  Doth tip these Words, which by my Fall were spoild;
And Dub with Gold dug out of Graces mine
  That they thine Image might have in them foild.
  Grace in thy Lips pourd out's as Liquid Gold.
  Thy Bottle make my Soule, Lord, it to hold.

Christ, as "the Word made flesh," is the "Golden Mint" that can foil Taylor's poetry in golden grace. The poem suggests, as Stanford's note remarks, that "Taylor hopes his words will be adorned with the golden image of Christ" but also that the spirit of grace and the Word are virtually synonymous. Taylor's words "foild" are tipped in the Word, in the Scriptures; despite his own fall, Taylor wishes to speak the Word of God—singing praise out of God's grace, pouring forth grace that depends on the Word.

This meditation on Ps. 45:2 establishes early in the several decades of *Preparatory Meditations* the essential poetic strategies of these poems. The meditation opens with the citation of the psalm, which is a wedding song, a royal psalm that praises a Hebrew king upon his wedding, advises and praises the bride, and calls for the perpetual celebration of the king.[13] In the headnote to the Geneva version, the principals as well as the spiritual meaning of the psalm are made explicit:

1 The maiestie of Salomon, his honour, strength, beautie, riches & power are praised, & also his marriage with the Egyptian being an heathen woman is blessed, 10 If; that she can renounce her people & the loue of her countrey and giue; her selfe wholly to her housband. Under the which figure the

> wonderful maiestie & increase of the kingdome of Christ and the Church his
> spouse now taken of the Gentiles is described. (244)

This Christological interpretation of the psalm, featuring Solomon as a
figure of Christ as well as the allegorical marriage of Christ and the
Church, is perhaps revealed to Taylor through the allusions in this psalm
to the Song of Solomon and understood in the half-verse Taylor does not
cite: "Thou art fairer than the children of men" (Ps. 45:2a).[14] So
construed, Psalm 45 reveals Taylor's favorite themes: the faith, hope, and
love of Christ necessary for the fruitful marriage of Christ and saint, for
sanctification and glorification.

In this poem, moreover, we find perhaps the first treatment of poetry
and poetics. The initial verse of Psalm 45 draws writing and singing
praise together: "My heart is inditing a good matter; I speak of the things
which I have made touching the king: my tongue is the pen of a ready
writer." The psalmist's invocation thus locates the source of the "good
matter" and overflowing heart in the king. The singer of the psalm sings
under the direct influence of Solomon or, typologically, Christ. In
Christographia, Taylor comments on this verse and directly connects
gold and the Word in the image of the "Golden tongue":

> All Scriptures of the Prophets are but the Ebullitions of this Authority, the
> Prophets say, as Ps. 45. I. My tongue is . . . a pen of a ready writer. Indeed
> every Writer of Scripture was the Golden tongue, and Spiritual Pen of this
> great prophet. (395)

Further, the second verse attributes to Solomon—and, through figuration
derived from the collated verse at Luke 4:22, to Christ—this unique
quality of speech: "gracious words which proceeded out of his mouth."
"Gracious words" are "Grace in thy Lips pourd out as Liquid Gold."
Allusion to these verses makes clear the connection between the Word
and "Liquid Gold"; grace is the ink in which Taylor hopes his own pen
and words will be "dubbed" and "tipped."

The process of grace's influence is explained in the meditation
literally and, with the collation of allusive passages, discursively. The
meditation does not quote Psalm 45 except in the repetition of the half-
verse cited at the beginning of the poem, "Grace in thy lips is pourd out,"
and again in lines 9 and 17. However, the key metaphor of the third
stanza, gold as the spirit of grace, as grace itself, alludes to the gold
wedding garment of the bride in verse 13 of the same psalm: "The king's
daughter is all glorious within: her clothing is of wrought gold."
Wedding garments receive a great deal of attention from biblical

commentators because of the parable of the unwilling guest (Matt. 22:1–14). As Keach explains, "By wedding garment is intended Christ's righteousness, or imputed righteousness, which is put on the soul by faith for justification" (473). The use of the garments and gold links these figures of grace. In his *Christian Dictionary,* Thomas Taylor specifically cites Ps. 45:13 as a metaphor; gold is "the most pure graces of the spirit; to wit, faith, hope and loue. *Psal. 45,10. Her cloathing is of broidred Gold*" (198). [15] Keach also expands on this figure of grace and may have been Taylor's source for the image of "Gold dug out of Graces mine:

> So those that would be enriched with the word of God, have much of it in their heads and hearts, must take pains; they must dig in these golden mines, as it were, for it. (573)

For Edward Taylor, as Norman Grabo tells us, the "wedden garment is absolutely necessary to the celebration of the wedden supper. . . . [The Lord's Supper is] styled a wedden feast" and "implieth the marriage of Christ and the soul" (37). Thus, the meditation must be seen as a natural continuation of the Canticles unit that precedes it; moreover, the poem also conflates several other scriptural texts and ideas.

Through meditation on Ps. 45:2, Taylor develops a multifarious description of grace and, ultimately, of the wine of the Lord's Supper. Christ's "Humane Frame" (echoing Ps. 103:14) contains the "Spirit of Grace . . . graciously distilld" (recalling Deut. 32:2, "my speech shall distil as the dew," and confirming Luke 4:21–22, "[21] This day is this scripture fulfilled in your ears. [22] And all bare him witness and wondered at the gracious words which proceeded out of his mouth"). As "the Word made flesh," Christ may convey grace to Taylor—through the Word and through the sacrifice. Grace "convay[ed]" imparts grace to the vessels into which it is poured; that grace restores the image of God within, which was besmirched by the Fall. Thus, the pouring forth of grace parallels the pouring of wine into the earthen vessel that is Taylor. With grace now in his heart, Taylor has "the tongue of a ready writer," "inditing a good thing"; his heart and words are foiled in grace, the image of God is restored to heart and word. [16]

While the poem moves through three ostensibly disparate images, we find in the scriptural yoking of grace and gold the unity of spiritual meaning that is important to Taylor and that clarifies the disparity. Christ's distillation of the Word produces "Heavenly choice drugs," a tincture of gold, a tincture of grace. Grace, in turn, mints new words with this "Liquid Gold," this ink of gold, a new wine put into Taylor's ink "Bottle" and his "Soule," alluding in the last line to Matt. 9:17 and maintaining a bifurcated imagery of containers with both scriptural and domestic sources.[17] Taylor's understanding of Psalm 45, and of the Scriptures generally, hinges on Scripture that interprets Scripture; his notion of poetry hinges on his understanding of the transformative potential of words dubbed "with Gold dug out of Graces mine."

Of course, Taylor is aware of the "inward beauty" Augustine found in the eloquence of the Scriptures, but he explores this inward beauty in ways that we seldom see in other Puritan poetry. In Meditation I.7, Taylor does use Scripture to interpret elements of Psalm 45, but he is not producing a new psalm that merely interprets the original Christologi-cally, although this is one effect of the intertextual patterning. Rather, Taylor's meditation takes the psalmist's invocation, which links the tongue and speech to the overflowing heart, and expands it by conflating scriptural allusions that are models of the action of grace: the bride puts on the "broidred gold" wedding garment; the Word is distilled; new wine is put in new bottles. These scriptural models of grace become personal models of the process of grace in the meditation. Thus, as models of language, the allusive key words and phrases extend the action of grace beyond the literal limits of the scriptural text: scriptural language, Taylor tells us, "give[s] Graces Tinctur in them where they go." We may further extend Taylor's transformation: we may say Taylor is "broidering" in gold his own "wedden" garment with the Word and his words of poetry. Without this speculative extension, Taylor's allusive strategies in *Preparatory Meditations* are at least an exploration of the Word's power to create spiritual meaning in the wider world of the poet's personal experience. Simply, Taylor, aware of the intertextual patterning of the Scriptures, applies the same principle to his own poetry: the Word inter-prets the Word, and the Word interprets Taylor's experience.

Series 1 Sequences

The extensive intertextual patterning of Meditation I.7 is not present in all the meditations. Often Taylor develops a single metaphor or, in Series 2 of the *Meditations*, a single type identified in the "title" of the meditation, in the biblical citation. This more straightforward allusive strategy recalls that of Michael Wigglesworth: the entire poem is derived from the biblical citation, perhaps with amplification from other biblical texts. The presence of these narrowly focused poems, especially at the beginning of the meditation "units," confirms Norman Grabo's and Barbara Lewalski's suggestions that the Series 1 units follow a program of meditation based on the *Treatise Concerning the Lord's Supper* (Grabo xx; Lewalski 396–97). While these poems initiate or complete the meditation "units" within Series 1 by presenting the paradigms on which the other poems in the unit depend, they are generally not dependent on allusive play or intertextual patterning for meaning or unity.

The "legal unit" meditations of Series 1 reveal the range of allusive strategies within these sequences as they follow this meditation program. In this case, the poems are but one exploration of "the contract celebrated in the 'wedden feast' of the sacrament" (Lewalski 396–97).[18] The legal aspects of the "contract" are not emphasized here; the opening meditation on 1 John 2.1, "An Advocate with the Father" (1.38), develops the figure of Christ as the "believing sinner's" advocate and thus refers most directly to the final judgment. While the biblical figure for Christ as advocate appears only in 1 John (the term "advocate" appears only once in the Bible), it is nevertheless an important figure. In Thomas Taylor's *Christian Dictionary,* the figural definition is the occasion for arguing against the "*Romish* Synagogue":

> [An advocate is] one, that pleadeth the cause of beleeuing sinners at the barre of Gods justice. Christ alone performes this office, by the euerlasting merite of his death. *I. John 2.2. We have an Aduocate with the Father, Jesus Christ the righteous.* Heere fals downe the multitude of Aduocates set vp in the *Romish* Synagogue, to Christ his great dishonor, who onely is our Advocate, because he alone is our Propitiator, or Reconciler. (6)

The figure is also developed extensively in Keach's *Tropologia* (408–13).

In a telling departure from these two commentators, Edward Taylor, in his *Treatise Concerning the Lord's Supper,* attributes the quality of advocacy not to Christ but to Christ's blood. The blood of Christ, writes Taylor, is

> advocating blood. Hence Christ is an advocate. He pleads their case with His Father in case of their sins. So that if the Accuser lay in any charge against them, He is ready to plead for them against the same, if I may speak after the manner of men, and He pleads for a pardon of their sins. This blood stands up and in effect saith, "I have paid their debts. I have in my hand an acquittance for their sin, and justice cannot seek nor receive her satisfactory pay at the hand both of debtor and surety." Thus doth this blood plead on the account of God's people as it is advocating blood, and this is sweet to contemplate. (209–10)

The logic of the exegesis in Thomas Taylor's *Christian Dictionary* suggests that the death of Christ results in his advocacy. Edward Taylor follows this logic, of course, but employs synecdoche (bloodshed in place of the sacrifice) from the beginning of his explanation. Furthermore, even here, in this relatively simple explanation, he employs *exergasia*: the blood is Christ, who is advocate; the blood "stands up" as advocate; and so on. Taylor attributes this function to the blood because the "new covenent [is] in My [Christ's] blood, and the soul's receiving of it imports the new covenent it's entered into with God in Christ" (204). As he explains in this section of his *Treatise Concerning the Lord's Supper*, the soul's "receiving" of the covenant is the soul's putting on the "wedden garment," a consistent metaphor used in the *Preparatory Meditations* and itself a figure of judgment. The intertextual patterning apparent here (Taylor juxtaposes scriptural passages throughout his *Treatise* arguments) he terms "the mystery of the Gospel" (205).

Despite this potential, the first meditation of the Legal Unit (1.38) demonstrates neither the exergasia nor the intertextual patterning of Meditation I.7. The poem proceeds through seven stanzas, each focused on a single aspect of the figure of the advocate. The language, with a few exceptions, derives from domestic sources: Law, Court of Justice, Pannellst, Bench, Bribe, Colourings, Pettifogger, Atturny. Some of the legal language does appear in the Bible; the language of the Lord pleading the case, repeated so often in the meditation, is repeated just as often in Psalm 119,[19] which expresses the link between the "uprightness of the heart" and submission to the law—a link not developed in this meditation, but one very important to Meditation I.40.

Other allusions lend little to this meditation. In the first stanza,

> Oh! What a thing is Man? Lord, Who am I?
>   That thou shouldst give him Law (Oh! golden Line)
> To regulate his Thoughts, Words, Life thereby.
>   And judge him Wilt thereby too in thy time.
>   A Court of Justice thou in heaven holdst
>   To try his Case while he's here housd on mould,

(I.38.1–6)

the term "golden Line" evokes a concept common to the Old Testament; the line is "a measuring rope . . . put for a country or tract of land, because it was measured by it, as Amos vii. 17" (Keach 6). Taylor uses the term as metaphor, which he may have found in 2 Cor. 10:15–16 and to which he adds the adjective "golden" to clarify the role of grace in the application of judgment. In the third line, "To regulate his Thoughts, Words, Life thereby," Taylor alludes to Col. 3:17.[20] These are the two most recognizable allusions (other than 1 John 2:1, cited in the title), yet neither is echoed or developed beyond the first stanza. The other six stanzas flesh out the advocacy metaphor in a manner strikingly similar to that of Keach, who lists an activity or quality of an advocate in one column and then applies that characteristic to Christ in a "parallel." In stanza 6, for example, Christ accepts no fees:

> This is his Honour, not Dishonour: nay
>   No Habeas-Corpus gainst his Clients came
> For all their Fines his Purse doth make down pay.
>   He Non-Suites Satan's Suite or Casts the Same.
>   He'l plead thy Case, and not accept a Fee.
>   He'l plead Sub Forma Pauperis for thee.

(I.38.31–36)

Keach argues that

> a good and worthy Advocate is of so noble and generous a disposition, that he will plead the cause of the poor out of pity, rather than they should miscarry. Parallel. The Lord Jesus stands not on fees, or gratuities, for indeed none are able to give unto him a reward for his work, but he acts on the same terms that God gives wine and milk, and that is, "without money, and without price. Whosoever will, may come" and take his advice. (410)

The advocacy metaphor, which is developed thoroughly in the poem's image, idea, and language, gives the poem the kind of unity we expect of the metaphysical poets.

Taylor employs this same metaphor in Meditation I.39 but uses allusion to bring intertextual patterning and greater depth and richness to the metaphor. While drawn once again from 1 John 2:1, the phrase Taylor chooses for the title is different and focuses on man sinning: "If any man sin, we have an Advocate." As is clear from the poem, the shift to "any man" helps focus the metaphor of advocacy in face of personal sin. Taylor's use of this as the primary metaphor of the poem is not so much an elaboration of Christ's advocacy as it is a direct application of the metaphor to Taylor's own condition.

Taylor employs, however, several other metaphors—ostensibly unrelated metaphors—in the making of Meditation I.39. The opening stanza is a typical and graphic description of sin:

> My Sin! my Sin, My God, these Cursed Dregs,
>   Green, Yellow, Blew streakt Poyson hellish, ranck,
> Bubs hatcht in natures nest on Serpents Eggs,

> Yelp, Cherp and Cry; they set my Soule a Cramp.
> I frown, Chide, strik and fight them, mourn and Cry
> To Conquour them, but cannot them destroy.
>
> (I.39.1–6)

The use of "dregs" that set the soul to cramping recalls several verses, primarily verse 8 of Psalm 75:

> (7) But God is the judge: he putteth down one and setteth up another.

> (8) For in the hand of the Lord there is a cup, and the wine is red; it is full of mixture; and he poureth out of the same: but the dregs thereof, all the wicked of the earth shall ring them out, and drink them.

Here, the wine bears grace, which acts against sin through wrath and affliction. Dregs then, the bitterest remains, the impurities within Taylor, are to be resisted but are the result of judgment. This allusion to Psalm 75 links dregs, sin, and the law and thus links dregs and advocacy in the poem.

The most important allusion, to James 3:1–3, provides the metaphor of bridle and reins:

> (1) My brethren, be not many masters, knowing that we shall receive the greater condemnation. (2) For in many things we offend all. If any man offend not in word, the same is a perfect man and able also to bridle the whole body. (3) Behold, we put bits in the horses' mouths, that they may obey us; and we turn about their whole body.

Taylor's selection of "If any man sin" in his citation of 1 John 2:1 emphatically echoes James 3:2. Taylor is this "any man," as he claims in the opening lines. The sin, however, is described in the mixed metaphor that at once relies on both a temporal and biblical referent—one elaborating the other in a confusion of dregs, bubs, eggs, and, in the second stanza, horselike imps and devils:

> I cannot kill nor Coop them up: my Curb
>   'S less than a Snaffle in their mouth: my Rains
> They as a twine thrid, snap: by hell they're spurd:
> And load my Soule with swagging loads of pains.
> Black Imps, young Divells, snap, bite, drag to bring
> And pick mee headlong hells dread Whirle Poole in.
>
> (I.39.7–12)

The metaphorical reins control the imps and devils; in James 3, they control "every kind of beasts" as well as man's body and especially his tongue and speech (which indicate the state of the soul):

> (6) And the tongue is a fire, a world of iniquity: so is the tongue among our members, that it defileth the whole body, and setteth on fire the course of nature; and it is set on fire of hell. (7) For every kind of beasts and of birds and of serpents, and of things in the sea, is tamed, and that been tamed of mankind: (8) But the tongue can no man tame; it is an unruly evil, full of deadly poison.

Taylor finds in the 1 John 2:1 citation the "rough" metaphor of James 3. In an additional play of allusion, Taylor puns on a homonym found in the Bible: "reins" is also the kidney, the seat of the affections. Keach explains: "The *heart* and *reins* are put for *inward thoughts* and *affections*. . . . 'God searches the heart and reins'" (14).[21] As poet and physician, Taylor must have been delighted to find this "spiritual meaning": the kidneys collect impurities of the body (flesh) and, in Taylor's use, relieve the soul that cramps with dregs, with sin.

In the later stanzas of Meditation I.39, Taylor employs images of the passion of Christ to describe in metaphor the atonement the sacrifice offers. Karl Keller calls them

> mixed and unclear metaphors in which Taylor finds the artful magic of Christ at work. On the anvil of life Christ can somehow hammer atoning nails out of flesh and blood that will hold man eternally. He can somehow use his blood for arguments out of his grave. Dying he can somehow live. These make little sense. It is left to Christ to make them more than mere fancifulness. (111)

Of course, these did make sense to Taylor, not only in the "artful magic of Christ" but, more accurately, in the magic of the Word. Keller refers to the blacksmith metaphor of the fifth stanza:

> I have no plea mine Advocate to give:
>   What now? He'l anvill Arguments greate Store
> Out of his Flesh and Blood to make thee live.
>   O Deare bought Arguments: Good pleas therefore.
>   Nails made of heavenly Steel, more Choice than gold
>   Drove home, Well Clencht, eternally will hold.

(I.39.23–30)

The metaphor is supported by the simile of the Word as both fire and hammer, as moved by the Spirit to break the stony heart of the sinner

(Jer. 23:29) and to fasten "the nails of conviction," leaving the "dreggy and impure part behind" (Keach 582, 578). The "Nails made of heavenly steel" leave an imprint of visible proof of the sacrifice that makes Christ's advocacy possible (John 20:25): "The words of the wise are as goads, and as *nails* fastened by the masters of assemblies, which are given from one shepherd" (Eccl. 12:11).

Clearly, the imagery of the poem's opening stanzas is an unusual, "inconsistent" mixing of dregs of wine, imps, and devils controlled with reins, curb, and snaffle; but it is imagery made consistent through the conflation of allusions to 1 John, James, Psalms, and Job. The closing stanzas similarly combine details of the passion of Christ with Old Testament passages that interpret those details and communicate both the need and the process of propitiation. Taylor's mixing of images and metaphors, his spiritual *exergasia,* relies on allusion to the Word for authority, meaning, and its own "peculiar eloquence"—the beauty of Taylor's "rough feet."

The final poem of this series, Meditation I.40, cites 1 John 2:2, "He is a Propitiation for our Sin," but Taylor moves away from the figure of Christ as advocate. Rather, he collates allusions to 1 John 1 and John 19, confessing his sin in images that are clearly domestic but that also recall details of the Crucifixion. Taylor acts on the wisdom of the epistle—"If we say that we have no sin, we deceive ourselves, and the truth is not in us" (1 John 1:8)—with the strategy of meiosis ("my sin is greater than thy grace" [l. 48]). As in other poems, Taylor employs exergasia, expanding on the filth of his heart, his sin, in a series of unrelated images:

> Still I complain; I am complaining still.
>> Oh! woe is me! Was ever Heart like mine?
> A Sty of Filth, a Trough of Washing-Swill
>> A Dunghill Pit, a Puddle of mere Slime.
>> A Nest of Vipers, Hive of Hornets; Stings.
>> A Bag of Poyson, Civit-Box of Sins.

$$(I.40.1-6)$$

Taylor's focus on his heart, so important throughout the *Preparatory Meditations,* is supported by the scriptural precedent in Psalm 119, to which Taylor alluded in Meditation I.38. The heart must be clean, upright in order for the Lord to "Plead my cause" (Ps. 119:154); thus, the filthy heart makes pleading the case all the more extraordinary.

In the following stanzas, however, the images for the heart change; the heart is now the site of games through which Satan "sheeres his fleece," teaches sin, and shuffles grace away.

Was ever Heart like mine: So bad? black? Vile?
    Is any Divell blacker? Or can Hell
Produce its match? It is the very Soile
    Where Satan reads his Charms, and sets his Spell.
    His Bowling Ally, where he sheeres his fleece
    At Nine Pins, Nine Holes, Morrice, Fox and Geese.

His palace Garden where his courtiers walke.
    His Jewells Cabbinet. Here his Caball
Do sham it, and truss up their Privie talk
    In Fardells of Consults and bundles all.
    His shambles, and his Butchers stale's herein.
    It is the Fuddling Schoole of every sin.

Was ever Heart like mine? Pride, Passion, fell.
    Ath'ism, Blasphemy, pot, pipe it, dance
Play Barlybreaks, and at last Couple in Hell.
    At Cudgells, Kit-Cat, Cards and Dice here prance.
    At Noddy, Ruff-and-trumpt, Jing, Post-and-Pare,
    Put, One-and-thirty, and such other ware.

Grace shuffled is away: Patience oft sticks
    Too soon, or draws itself out, and's out Put.
Faith's over trumpt, and oft doth lose her tricks.
    Repentence's Chalkt up Noddy, and out shut.
    They Post, and Pare off Grace thus, and its shine.
    Alas! alas! was ever Heart like mine?

The shift to these temporal images seems to have little to do with law, advocacy, and propitiation; the only possible link is to the casting of lots for Christ's garments in John 19:24:

> They said therefore among themselves, Let us not rend it, but cast lots for it, whose it shall be: that the scripture might be fulfilled, which saith, They parted my raiment among them, and for my vesture they did cast lots.

The gambling fulfills the prophecy of Psalm 22, just as the confession of sin, according to 1 John, is necessary for atonement. The gaming imagery, however, need not be linked directly to this possible allusion; the conflation of games in this description of Satan's play upon the soul demonstrates Taylor's propensity for applying the method of scriptural eloquence to nonscriptural materials. Here, Taylor mixes what Robert D. Arner identifies as folk images and metaphors with commonplace "scriptural" language (the words "sin" and "Hell," the phrase "sheeres his fleece," and the characterization of Satan engaging the players "Grace," "Patience," "Faith," and "Repentence"). Taylor conflates different games and gaming activities, puns on the names of the games, and develops Satan's activities in both folk images and spiritual terms. We should see this as exergasia of a different sort, a "temporal" exergasia, and as an extension of the special eloquence of scriptural language into temporal language.

The remaining stanzas of Meditation I.40 describe the action of grace as a result of atonement; here, Taylor conflates images in 1 John 1:7 of light and cleansing ("But if we walk in the light, as he is in the light, we have fellowship one with another, and the blood of Jesus Christ his Son cleanseth us from all sin") and the language of John 19:34 ("But one of the soldiers with a spear pierced his side, and forthwith came there out blood and water"). The blood and water is the "clear stream" necessary to bleach Taylor's soul clean in "Zions Bucking tub."

> And let thy Sun, shine on my Head out cleare.
>   And bathe my Heart within its radient beams:
> Thy Christ make my Propitiation Deare.
>
>   (I.40.61–63)

The meditation is the required confession of sin that will allow this cleansing to occur. Thus, the Legal Unit concludes with the *application* of the scriptural text to Taylor's personal life. Taylor actively answers the question of Meditation I.39: "What shall I doe, my Lord? what do, that I / May have thee plead my Case?" In the process, he moves from the uncomplicated articulation of the initial figure of Christ as advocate, through the articulation of the need and process of propitiation in the middle meditation, to the final hopeful confession. The play of allusion, particularly in Meditation I.39, is Taylor's method for understanding the potency of the Word and Christ (as "the Word made flesh"); he understands the paradigm through the "mystery of the Gospel."

Series 2 Typological Poems

As a significant number of the *Preparatory Meditations* in Series 2 are based on types of Christ, Karen Rowe is justified in arguing that "Taylor's typological vision is at the very heart of his poetic creativity, there by distinguishing him from tropological poets" (xiv). Using Taylor's *Upon the Types of the Old Testament,* Rowe analyzes sermons and corresponding *Preparatory Meditations* in Series 2 and argues that the

sermons and *Preparatory Meditations* are the last formal work on typology in England or America. Although in her final chapter Rowe suggests
Taylor's poetry is best when it ventures beyond typology into tropology,
her primary interest is in demonstrating Taylor's use of types. Even Taylor's distinctly typological poems, however, are enriched by the use of
allusions not directly associated with the specific type of meditation—
that is, he still uses the poetics developed in Series 1 in this more narrow
poetic context.

Throughout the early Series 2 *Meditations*, Taylor seems to be struggling with meditation on the type. Meditation II.6, on Jacob as a type of
Christ, is such a poem. It opens with Taylor's preferred structure, a confession of sin and a shift to meditation on a type:

> I fain would praise thee, Lord, but finde black Sin,
>   To stain my Tunes my Virginalls to spoile.
> Fetch out the same with thy red blood and bring
>   My heart in kilter, and my Spirits oyle.
>   My Theme is rich: my Skill is poore untill
>   Thy Spirit makes my hand its holy quill.
>
> I spy thyselfe, as Golden Bosses fixt
>   On Bible Covers, shine in Types out bright,
> Of Abraham, Isaac, Jacob, where's immixt
>   Their streaming Beames of Christ displaying Light.
> Jacob now jog my pen, whose golden rayes
>   Do of thyself advance an holy blaze.

Although the metaphor of the quill or pen of grace may be found in
Psalm 45 (to which Taylor alludes in Meditation I.7), Taylor does not
allude to any distinct scriptural text in these two stanzas beyond the use
of proper names.

In the next three stanzas, Taylor develops Jacob as type. As Rowe
points out, Taylor "relies upon *manifest* analogies between the Old and
New Testaments" (67).[22] Thus, little in the poetic description of Jacob as
type goes beyond what we find in either Samuel Mather's or Benjamin
Keach's expressions of it. Mather, like Taylor, cites Isa. 49:3 as the pas-
sage that "intimates" that Jacob is a type of Christ; he interprets Jacob's
"Sojourning" and "Wrestling" as the two points of comparison, noting
Jacob's travel to and from Egypt "by Joseph's hand" and his purchase of
"his two Wives," as well as Jacob's taking "of the Name of Israel."[23]
Keach cites these same comparisons organized by different headings.
Keach, Mather, and Taylor often allude to or cite the same verses as
sources of these comparisons; for example, Taylor's lines "The Name of

Israel in Scutcheons shows / Thou art Gods Prince to batter down his Foes" (ll. 17–18) allude to Gen. 32:28, to which Keach also alludes and which Mather cites.[24] Finally, Taylor's expression of the type does not elaborate on either commentator's work, and, of course, Taylor may have used Mather's description as a source. Indeed, the second stanza as an introduction to the type, suggests that the poem is not an exploration of type but instead a poem about meditating on types, which is confirmed by the sixth stanza:

> In all those Typick Lumps of Glory I
>   Spy thee the Gem made up of all their shine
> Which from them all in thickest glory fly
>   And twist themselves into this Gem of thine.
>   And as the Shine thereof doth touch my heart,
>   Joy sincks my Soule seeing how rich thou art.
>
>   (II.6.31–36)

In this stanza we also find the introduction of disparate images that have little connection to the type but have source texts in the Bible. The opening line links the image of the stem and branches in the previous stanza with the image of lumps in Rom. 11:16, "For if the firstfruit be holy, the lump is also holy: and if the root be holy, so are the branches." The next metaphor, the "Gem made up of all their shine," is more difficult to trace to a specific source text, but Keach describes the "metaphorical mentions of gems" as a "description of the glory and inward splendour of the church of Christ" (130) and identifies the source in Isa. 54:11–12,

> (11) . . . I will lay thy stones with fair colours, and lay thy foundations with sapphires. (12) And I will make thy windows of agates, and thy gates of carbuncles, and all thy borders of pleasant stones.[25]

Taylor's use of carbuncles and gems confirms this; he often employs the metaphor, using these terms interchangeably, as he does in Meditation II.34.[26]

The play of allusions is no different from that in the Series 1 *Meditations*. Only one allusion linked to Jacob as a type lends any intertextual patterning to the poem. When he is met by other principal figures in Genesis, Jacob is embraced by them (Gen. 29:13, 33:4, 48:10).[27] In the final stanza of Meditation II.34, the phrase "mine Embraces shall thy worship be" suggests that Taylor embraces Christ as the figures of the Old Testament embraced Jacob; the embrace is not typological but figural. As Rowe correctly suggests, Taylor uses types because "he seeks inclusion in the New Testament dispensation" (250); however, this is the same motivation for the earlier *Preparatory Meditations.* While Rowe sees typology as central to Taylor's "poetic creativity," Meditation 2.34 suggests that the typological element of Taylor's "poetic creativity" is overestimated. Rather than "*manifest* analogies between the Old and New Testament," Taylor seems more reliant on manifest tropes of grace. At this point in the *Meditations,* Taylor has developed an exergasia of images of grace: light, flame, golden light, lines of light, beams, golden ladders, lines of gold, lines written with a tincture of gold, jewels and gems of light, and jewels and gold woven into the wedden garment. In this meditation on a type, Taylor depends in every stanza on images he has already developed elsewhere.

Not all poems depend on this cluster of tropes; other patterns evolve—especially in Series 2. When Taylor turns to the ceremonial types, he explores images and metaphors that the personal types do not offer. In these poems, Taylor demonstrates the widest range of allusive strategies of any of the Puritan poets: his poems employ quotation, echo, and paraphrase not only of disparate biblical passages but also of typological conceits that are independent intertextual constructions.

One such typological conceit is manifested in Meditation II.27, which uses the purification ritual of the Old Testament to interpret Heb. 9:13–14. The meditation begins with the usual scriptural citation followed by a phrase from the verse. In this case, Taylor takes only the phrase "How much more shall the Blood of Christ etc." from Heb. 9:14, but it is clear from the poem that he has a series of verses in mind—specifically, Heb. 9:13–15:

(13) For if the blood of bulls and of goats, and the ashes of an heifer sprinkling the unclean, sanctifieth to the purifying of the flesh:

(14) How much more shall the blood of Christ, who through the eternal Spirit offered himself without spot to God, purge your conscience from dead works to serve the living God?

(15) And for this cause he is the mediator of the new testament, that by means of death, for the redemption of the transgressions that were under the first testament, they which are called might receive the promise of eternal inheritance.

Initially, then, Taylor uses one form of allusion, the direct quotation, to cite not just the single verse but the entire concept of justification and sanctification made possible through the sacrifice of Christ. Additionally, these verses themselves allude to other biblical verses—Lev. 16:14 ("the blood of bulls and of goats"), Num. 19:2 ("ashes of an heifer") and 1 John 1:7 ("the blood of Christ cleanseth"). Later in the chapter, the writer (traditionally considered to be Paul) alludes to Lev. 14:4, to the cleansing ritual that Taylor employs at length in this meditation; thus, the typological conceit is explicit in the Scriptures. The Bible itself provides some play of allusion, bringing verses together to form a concept in the process Cotton terms "Scripture interpreting Scripture." Taylor develops the biblical play of allusion, this intertextual play, in his use of leprosy as a metaphor for inward filthiness, for sin, and in his use of the purification rituals described in Lev. 13 and 14, as both types and metaphors for the cleansing of the soul by the blood of Christ.[28] Beyond the typological conceit, however, is allusion to other biblical texts, collated to amplify the typological conceit.

In the opening stanza of Meditation II.27, Taylor contemplates Christ in New Jerusalem, "Bedeckt . . . with Glories shine alone":

My mentall Eye, spying thy sparkling Fold
  Bedeckt, my Lord, with Glories shine alone,
That doth out do all Broideries of Gold:
  And Pavements of Rich Pearles, and Precious Stone
  Did double back its Beams to light my Sphere
  Making an inward Search, for what springs there.

(II.27.1–6)

The allusion to Rev. 21 illuminates the point of comparison in the poem.[29] Upon glorification (in heaven), the image of God on the individual soul is free of impurities, is restored completely. Taylor, with his "mentall Eye," compares the clothes of glory with the issues of leprosy he presently wears.

The clothing theme is maintained through the poem by other allusions. In line 49, "And put it Gold-Ring-like on my Right Thumbe," Taylor conflates the cleansing ritual of Leviticus with a passage in James 2:2 in which the disciples are instructed to make no distinction between those outwardly clothed in affluence, for they are as in need of the Gospel as those poorly arrayed. As in previous poems that allude to the "wedden garment," being clothed with the gold ring and gems (of Christ's blood) is being clothed with grace itself. Further, Taylor alludes in the final stanza of this poem to Exod. 19:10–14, in which Moses links sanctification and the cleansing of clothes; Taylor writes, "And clothe my heart and Life with Sanctity."

In another allusion to the cleansing process, Taylor invokes "Gospells Razer":

> Sprindge Lord mee With it. Wash me also in
>   The Poole of Shiloam, and shave mee bare
> With Gospells Razer. Though the Roots of Sin
>   Bud up again, again shave off its hair.
>   Thy Eighth dayes Bath, and Razer make more gay,
>   Than th'Virgin Maries Purifying day.
>
> (II.27.37–42)

By using the term "Razer," Taylor alludes not to Leviticus—the term does not appear there—but to any of a number of Old Testament sources.[30] In most of these passages, the razor is used to remove the hair, which itself is an indication of strength. In the seventh stanza the "Gospells Razer" removes sin—sin so strong the razor must be used twice.

In the same stanza, Taylor's "Wash me in / The Poole of Shiloam," an echo of John 9:7–11, is quite typical of his poetry. Yet it seems out of place, the odd line that doesn't fit the overall conceit. Yet, when we examine the allusion, we find it refers to a passage in John which retells the miracle that affirms Jesus as "a Prophet" or messenger of God. Jesus spits on the ground and with the spittle makes a clay. Spreading the clay on a blind man's eyes, he tells him to wash in the Pool of Siloam. Cleansing his eyes, the man recovers his sight. Applied here, this is the "Miracle" that Taylor calls for in lines 19 and 20 of Meditation II.27, "Woe's mee. Undone! Undone! my Leprosy! / Without a Miracle there is no Cure." The sanctifying spittle contrasts with his own "uncleane Spittle"; it is the cleansing that brings eternal life. Thus, Taylor's allusive strategies are not limited to the use of typological conceits, even in poems that correspond to the sermons on the use of types. Taylor conflates passages from throughout the Word to confirm the power of the "Scripture to interpret Scripture" and to reveal the "poetry" of the Word. More importantly, we see in this poem (and throughout Series 2) that Taylor has developed *intratextual* strategies: he echoes himself, alludes to an image of grace but invokes the entire cluster of images, and is able within a single poem to refer to several images of grace in successive stanzas, even though the poem is controlled not by images of grace but by the cleansing metaphor. Furthermore, he applies these strategies not only to scriptural allusions but also to temporal imagery as well, conflating disparate images to describe better the overwhelming emotional or spiritual state in which he finds himself.

The "peculiar elegance" of Taylor's poetry depends, first, on his awareness and use of the paradoxical injunctions of Paul, as developed by Augustine and later Protestant exegetes, and, secondly, on Taylor's ability, as poet, to recast biblical allusions to create intertextual patterning, to create new meaning in new contexts, to create new songs according to the prescription of Cotton's *Singing of Psalmes*. In reading Taylor's poems, we need to recognize the spiritual significance that unifies the "mixing of language," both spiritual and temporal, to recognize the moments when Taylor makes biblical allusion into images of a personal vision. While for Taylor the creation of new meaning is still explicitly the work of grace, the "Golden mint of words," and the "pouring forth of grace," the intertextual and intratextual play within his poetry results from a sophisticated understanding of language that he brings to the making of new poems. In this regard, Taylor is clearly the most sophisticated of the Puritan poets, but his "peculiar elegance" points to a new understanding of what is poetic about Puritan poetry.

Notes

1. Cotton, Preface (1640), Sig. **4. Throughout, I have retained the original spelling in quotations of original texts.

2. Both passages cited on psalter title pages come from Pauline Epistles (Colossians and Ephesians); the Pauline injunction for "great plainness of speech" comes from 2 Cor. 3:12. Compare also Paul's distinction between man's "excellency of speech and of wisdom" or the "enticing words of man's wisdom" and the power of the "Spirit" in 1 Cor. 2:1–5.

3. Ainsworth provides both verse and prose translations of the Psalms as well as annotations, which were intended for those trained in Hebrew and for "general use" (Sig. **2). Ainsworth's preface, which is significantly shorter than the Bay Psalm Book preface, nevertheless treats most of the same issues—and significantly for my argument, Ainsworth devotes the bulk of it to "aesthetic" issues.

4. *Singing of Psalmes, a Gospel Ordinance* was published in London in 1647 and 1650. Much of the material in his preface to the Bay Psalm Book is contained in this treatise, although the admonition against polishing God's altar is not. Published in London just as the second edition of the Bay Psalm Book was going to press in New England, the treatise was published again as the Dunster-Lyon revision was going to press and may be seen, therefore, as a defense of both the first and second psalters, especially in light of Cotton's reference to the revision late in the treatise.

Although I refer to John Cotton throughout, the authorship of *Singing of Psalmes* is open to speculation. Everett Emerson indicates in *John Cotton* that Thomas Shepard shared in the writing of the treatise (11). Zoltán Haraszti cites a note (124 n. 6) in Cotton's edition of the treatise written by the younger Thomas Shepard, who quotes pastor Edward Buckley quoting Cotton as having attributed "the chief hand" in the treatise to Thomas Shepard.

5. Expressed here in the words of the translators of *The Holy Bible* (King James Authorized Version) in "The Translators to the Reader."

6. For the comments on style and phrasing ("bee so full and perfect"), see ibid.

7. In studies of his sermons and exegesis, various critics have demonstrated Cotton's awareness of the "elegancy of the Holy Ghost" in sermons, which derives from the Protestant belief in the Bible as "a single composite whole" and a desire to allow the language of the Scripture to explain the sense of the Scripture. Edward H. Davidson sets out Cotton's training in the Protestant exegetical tradition in "John Cotton's Biblical Exegesis: Method and Purpose." Two other recent works have examined the "logic" of Cotton's exegesis and found it less than logical. Teresa Toulouse finds that Cotton brings scriptural passages together as "images" and allows his audience to find or build the meaning out of the juxtaposition of those scriptural images (see "John Cotton and the Shaping of Election," 13–45). Eugenia DeLamotte argues for Cotton's "subtle technique of illuminating signs by juxtaposing them with the abstractions they signify, but without allowing the translations to supplant the actual language of the Biblical text" (51).

8. Not unique to Cotton or Puritans, the practice of bringing scriptural verses together to form new edifying works was common in the sixteenth century. In *English Metrical Psalms: Poetry as Praise and Prayer, 1535–1601,* Rivkah Zim cites works by John Fisher, Thomas Rogers, Henry Bull, and Anthony Cope, all of whom compile verses from Psalms (29–30). In addition, George Herbert argues for a similar exegetical practice in *A Priest to the Temple*: "The third means is a diligent Collation of Scripture with Scripture" (Stewart 61).

9. Although Cotton is not directly addressing the writing of poetry, he does argue that "all men are likewise bound to sing to the praise of God in their deliverances, and comforts"—to quote just one short passage from chapter 9. The chapter suggests that even those without the spiritual gifts "necessary to make melody to the Lord in singing" have a duty to sing anyway. Spiritual songs composed "in faith" are acceptable because praise is a duty and also because praise or thanksgiving is not "an opening of the Word" of God to man but "an opening of the heart" of man to God (44).

10. Both Jeffrey Hammond, in "Reading Taylor Exegetically: The *Preparatory Meditations* and the Commentary Tradition," and Michael Schuldiner, in "Edward Taylor's 'Problematic' Imagery," refute the notion of Taylor's inconsistent imagery and suggest that Taylor's poems are better understood in the context of his resource materials: texts in Taylor's library and exegetical works of various (chiefly Protestant) commentators. Arguing for specific types of source materials, various critics find Taylor consistent within a particular poetic or religious tradition: Lewalski's *Protestant Poetics and the Seventeenth-Century Religious Lyric* on Taylor's use of the traditions of religious meditation; E. F. Carlisle on the "deep structures" of Puritan rhetoric that give form to Taylor's "Puritan poetry" in "The Puritan Structure of Edward Taylor's Poetry"; Norman S. Grabo's *Edward Taylor,* as well as his introduction to *Edward Taylor's Christographia,* for the importance of the sermon to Taylor's poetic and the structure of the *Preparatory Meditations;* Karen E. Rowe's *Saint and Singer: Edward Taylor's Typology and the Poetics of Meditation* for the influence of scholastic typology, meditations, and sermons on types in Series 2 of *Preparatory Meditations*.

11. In Clark, Taylor is the study example. As in Cotton's arguments for the singing of spiritual songs, formulations of exegetical method and "plain style" are crucial to the

Puritans' and Taylor's poetics. As a minister, Edward Taylor was acutely aware of the power of verbal relationships within the Bible, of the power of Scripture that interprets Scripture. In commentary on the Puritan exegesis, Clark argues that the exegetical method of the Puritans "echoed their psychology by divesting the scriptural image of its temporal dimension" ("'The Crucified Phrase'" 287). Divestiture of the temporal bonds of the image is but one step in the "exegetical process" of the poems. The Word in the new context still bears the image of Christ and thus carries the promise of grace to the new context.

12. Hammond's "biblical metatext" might be said to contain this "spiritual significance." I wish to focus upon Scripture's special eloquence as the license by which the Puritan poet, and specifically Taylor, may modify the biblical metatext by creating new meaning in new contexts. Additionally, Taylor applies the method of special eloquence to temporal language as well, creating new meaning in nonbiblical tropes and imagery.

13. "Royal Psalm," in *Die Psalmen,* is Hermann Gunkel's classification; see also McCullough 6–7.

14. Taylor had already written several meditations on Canticles by this time (Meditations I.2–6); verses 8 and 14 echo Song of Solomon 1:3–4. Keach cites Ps. 45:2 in his exposition of the figural "Church compared to a Wife" (689–92): "The Church, and every true believer, by being espoused and married to Christ, the Lord Jesus, hath a near, a dear, a strong, and most precious complacency in Christ; he is more than father, mother, sons, or daughters. 'He is fairer that the sons of men' (Ps. 45.2)" (691).

15. Thomas Taylor cites verse 10 but quotes 13.

Keach also describes the scriptural use of gold as simile for the Word: "The word of God most gloriously decks and adorns every true Christian, that hath store of it in his heart, in whom it dwells richly. The Church is said to be clothed with wrought Gold; the word of God, and the graces thereof, are doubtless intended thereby" (573). Although Keach does not cite Psalm 45 as one of the source texts, the language of his description echoes this text convincingly.

16. Scheick best delineates Taylor's views concerning grace and faculty psychology, particularly as they appear in the poetry.

17. The container images are typical of the *Preparatory Meditations,* of course, and each container has both a domestic and scriptural source. Scriptural sources for these images are cited in previous paragraphs.

18. See also Lewalski's discussion of this theme at 176–77.

19. Karl Keller suggests that Taylor intentionally misuses the Scriptures, confusing the roles of the lawyer and advocate in Meditation I.39. However, Taylor's source of "confusion" is likely Psalm 119. See Keller 110.

20. "And whatsoever ye do in word or deed, do all in the name of the Lord Jesus, giving thanks to God and the Father by him."

21. The phrase "heart and reins" appears in Psalms (7, 26, 51, 73), Proverbs (23), and Jeremiah (11, 17, 20).

22. Rowe indicates that "Taylor's poetic rendering virtually glosses" the typological sermon in his *Upon the Types of the Old Testament* (66).

23. See Mather 85–86.

24. See Keach 974–75; Mather 86. As Gen. 32:28 notes, Israel means "God's prince."

25. Neither "gem" nor "gems" appears in the Bible.

26. See lines 3 and 21.

27. "Embraced" is sparingly used in the authorized Bible; these verses are the word's first three appearances. Taylor also uses "to embrace," most often in meditations on Canticles, where the verb also appears (2:6; 8:3).

28. Rowe discusses the types in this poem (135 ff.).

29. Rev. 21:23 describes the city, which "had no need of the sun, neither of the moon, to shine in it: for the glory of God did lighten it, and the Lamb is the light thereof."

30. See Isa. 7:20, for example: "In the same day shall the Lord shave with a razor that is hired, namely, by them beyond the river, by the king of Assyria, the head, and the hair of the head: and it shall consume the beard." The razor metaphor is described by both Keach (177) and Thomas Taylor. The latter's definition includes the reference to Isaiah, and he interprets razor to mean "a fierce and cruell enemy, which destroyes and cuts downe all, as a sharpe Rasor shaues and cuts all bare" (389). See also Num. 6:5, Judg. 13:5 and 16:17, 1 Sam. 1:11, and Ps. 52:2.

Works Cited

Ainsworth, Henry. *The Book of Psalmes: Englished both in Prose and Metre.* Amsterdam, 1621.

Arner, Robert D. "Edward Taylor's Gaming Imagery: 'Meditation 1.40.'" *Early American Literature* 4 (1969): 38–40.

———. "Folk Metaphors in Edward Taylor's 'Meditation 1.40.'" *Seventeenth Century News* 31 (1973): 6–9.

Augustine, Bishop of Hippo. *Confessions.* Translated by J. G. Pilkington. Vol. 14 of *The Works of Aurelius Augustine, Bishop of Hippo,* edited by Marcus Dods. Edinburgh: Clark, 1876.

———. *De Doctrina Christiana.* Translated by Marcus Dods. Vol. 9 of *The Works of Aurelius Augustine, Bishop of Hippo,* edited by Marcus Dods. Edinburgh: Clark, 1873.

[The Bay Psalm Book.] *The Whole Booke of Psalmes Faithfully Translated into English Metre.* Cambridge, Mass., 1640. Facsimile edited by Zoltán Haraszti. Chicago: University of Chicago Press, 1956.

The Bible and Holy Scriptures conteyned in The Olde and Newe Testament. Geneva, 1560. Facsimile edited by Lloyd E. Berry. Madison: University of Wisconsin Press, 1969.

Carlisle, E. F. "The Puritan Structure of Edward Taylor's Poetry." *American Quarterly* 20 (Summer 1968): 147–63.

Clark, Michael. "'The Crucified Phrase': Sign and Desire in Puritan Semiology." *Early American Literature* 13 (1979): 278–93.

———. "The Subject of Text in Early American Literature." *Early American Literature* 20 (1985): 120–30.

Cotton, John. Preface to The Bay Psalm Book. Cambridge, Mass., 1640. Facsimile edited by Zoltán Haraszti. Chicago: University of Chicago Press, 1956.

———. "The Preface to the Bay Psalm Book: Richard Mather's Original Draft in the Boston Public Library, now First Published." *More Books: The Bulletin of the Boston Public Library* 4 (1929): 223–29.

————. *Singing of Psalmes, a Gospel Ordinance*. London, 1650.

Davidson, Edward H. "John Cotton's Biblical Exegesis: Method and Purpose." *Early American Literature* 17 (1982): 119–38.

Davis, Thomas M. *A Reading of Edward Taylor*. Newark: University of Delaware Press, 1992.

DeLamotte, Eugenia. "John Cotton and the Rhetoric of Grace." *Early American Literature* 21 (1976): 49–74.

Emerson, Everett. *John Cotton*. Boston: Twayne, 1990.

Fithian, Rosemary. "'Words on My Mouth, Meditations of My Heart': Edward Taylor's *Preparatory Meditations* and the Book of Psalms." *Early American Literature* 20 (1985): 89–119.

Gelpi, Albert. *The Tenth Muse: The Psyche of the American Poet*. Cambridge, Mass.: Harvard University Press, 1975.

Grabo, Norman S. *Edward Taylor*. New York: Twayne, 1961. Rev. ed., Boston: Twayne, 1988.

Gunkel, Hermann. *Die Psalmen*. Göttingen: Vandenhocck & Ruprecht, 1926.

Hammond, Jeffrey A. "Reading Taylor Exegetically: The *Preparatory Meditations* and the Commentary Tradition." *Texas Studies in Literature and Language* 24 (1983): 347–71.

————. *Sinful Self, Saintly Self: The Puritan Experience of Poetry*. Athens: University of Georgia Press, 1993.

Haraszti, Zoltán. *The Enigma of the "Bay Psalm Book."* Chicago: University of Chicago Press, 1956.

The Holy Bible. Authorized King James Version, 1611.

Keach, Benjamin. *Tropologia; A Key to Open Scripture Metaphors, together with Types of the Old Testament*. London, 1681. Facsimile reprint. *Preaching from the Types and Metaphors of the Bible*. Grand Rapids, Mich.: Kregel, 1972.

Keller, Karl. *The Example of Edward Taylor*. Amherst: University of Massachusetts Press, 1975.

Lewalski, Barbara Kiefer. *Protestant Poetics and the Seventeenth-Century Religious Lyric*. Princeton, N.J.: Princeton University Press, 1979.

Mather, Samuel. *The Figures or Types of the Old Testament*. 2nd ed. Edited by Mason I. Lowance, Jr. 1705; rpt. New York: Johnson Reprint Corporation, 1969.

McCullough, W. Stewart. *Introduction to Psalms*. Vol. 4 of *The Interpreter's Bible*. Nashville, Tenn.: Abingdon, 1955.

[The New England Psalm Book.] *The Psalms Hymns And Spiritual Songs of the Old and New Testament, faithfully translated into English metre*. Edited by Henry Dunster and Richard Lyon. Cambridge, Mass., 1651.

Rowe, Karen E. *Saint and Singer: Edward Taylor's Typology and the Poetics of Meditation*. New York: Cambridge University Press, 1986.

Scheick, William J. *The Will and the Word: The Poetry of Edward Taylor*. Athens: University of Georgia Press, 1974.

Schuldiner, Michael. "Edward Taylor's 'Problematic Imagery.'" *Early American Literature* 13 (1978): 92–101.

Shucard, Alan. *American Poetry: The Puritans through Walt Whitman*. Boston: Twayne, 1988.

Stewart, Stanley. *George Herbert*. Boston: Twayne, 1986.

Taylor, Edward. *Edward Taylor's 'Christographia.'* Edited by Norman S. Grabo. New Haven: Yale University Press, 1962.

————. *Edward Taylor's Minor Poetry: Volume 3 of the Unpublished Writings of Edward Taylor*. Edited and with an introduction by Virginia Davis and Thomas M. Davis. Boston: Twayne, 1981.

————. *Edward Taylor's Treatise Concerning the Lord's Supper*. Edited by Norman S. Grabo. East Lansing: Michigan State University Press, 1966.

————. *The Poems of Edward Taylor*. Edited by Donald E. Stanford. New Haven: Yale University Press, 1960.

Taylor, Thomas. *Christian Dictionary Opening the signification of the wordes dispersed generally through [Holie] Scriptures of the Old and New Testament tending to increase Christian knowledge*. London, 1612.

Toulouse, Teresa. *The Art of Prophesying: New England Sermons and the Shaping of Belief*. Athens: University of Georgia Press, 1987.

Zim, Rivkah. *English Metrical Psalms: Poetry as Praise and Prayer, 1535–1601*. New York: Cambridge University Press, 1987.

Part 2
Gods Determinations

Puritan Casuistry and the Character of the Three Ranks of Soul in Edward Taylor's *Gods Determinations*

MICHAEL SCHULDINER

The importance of the casuistic tradition for understanding *Gods Determinations* might be anticipated by the fact that at about the same time Edward Taylor began writing *Gods Determinations* in 1679, he was also confronting the prospect of gathering a church in Westfield, Massachusetts, with barely the requisite number of members in full communion. Taylor's major problem as he started work on *Gods Determinations* was how to increase the number of communicants in Westfield, and two solutions existed: lower the requirements for admission to the Supper, as rumor had mistakenly assumed Stoddard had undertaken in nearby Northampton, or find the means to bring the baptized elect to recognize their conversion and apply for admission to the Sacrament. As Thomas M. Davis points out in *A Reading of Edward Taylor* (1992), *Gods Determinations* makes hardly any reference at all to the Lord's Supper; instead, Taylor presented in *Gods Determinations* the different ways "to encourage the reluctant, backward elect to recognize their election, to come forward and to accept what was rightfully theirs" (32). The main source for discussion of the impediments that the elect placed in the way of acceptance of their election, as well as how these impediments might be overcome, was Puritan casuistry.

In fact, in his study *Gracious Laughter*, John Gatta suggests that *Gods Determinations*—especially the long middle portion of the poem—can be read as a study in case divinity.[1] There is no question but that Gatta is correct. The dilemmas experienced by the several ranks of soul in *Gods Determinations* are precisely the kind that one would expect to find in a casuistical work. However, the extent of the indebtedness of *Gods Determinations* to Puritan casuistry has not been fully appreciated. Much of what is otherwise obscure in Taylor's poem is clarified through a familiarity with certain casuistical works with which Taylor would have been familiar. The precedent for dividing elect souls into three ranks can be found in Puritan works of casuistry, but, more importantly, these studies in case divinity help the reader of *Gods Determinations* understand the different spiritual and moral character of the several types of soul being presented and thus provide the reader with another glimpse into the spiritual life of the seventeenth-century New England elect, a glimpse from the point of view of the minister-poet.

As will be explained, Taylor was familiar with Puritan studies in casuistry such as David Dickson's *Therapeutica Sacra*, which discussed the nature of those dilemmas that individual souls confronted in their spiritual development. In fact, the particular source for Taylor's division of spiritually distraught souls into three ranks in *Gods Determinations* appears to be Dickson's *Therapeutica Sacra*. Moreover, within the context of each of these three ranks, Dickson identified more precise character "types" whose progress in the faith would have to be nurtured in different ways. Of these types, Taylor selected several for special attention in *Gods Determinations*, and it is instructive to discover which character types Taylor singled out. However, before proceeding to discuss the manner in which our understanding of *Gods Determinations* benefits from familiarity with Dickson's *Therapeutica Sacra*, it would be useful to provide a brief discussion of Puritan casuistry in general, especially since no modern full-length treatment of specifically *Puritan* casuistry exists. Such an explanation will help us understand something of the casuistical tradition in which Taylor is working and why Taylor would turn to Dickson's casuistical study for guidance.

Puritan Casuistry and David Dickson's *Therapeutica Sacra*

According to Camille Wells Slights's study of English casuistry and British literature, the kinds of questions that typically concerned the English casuist of the late sixteenth and seventeenth century had to do with largely legal and moral matters: "Whether a man is obligated by a rash vow to disinherit his disobedient daughter, whether it is lawful to change interest on a loan," or "whether Christians may lawfully seize the lands of pagans by force." Such questions or "cases," says Slights, were typically to be found in the writings of English casuists such as Joseph

Hall and Thomas Barlow. Puritan casuists, says Slights, "in addition to cases of this sort . . . include cases that solely concern the spiritual life of the individual. They [Puritan casuists] treat such questions as how a man may be assured of his salvation and how a man may attain true faith in Christ" (31). Slights is quite correct about Puritan casuistry, as far as she takes the matter.[2]

It is true that in the casuistical studies of such Puritans as William Perkins and William Ames, one finds both moral questions as well as questions of faith dealt with at length. But the questions of faith were not simply tacked on to these casuistical studies as one might mistakenly assume from Slights's comments. The matter of faith was at least as important a concern as moral conduct for Puritan casuists, who in their books presented first matters of faith and only afterwards matters of moral conduct. In fact, one might argue that for some Puritan casuists moral conduct assumed an importance largely because the central statement in the work of Puritan casuistry was that in which the order of faith was delineated, and the order of faith for these Puritan casuists included within it, in a very prominent way, morally and doctrinally sound conduct.

Indeed, one might view the Puritan casuist's presentation of the order of salvation as the context within which he preferred to deal with questions of faith and obedience. In Perkins's *The Whole Treatise of the Cases of Conscience*, for example, the order of salvation is presented in the first of his three books. In that first book, Perkins begins by presenting his prefatory material on the need for confession, the nature of goodness and sin, and the types of conscience. Perkins then presents the order of salvation in the form of answers to specific cases or questions, as a brief glance at the first two question headings suggests: "I. Question. *What must a man doe, that he may come into Gods favour and be saved?*" (1:30); "II. Question. *How a man may be in conscience assured, of his owne salvation?*" (1:43). Perkins's answers to these first two questions present of course the development of faith, including the requirement of "*New obedience*" (1:38–43). The question that follows, the third question, now provides a basis for transition from discussions of faith to discussions of moral conduct, while still speaking within the framework of the order of salvation: "III. Question. *How a man being in distresse of minde, may be comforted and relieved?*" (1:52). Question 3 asks how the "distresse of minde"—created by one's own sense of disobedience and sin—which undermines one's faith can be remedied. Having answered this question in a very general sort of way for question 3 of book 1, Perkins can then go on in books 2 and 3 of his study to discuss in a more particular fashion the right conduct toward God and man which remedies that "distresse of minde" due to that disobedience which weakens one's faith. Hence, solutions to cases or questions regarding man's obedience to the Law, both insofar as his relationship to God and his relation to other men are concerned, become relevant (or remarkably irrelevant, as in the case of *adiaphora*) to the matter of one's progress in the faith, assuming of course that the case is one in which regeneration appears to be taking place. Answers to such questions as "Whether ornaments of Gold, Silver, pretious Stones, Silkes and Velvets, & c. may not lawfully be used?" might be useful in assuaging the soul of the regenerate, and they even become relevant for determining the state of his soul. However, the answers provided to such questions about conduct might also be of use to individuals who are not regenerate, or who are not in any course that would suggest regeneration, even while earlier questions concerning the nature of regeneration would *not* be of value to these same unregenerate individuals.

In William Ames's *Conscience with the Power and Cases Thereof,* it becomes still more apparent that the order of salvation forms the preferred context in which cases or questions of conscience are solved. Ames's introduction consists of a discussion of the general theory of conscience. He then provides the reader, much as Perkins had, with "cases" or questions regarding man's progress in his faith, as well as the temptations to that faith that the individual might meet with along the way. He then presents cases or questions regarding man's obedience, both insofar as man's relationship to God and man's relationship to other men are concerned. Unlike Perkins, however, Ames is explicit at the outset of his discussion of obedience or moral conduct about a common soteriological context that both questions of faith and questions of obedience share. According to Ames,

> every question, or case of Conscience (as the nature of the thing it selfe, and experience sheweth) is either about the state of man before God, or about those actions which in that state he doth put forth, and exercise. (2:2)

Cases or questions of conscience always proceed from a context that assumes that man is in a certain "state" or relationship with God, whether it is one of reprobation, weak faith, or assurance. Some questions of conscience concern that state or relationship itself; other questions concern the "actions" or obedience that is to be rendered by man in those states. However, the context for discussion of that obedience remains one's state or place in the order of salvation. Nonetheless, Ames separates matters of faith from questions of obedience, much as Perkins had, thus permitting one to extricate questions of obedience from the larger context of the order of salvation, if one chooses to.

However, in David Dickson's *Therapeutica Sacra,* the order of salvation quite explicitly provides the context for all the cases of conscience that he presents. As he makes quite clear, he is only concerned with cases of conscience that appear during the course of regeneration. Having identified some of the various types of "common Cases of Conscience" and distinguished those "that specially concern Regeneration," Dickson makes plain that he will concern himself exclusively with those cases that concern the elect: "Of this hudge great Tree, we take but only one branch to speak of, so far as maketh for our purpose concerning Regeneration" (17). Like Taylor, Dickson is concerned only with God's determinations concerning His elect.

The better portion of the introductory book 1 of the *Therapeutica Sacra* (some two hundred pages, each measuring 19 cm. in height) is given to discussion of the Covenant of Redemption, the Covenant of Works, and the Covenant of Grace, largely in order to explain the manner in which these covenants, in particular the Covenant of Works and the Covenant of Grace, are applicable to the regeneration of the elect. What emerges is a covenantally oriented presentation of the order of salvation: the elect individual gradually discovers the demands of the Covenant of Works; he then realizes that he cannot meet the conditions of the Covenant of Works; and so, by the will of God and the office of the Holy Spirit, he becomes engaged in the Covenant of Grace. It is a covenantal soteriology that Dickson presents, eminently suitable for a church society such as that of seventeenth-century Massachusetts, where, of course, the idea of the covenant played such a key role.

The remainder of the *Therapeutica Sacra* (over five hundred pages in addition to the two hundred mentioned above) is given over to presenting cases of conscience, specifically those that might be confronted by individuals struggling with their salvation. The very order in which Dickson presents his cases is indebted to his view of the order of salvation. Dickson first presents cases in which the individual is confronted by circumstances that prevent regeneration from taking place. He next presents cases in which those undergoing the process of regeneration confront circumstances that make them doubt whether they are of the elect and regenerate. Finally, he speaks of those cases of individuals who are indeed regenerate but whose regeneracy is obscured for a time. In effect, Dickson's order of presentation takes the reader from the very beginnings of the process of regeneration onward to about as far as one can go in this world.

The Covenant of Redemption and Covenantal Soteriology

The casuistical studies of both Ames and Dickson are particularly relevant to a discussion of *Gods Determinations* since these were the two casuistical studies that one can be fairly certain were available to Edward Taylor. Ames's *Cases* was found in Taylor's personal library when his effects were inventoried after his death and after his relatives had probably already taken a good many of the books (Johnson 211). Both Ames's *Cases* and Dickson's *Therapeutica Sacra* have been identified as texts or reference books at Harvard College when Taylor was a student there in the seventeenth century (Norton 384, 403). Of the two works, however, Dickson's is the more relevant for this investigation of Taylor's *Gods Determinations*.

There are any number of reasons why Taylor might have been drawn to Dickson's study in case divinity. Perhaps the most attractive aspect of Dickson's study, however, was that it presented its cases in fuller, more dramatic terms than did other casuistical studies written by Puritans. Early Puritan studies in case divinity such as those of William Perkins and William Ames did not actually present "cases"; that is, a "case" in the works of Perkins and Ames was not presented as a narration about an individual in a given set of circumstances for which the proper course of action is debated. Instead, the works of Perkins and Ames presented "questions," for each of which a lengthy answer or series of short alternative answers was given. In effect, the early Puritan works of casuistry, such as those of Perkins and Ames, more closely resembled sophisticated catechisms than case studies, at least as one might today think of case studies. If any actual cases were presented, it was in the biblical illustration used to demonstrate the scriptural warrant upon which the answer(s) rested. The point to presenting general questions was to provide "guidance" for the minister; some casuists believed that the actual number of different cases of conscience was simply too large to attempt to catalogue. Dickson's study, however, was stylistically much different. Dickson actually presented a case which, while somewhat generalized, described the circumstances which made for the anxious situation that the individual soul confronted. In some instances there even appeared the voice of the distressed individual, confronted with a choice and complaining of his bewilderment. The voice of that distressed individual did not vary from one perplexity to the next, but Dickson clearly thought the drama of a given case worth presenting in a way that Perkins and Ames did not.[3] It would be Taylor, however, who would fully realize the dramatic potential of the study in case divinity in *Gods Determinations*.

In Dickson's work, the covenants are the basis for the paradigm of spiritual growth that he presents. So too do the three covenants form the overarching structure of *Gods Determinations*. Moreover, within the context of each of the covenants, the related stage (or stages) of spiritual growth is presented. Like Dickson, Taylor views the Covenant of Works as the context within which the elect experience God's work of conviction for sin that is preparatory to conversion, and the Covenant of Grace becomes the context in which the faith of the elect grows to the point at which the elect are able to claim their right to the Lord's Supper and full membership in the church. Both stages of spiritual growth are, of course, comprehended in the Covenant of Redemption, which comprises the Covenant of Works and the Covenant of Grace. To explain the manner in which *Gods Determinations* presents the three covenants, the related spiritual developments, and the specific cases of conscience common to the particular stages of spiritual growth would require nothing less than a full-length monograph. I will focus here on Taylor's presentation in *Gods Determinations* of the Covenant of Redemption, which, as Norman Grabo pointed out (162 [1961 ed.]), is presented by Taylor in "A Dialogue between Justice and Mercy" and, one might emphasize, comprises the two covenants of works and grace as well as the related soteriological developments in the context of which Taylor presents his various types of elect soul. [4]

As Dickson explains the Covenant of Redemption made between God and Christ before time began, the covenant contained many points of agreement or "articles," but four of them were especially important for Dickson's study because they concerned the redemption of the elect by Christ (49). These four articles concerned 1) "the Persons Redeemed," 2) "the Price of redemption to be payed by Christ in the fulness of time," 3) "the gifts and Benefits purchased for, and to be given unto, the persons redeemed," and 4) "the Means and Ways whereby the Gifts and benefits purchased, may be wisely, orderly and effectually applyed to the Redeemed" (50). With some modification, largely for dramatic purposes, Taylor presents these four articles of the Covenant of Redemption in his poem "A Dialogue between Justice and Mercy."

In "A Dialogue," Christ is portrayed as Mercy and God the Father as Justice, and it is as Justice and Mercy that the Father and the Son argue over the articles or conditions of the Covenant of Redemption. The first article of the covenant, as identified by Dickson, the actual redemption of man by Christ from the penalties of the Law threatened by the Father, is insisted upon by Mercy. She explains that, as the very embodiment of mercy, she must show mercy to sinful man, however deserving of punishment he might be (ll. 1–26). The second article of the Covenant of

Redemption, as Dickson identifies it, the price paid for the redemption of man, then becomes the topic of discussion as Mercy agrees to stand in the place of the elect and suffer for the sins of man. Justice responds by agreeing to stay his hand against the elect, but he specifies the suffering that Mercy must undergo if man is to be redeemed: Mercy must be incarnated as man and suffer the Passion (ll. 26–48).

Dickson's discussion of the third article of the Covenant of Redemption, concerning the gifts and graces purchased for man by Christ, does not attempt to present all the particular graces (charity, patience, prudence, etc.). Instead, Dickson, employing more general terms, focuses on "chiefly Three: The First is regeneration, or turning of the Man toward Himself [conversion to God]: The Second is the Gift of saving Faith: The Third is perseverance" (83). In the lines that follow Taylor's presentation of the price paid for the redemption of man, Taylor also specifies three gifts purchased by Mercy which are indispensable to man if justice is to be appeased. But these three gifts differ slightly from those identified by Dickson. The dramatic context of Taylor's presentation of the gifts purchased for man by Christ is a debate in which Justice argues that Mercy cannot do enough for man to mitigate the sin he's prone to. Given this context, one would expect to find among the gifts bestowed upon mankind by Mercy the very matter of justification for sin, and that in fact is the first gift that Mercy speaks of (ll. 49–60). Says Mercy, "I'le free him from his Sin, and Set him free / From all those faults the which he's subject to" (ll. 57–58). That in itself is insufficient, argues Justice. It is not enough to be justified for sin; man will also have to demonstrate some measure of inclination toward the performance of the good, or regeneration. "None are sav'd without Inherent grace," argues Justice. Mercy therefore confers upon elected individuals a second gift, regenerate inclinations toward performance of God's law, the inherent grace that Justice says will be necessary (ll. 61–72).

Justice, however, has still one more argument to make, and Mercy, one more gift to bestow upon man (ll. 73–84). Despite the newly regenerate inclinations, there will still reside within man the tendency to sin, and man, says Justice, will fall away from the graces he has been regenerated with unless that regeneration is nurtured and strengthened. Says Justice, "he'l fall / For want of hands to hold himself withall" (ll. 77–78). To this, Mercy responds with the gift of saving faith in Christ's redemption of man, which furthers and nourishes regeneration and prevents one from lapsing entirely into sin. "I'le make him hands of Faith to hold full fast," says Mercy (l. 83). In effect, Taylor is presenting here not only the gift of faith; he is also presenting that other gift that

Dickson speaks of, perseverance. For Taylor, at least in this poem, saving faith and perseverance are not separate. It is by virtue of saving faith that one is able to persevere in a regenerate course. The point, however, is that Taylor presents here the same three gifts of Christ to man that Dickson does: regeneration, saving faith, and perseverance, although Taylor adds to this list the matter of justification.

Dickson's fourth article of the Covenant of Redemption contracted between God and Christ has to do with "the Means and Ways" by which the gifts purchased by Christ are to be applied to the elect. Here, Dickson speaks of the manner in which "the Elect shall be called forth from the Perishing World, and be effactually called and turned unto God." It is the order of salvation that Dickson is speaking of here. Moreover, he speaks also of the instruments by which this spiritual development is to be accomplished, specifically the hearing of the Word, entrance into the federal covenant, baptism, and the Lord's Supper (100–102).

In "A Dialogue between Justice and Mercy," Taylor also has a section in which he presents the manner in which "the Elect shall be called forth from the Perishing World, and be effactually called and turned unto God." What's more, the "means" by which such spiritual growth is to be furthered is the application of the very covenants themselves. Justice agrees to apply the Covenant of Works, and Mercy to apply the Covenant of Grace to the elect in order to further their conversion. One example from this section will suffice to demonstrate this very basic covenantal paradigm for spiritual development. In this instance, Justice and Mercy explain how they will generally incite the soul to the work of preparation and proceed to instill within him the grace of faith. Justice first explains how he will see to it that the soul experience the preparatory conviction for sin that will make the soul a fit receptacle for grace. The means by which Justice will convince man of his sin is by holding up to man the Covenant of Works so he can plainly see that, in the terms prescribed by the Covenant of Works, man is worthy only of damnation. Says Justice,

> I'le steping in
> Convince him by the Morall Law, whereby
>   Ile'st se in what a pickle he is in.
>   For all he hath, for nothing stand it shall
>   If of the Law one hair breadth short it fall.

                                                    (ll. 140–44)

Mercy will then be in a position to apply the Covenant of Grace—to offer the soul that grace of faith by which it is able to take up Christ and rely on Him for justification of his sin. As Mercy then explains,

Nay I to him will hold out in my hand
   The golden scepter of my Rich-Rich Grace.
   Intreating him with smiling lips most cleare
   At Court of Justice in my robes t'appeare.

(ll. 147–50)

The point here is that Taylor in "A Dialogue" not only presents the four articles of the Covenant of Redemption as Dickson had spelled them out, Taylor also presents a version of the order of salvation based upon the Covenant of Redemption.

However, Justice and Mercy will apply the covenants of works and grace differently toward different types of souls, and before presenting the different ways in which different types of souls will have the covenants applied to them and be converted by Justice and Mercy, Taylor first presents the different types of souls and the different obstacles they will meet with. In so doing, Justice and Mercy present different "cases" of souls, similar if not identical to those presented in Puritan works of casuistry such as David Dickson's.

Cases of Conscience and the Three Ranks of Soul

As indicated, the passage cited above in which Justice and Mercy explain how they generally perform the work of preparation and conversion in the elect is part of a larger section of "A Dialogue." That section begins by presenting the cases of three different types of elect individuals who put different impediments in the way of their conversion and concludes with a discussion of how these elect are dealt with by Justice and Mercy in order to undergo preparation and conversion. The different types of elect individuals that are defined in the cases presented in this section of "A Dialogue" emerge in later poems as the three ranks of soul. However, it is of special interest to note here not only the particular types of circumstances that the several types of soul suffer under but also the manner in which particular cases are treated by Mercy and Justice, who no doubt are to be emulated by those of this world who are charged with care for the souls of others.

According to Justice and Mercy, there are fundamentally three different ways in which man puts off his regeneration and finds excuses for not immediately taking up the "hands of Faith." Some will be so proud of their own accomplishments and abilities that they will scorn the need for salvation through Christ; some, while they might recognize the need for salvation, will simply be too consumed with worldly concerns to take up the matter of their salvation; and some will feel their sin so strongly that they will not take up the matter of their salvation for fear they are beyond reclamation (ll. 97–132). The proud, the distracted, and the despairing or excessively humble—these are the three types of individuals that Justice and Mercy find unwilling to begin the work of preparation, and so Justice and Mercy identify the manner in which *they* will have to begin the work of preparation in these souls.

Dickson, in the *Therapeutica Sacra*, earlier presented the same three cases of the elect who lay down impediments to the work of preparation in their soul, as Taylor does. For the sake of easy exposition, Dickson classifies these impediments according to the different type of individual that is likely to experience them:

> We therefore, that we may follow the easiest course, shall divide all Unregenerat Men, impeding their own Regeneration, in three Ranks. The First Rank shall be of those who eshew, so far as they can, all Examination of their own Conscience, lest it should pronounce Sentence of their state and disquiet them. The Second Rank shall be of those who do judge themselves indeed according to the Law of God, but after Examination do despair of any Remedy. The Third Rank shall be of those, who make a slight Examination of themselves, and upon some slight pretence give out Sentence of Absolution of themselves which God will not allow. (229)

Those souls who are met with first in Taylor's "A Dialogue," and are so proud of their own worth that they scorn the need for salvation, are listed by Dickson among his third rank of soul. As Dickson goes on to explain about this third rank of soul, the reason they are so quick to absolve themselves of sin is that their sense of self-worth is actually based on their worldly riches. This rank of soul perform only a superficial examination and "do absolve themselves in their own Conscience, by their good Works and Obedience done to the Law," says Dickson. He goes on to explain what he means by presenting an illustration from the Bible:

> Such was the rich young Man in the Gospel, who said to Christ, that he had keeped all the Commands from his Youth up, till Christ did prove him a covetous Idolator, who put a higher Price on his Riches than upon Christ and the Kingdom of Heaven. (271)

This rank of soul described by Dickson is the same as the proud soul that Taylor presents in "A Dialogue," whose pride like that of Dickson's third rank of soul rests in his sense of wealth and hence self-worth. As Justice complains,

> . . . I foresee Proude man will me abuse.
> Judging his Shekel is the Sanctuaries.

(ll. 103–4)

In both cases—Dickson's third rank of soul and Taylor's proud soul—the souls perform a superficial examination of themselves and proclaim themselves saved. If the self-examination were anything other than superficial, of course, the individual would have realized that no works or wealth of his own could possibly redeem him of his sin.

Taylor next presents the case of individuals who so distract themselves with worldly pursuits that they are able to ignore the dire consequences of the sinful life they lead. These individuals take their time getting round to examining their souls. In the words of Mercy,

> Some will have Farms to farm, some wives to wed:
> Some beasts to buy; and I must waite their Will
> Though they scrape their naile, or scratch their head
> Nay though with Cap in hand I Wooe them long
> They'l whistle out their Whistle e're they'l come.

(ll. 110–14)

Moreover, not only do these individuals generally ignore their sinful state, when they do think of their sin, says Justice, "most will count me blinde" (l. 116) or "they more just than mee" (l. 118), and they will continue unheedful of their spiritual needs. These of course correspond to Dickson's first rank of soul, those who, to use Dickson's words "eshew, so far as they can, all Examination of their own Conscience, lest it should pronounce Sentence of their state and disquiet them."

Taylor's third case of elected individuals who temporarily impede the beginnings of their regeneration is that of the soul who feels that his sins are too great to be pardoned by God. As Mercy explains, "I fear the Humble Soul will be too shie; / Judging my mercy lesser than his Sin" (ll. 121–22). In fact, this type of soul has such a keen sense of its sin that it believes itself worthy only of God's vengeance. The complaint of Justice to Mercy is that "The Humble Soul deales worse with me, doth Cry / If I be just, I'le on him Vengeance take" (ll. 127–28). What Taylor describes here is, in Dickson's terms, "the Second sort or rank of those who hinder their own Conversion" (256). These are the rank of soul who

> comparing the Justice of God's Judgment with their Sins, and, laying aside all
> thought of a Remedy from God's Mercy they flatly Despair, as if there had

been no Remedy provided in the Word of God for them, or as if the Threatenings had been pronounced, as Sentences pronounced absolutely without exception of their Repentance. (259–60)

It is also worth noting here, of course, that Dickson is not only identifying in his presentation of this rank of soul precisely the case that Taylor presents in "A Dialogue," he is also speaking in terms of "Justice" and "Mercy," the attributes of God the Father and Christ that are personified in Taylor's poem and who carry on the discussion of the three cases of individuals who impede their own regeneration.

The remainder of "A Dialogue between Justice and Mercy" discusses the manner in which Justice and Mercy will attend to the different individuals—the distracted, the excessively humble, and the proud—who experience the three types of impediments to preparation for conversion. This section of the poem begins with Mercy asking Justice what can be done about the "cases" of these three ranks of soul who will put impediments in the way of their own salvation.

> But in this Case alas, what must be done
>   That haughty souls may humble be, and low?
> That Humble souls may suck the Hony Comb?
>
> (ll. 133–35)

What follows is a series of six cases of different types of impediments that the three ranks of soul might confront; for each of these six cases, Justice and Mercy identify the specific manner in which the soul will be prepared and, in most instances, initiated into the conversion process.

Taylor first presents the manner in which Justice and Mercy generally operate to prepare for and begin the work of conversion of those individuals who "in Sin securely ly, / And do neglect Free Grace" (ll. 139–40; see p. 113). This general discussion is then followed by five specific cases. In the first three, Justice and Mercy tell how they will bring to conversion two different types of the distracted soul—those who perform no self-examination—and one type of the proud soul—those who perform some self-examination for sin but absolve themselves instead of relying on Christ for absolution.

The first case is that of the individuals who not only "in Sin securely ly," but "after Satans Pipes do Caper" (l.151), who are entirely consumed by worldly lusts and distracted from performing any self-examination. This case is described by Dickson as one found among his first rank of soul. As Dickson explains the problem, these individuals give themselves over to their "Brutish Lusts" and "beastly Affections," and so "by

frequent sinning have extinguished all sense of sin" (243). Therefore they
do not examine themselves. For this type of individual, says Justice,

> Red burning Coales from hell in Wrath I gripe,
>   And make them in his face with Vengeance Vaper,
>   Until he dance after the Gospell Pipe.

(ll. 151–53)

Nothing less than the vivid threat of hell and damnation will be sufficient
to convince this type of sinful individual of his need for Christ.

But this individual's case is not so bad that Mercy cannot foresee a
point at which he will demonstrate conviction for sin and will thus have
readied himself for grace, the "Musick of the Gospell Minsterill." Says
Mercy,

> When any such are startled from ill,
>   And cry help, help, with tears, I will advance
> The Musick of the Gospell Minsterill,
>   Whose strokes they strike, and tunes exactly dance.

In fact, the suggestion here is that these one-time profligates will make
especially dutiful Christians, dancing "exactly" to the "tunes" of the
"Gospell Minsterill."

The next case presented by Taylor is from among the rank of soul
identified earlier as the "proud" soul. This rank might perform some
examination but will absolve itself rather than seek absolution in Christ.
The specific case presented by Taylor here is that of the individual who
looks to his good works as meriting salvation. While the inclination to
the performance of the good might provide some "evidence" that
regeneration has already taken place, the works of man can never be so
perfect as to satisfy the demands of the Law and "merit" salvation. Yet,
as Dickson explains, there are some who perform a superficial self-
examination "and do absolve themselves in their own Conscience, by
their good Works and Obedience to the Law" (271). Of the works of
these individuals, Justice will perform his own evaluation and make his
own determination as to whether the individual's works might "merit"
salvation. Says Justice,

> The Works of Merit-Mongers I will weigh
>   Within the Ballance of the sanctuary:
> Their matter, and their Manner I will lay
>   Unto the Standard-Rule t'see how they Vary.

(ll. 163–66)

These individuals who count themselves saved on the basis of the merit of their good works do not take into account that the Law demands *perfect* obedience of them. It may also be that these individuals do not accurately try their works to see how they vary from the perfect obedience demanded by the Law. If they did judge correctly, these individuals would discover that their works cannot conform to the demands of the Law. But the suggestion here is that these individuals intentionally do not accurately assess the conformity of their works to the demands of the Law. They want to delude themselves into thinking that their works merit salvation and that they are saved. However, Justice will weigh the works of these individuals for them and discover to them how their works "Vary" from the "Standard-Rule." To trust to one's own works for salvation is, after all, the Arminian heresy. To look to one's own works for redemption is to count for nothing the redemptive work of Christ.

After Justice has convinced these individuals that their works cannot approximate the perfect obedience demanded by the Law and therefore cannot merit salvation, Mercy's role will then be to offer these individuals salvation through the merits of Christ's redemptive act. Says Mercy,

> Yet if they'l onely on my Merits trust
> They'st in Gods Paradise themselves solace. . . .

> (ll. 169–70)

Mercy will offer her own merits, the merits of Christ's work of redemption, for salvation. All these individuals will need to do is trust in Christ's merits. However, once these individuals have placed their trust in Christ, "perfumes shall from them flow," says Taylor (l. 174). These individuals will now be able to give praise to God and perform such works as are acceptable in God's sight, even though their works still will never approximate the perfect obedience demanded of the Law.

The next case, like the first described here, is also of a type of individual that I include among the rank of those that I have labeled the "distracted," but it is not really accurate to say that the individual that Taylor presents in this next case is distracted from performing an examination of his soul in the usual sense of the word "distracted," that is by something in the world outside himself. Rather, it would be more accurate to say that this individual is "distracted" in the sense that he is so oblivious to what is going on around him that he does not even think of sin as in any way threatening or anything to be avoided. He is, in the words used by Taylor, "ignorant" of sin—a "simple" soul. This individual is found in Dickson's case studies among his first rank of soul who perform no examination of themselves due to "gross Ignorance" of the "Rudiments of Saving Knowledge" (232).

The role of Justice in this case will be, of course, to distinguish for the individual between good and evil and to explain to the individual that all but saints will experience eternal damnation. Says Justice,

> Those that are ignorant, and do not know
>   What meaneth Sin, nor what means Sanctity,
> I will Convince that all save Saints must go
>   Into hot fire, and brimstone there to fry.

(ll. 175–78)

The soul having been sufficiently brought forth from ignorance and darkness by Justice to realize its sin and need for salvation, Mercy will then do its work, instilling within the soul the everlasting wisdom and light of salvation through Christ:

> Though simple, learn of mee. I will you teach,
>   True Wisdom for your Souls Felicity,
> Wisdom Extending to the Endless reach
>   And blissful end of all Eternity.

(ll. 181–86)

The wisdom that the soul will learn—that "Wisdom" which is the "Souls Felicity"—is the reason why God created the world, and, as every Puritan knew, the reason why God created the world is so that man might praise Him. But the sort of wisdom that Taylor is speaking of here is of course also an affective knowledge that not only "knows" that praise of God is the end for which the world was made but actually permits one affectively to praise God. In fact, in each of the three cases presented above, Justice promises to perform its role of convincing man of sin, and Mercy then offers to begin that work upon the soul that will eventually make the soul able to praise God for the grace of faith received.

In each of these three cases—the distracted individual who will be turned from his passions for things of the world to a love of Christ, the proud individual who will learn to rely on Christ's merits rather than trust his own works for salvation, and the distracted individual who will awaken to his sin and need for pardon through Christ—Justice and Mercy will have a distinctively different work to perform in order to bring the individual to a converted state. Justice will assist in the work of preparation, which in Taylor's terms consisted of conviction for sin by

Justice, as well as man's work; Mercy will then begin the work of converting these individuals and providing them with the grace of faith by which they are able affectively to praise God.

The two cases that conclude "A Dialogue between Justice and Mercy" differ significantly from the cases that preceded them in that Justice and Mercy do not perform the roles that we have become accustomed to seeing them perform. In the first case that follows, Mercy has hardly any mercy, or grace, for the individual; in the second case, Justice has no need to convict the individual soul of sin.

The first case is from among that rank of soul that I have designated the proud, those who perform some slight examination of themselves and absolve themselves of sin rather than seek absolution through Christ. The proud individual presented earlier in the poem thought that his works were sufficient to merit redemption. The proud individual in the case discussed here does not look to his works to merit redemption; instead, he extenuates his sin—he thinks his sin so little that God will not deny him salvation on so small an account. As Dickson explains this case, there are some who

> do think in their Heart that none are in danger [of damnation] except gross flagitious and notorious Sinners; but as to themselves, they conceive because they are not the worst of Men, they are without the reach of Divine Justice, especially if their Conversation be according to humane Laws, so regulated as they have the Reputation of honest Neighbors. (270)

But Justice has other news for such individuals:

> You that Extenuate your sins, come see
>   Them in Gods multiplying Glass: for here
> Your little sins will just like mountains bee,
>   And as they are just so they Will appeare.
>   Who doth a little sin Extenuate
>   Extends the same, and two thereof doth make.
>
> (ll. 187–92)

There is no such thing as a little sin, Justice will explain to the soul that counts its sins small. What is more, Justice will explain how extenuation of sin is itself sin and so compounds the offense in God's eyes. In this manner, Justice will perform the preparatory work of conviction.

What is surprising is that, in the stanza that follows the one above, Mercy does not explain how Mercy will offer consolation to the individual made contrite and humble by the convicting words of Justice.

In all the previous hypothetical cases presented by Justice, Mercy had foreseen the occasion to proffer mercy to the individual who would be distressed by Justice's conviction for sin. But that is not the case here. In this case, Mercy foresees how she will have to *further* the work of conviction started by Justice:

> A little sin is sin: and is Sin Small?
>   Excuse it not, but aggrivate it more.
> Lest that your little Sin asunder fall
>   And two become, each bigger than before.
>   Who scants his sin will scarce get grace to save.
>   For little Sins, but little pardons have.

(ll. 193–98)

Mercy's reply to this individual will not be an offer of justification through Christ. The individual will simply not be ready; he will still not be sufficiently contrite and humble. Mercy therefore will have to counsel the individual to more conviction for sin. In language that would seem more appropriate coming from the mouth of Justice, Mercy will tell this individual that, far from excusing himself for sin, the individual should "aggrivate" his sin—permit sin to fester in his conscience—for "Who scants his sin will scarce get grace to save." Those who extenuate their sin are not ready for the grace that Mercy would bestow.

The most difficult case, according to Taylor, is the individual who rationalizes away his sins as small. The others—the individuals distracted by the pleasures of the world or the distractedly ignorant or simple, or even the proud Arminians who think their works might merit salvation—none of these present so difficult a case as those proud individuals who extenuate their sins. All others presented in "A Dialogue" will be sufficiently convicted of sin by Justice so that Mercy can proceed to offer those souls kind words and redemption through Christ. The case of those who extenuate their sin is different. Mercy has no mercy, or hardly any, for these individuals, even though they are of the elect. It is more the convicting work of Justice that they require. For these individuals, providing additional conviction for sin is the most merciful act that Mercy can perform.

While in the first of the two cases that conclude "A Dialogue between Justice and Mercy" Mercy has no mercy for the individual, in the second of the two cases, Justice has no convicting work of justice to produce contrition and humiliation within the individual. This individual is from among Dickson's second rank of soul, the soul who performs a slight examination and thinks his sin too great to be redeemed by Christ and so is likely to discontinue entirely the work of preparation (256). He is from among the rank of soul that I call here the excessively humble. In the words that Taylor places in the mouth of Justice, this individual is "the Humble Humble Soule" whom Justice—sounding at this point more like Mercy—will counsel "Cheer up, poor Heart, for satisfi'de am I. / For Justice nothing to thy Charge can lay" (ll. 199–201). Mercy beckons this individual to hasten to her with the words

> My Dove, come hither linger not, nor stay.

> (l. 205)

It is this rank of soul who is ready to receive the testimony of Christ and put forward its first act of faith in Christ, if it can be prevented from entirely despairing of salvation.

Taylor at this point has provided such details about the original three ranks of soul—the proud, the distracted, and the excessively humble— that categories based on the manner of their conversion can begin to emerge in "The Frowardness of the Elect in the Work of Conversion" and finally appear in "Satans Rage at them in their Conversion." Also, in "A Dialogue," Mercy and Justice have been creating the Covenant of Redemption, explaining who the ranks of soul would be and how they would be dealt with. In "The Frowardness of the Elect in the Work of Conversion," the actual process begins by which the prepared souls are converted and brought to the point at which they can claim their place at the Sacrament.

The excessively humble soul identified last in "A Dialogue"—the soul who thinks his sin too great to be redeemed and who obviously does not require any more of the convicting work of Justice in order to be converted—is captured by Mercy alone in "The Frowardness of the Elect" and thus becomes the First Rank Soul of *Gods Determinations*. The proud soul who extenuates its sin, requiring additional conviction for sin—which is properly the work of Justice—in order to achieve its conversion, will be captured by Justice alone and become the Second Rank Soul. The other souls—those distracted by lust, the distractedly simple, as well as the proud Arminians—will be captured in more common fashion by the convicting words of Justice, followed by the consoling words of Mercy, and become the Third Rank Soul of *Gods Determinations*.

In "The Frowardness of the Elect in the Work of Conversion," Taylor begins the actual presentation of the first part of the process of the conversion of the three types of soul presented earlier in "A Dialogue."

Here, the excessively humble, the proud, and the distracted elect souls receive the infusion of the *principle* of grace by virtue of which the individual's reversion to God takes place and he is turned to saintliness. The work of conversion in them is thus begun (the first act of faith will appear afterward and saving faith still later). "The Frowardness of the Elect" illustrates the manner in which the three types of soul are not just passive in their reception of the principle of grace but actively try to resist the entreaties of Mercy and the threats of Justice to turn to God and follow His ways. The several types of soul flee from those entreaties and threats that are for the purpose of converting these souls to God, although all the souls are eventually "captured" and become followers of Christ, thus demonstrating, as Norman Grabo first pointed out (163), the manner in which grace is irresistible. However, since the substance of the entreaties and threats used by Mercy and Justice to convert these souls to God's ways has already been presented in "A Dialogue," what is presented in "The Frowardness of the Elect" is simply the imagery of the several types of soul fleeing from Mercy and Justice, without any discussion of the substance of the entreaties or threats used to finally capture the souls and turn them to the good.

In "The Frowardness of the Elect," Mercy is the first to go after those of the elect who are followers of Satan, who now resist grace and run away (l. 19). The individuals that Mercy will capture are, as explained above, the excessively humble—the individuals who think themselves too sinful to warrant salvation. These would be brought to the brink of despair if they were pursued by Justice and suffered further threats of damnation. Instead, Mercy alone pursues these individuals with her entreaties to turn to Christ. Thus pursued, these souls eventually "Cast down their arms" and "Cry Quarter, Grace," or "Chased out of breath drop down with feare / Perceiving the persuer drawing neer" (ll. 20–22). Some of these souls throw down their weapons used in Satan's service and turn to Christ shortly after they experience the entreaties of Mercy; others run until out of breath and drop, still fearful, despite Mercy's entreaties, that they are not sufficiently worthy to serve Christ. However, both of these types of First Rank Soul find grace irresistible and, having been captured by Mercy, are regenerated with a new inclination to the performance of the good. These souls, however, will still have to put forward a first act of faith before they can be thought of as in any sense converted.

Justice now enters the fray and, with threats of damnation for those who do not turn to God, "doth persue as hot as sparkling fire" the rest of the souls, who divide into two ranks (ll. 23–26). The first of these two ranks of soul runs up against a barricade. "They're therefore forc'd to face about . . . Their spirits Queld" (ll. 29–30). They thus surrender to Justice. These are the once proud and sin-extenuating souls presented in "A Dialogue." Justice's threats of damnation subdue the vanity of these souls and, "Their spirits Queld," they "Quarter Crave." These become the Second Rank Soul.

Justice next pursues the other souls, those who will become the Third Rank Soul. These souls are chased out onto a peninsula, where they are forced to make a stand that, if it fails, will lead to one of three consequences: being forced "into the Infernall Gulfe alive," being "hackt in pieces," or being taken captive by Justice. These souls, seeing Mercy standing beside Justice, decide, like many of the First Rank, to "Cast down their Weapons, and [to Mercy] for Quarter pray" (l. 40). Threats of damnation make these souls turn to Christ not in order to serve him in faith but for relief from the persecutions of conscience represented here by Justice.

The "lives" of these Third Rank Souls are thus spared, but they do not become Mercy's captives, as the First Rank did. They do not receive relief from the persecutions of conscience. These souls become the captives of Justice, just as the Second Rank became the captives of Justice. This Third Rank Soul comprises the majority of souls— designated earlier as the distracted (and some Arminians)—who are for the most part so preoccupied with other matters that they do not find time to concern themselves with the state of their souls. It is the threat of the "Infernall Gulfe" or of being "hackt in pieces" that makes these souls "Cast down their Weapons" and change their ways as the threats of damnation and a guilty conscience overwhelm them.

All the several ranks of souls, having however been turned to the ways of God, or "captured," and having acquired the principle of grace, can now put forth the first act of faith. These souls will also thereafter receive the testimony of Christ. The poem "Satans Rage at them in their Conversion" serves two important functions in terms of the larger development of *Gods Determinations*: first, "Satans Rage" provides the context in which the three ranks of soul are first identified as such; secondly, "Satans Rage" provides the several ranks of soul with the motivation for calling upon Christ and putting forward the first act of faith in the poem that follows, "The Souls Address to Christ against these Assaults."

Having been captured by the forces of Christ, the souls are now attacked for the first time by their former captain in "Satans Rage at them in their Conversion." Satan's basic line of attack is to accuse the souls of being unreliable converts. Just as the souls turned from Satan to Christ, so too they will turn back again when it suits them, says Satan. In the

course of presenting his attack, however, Satan also identifies the several
ranks of soul for the first time:

> You're the first Van that fell; you're Traitors, Foes,
> And Unto such Grace will no trust repose.
> You Second Ranck are Cowards, if Christ Come
> With you to fight his field, you'l from him run.
> You third are feeble-hearted; if Christs Crown
> Must stand or fall by you, you'l fling it down.
>
> ("Satans Rage," ll. 19–24)

The First Rank soul are those excessively humble souls who were
captured by the entreaties of Mercy after experiencing profound
humiliation and thinking themselves unworthy of Christ. This is the rank
of soul that, in effect, had always wanted to be one of Christ's soldiers
but had never thought itself good enough. Satan appropriately designates
these souls as "Traitors" whose conversion to Christ has been most fully
accomplished, having experienced both Justice's conviction for sin and
Mercy's consolations.

The other two ranks—the once-proud and the formerly distracted—
were captured by the threats of Justice. While they now both "sue for
Pardon do at Mercies Doore" ("Satans Rage," l. 7), the conviction for sin
that they experienced has not yet been assuaged by the consolations of
Mercy. These are the souls who will not know what to do later in the
poem when confronted with Satan's assaults, and they experience the
hope-fear dilemma (although of course they will eventually seek the
counsel of Saint). These Second and Third Rank Souls are appropriately
designated "Cowards" and the "feeble-hearted." Although they will not
actually run from Christ, as Satan here says they will when he later
confronts them and they experience the hope-fear dilemma, the faith of
these ranks of soul will be too weak actually to call on Christ, and so they
will eventually look to counsel from Saint.

At this point, however, the three ranks of soul experience the first
attack by Satan, which has been of sufficient alarm that, now, acting
collectively, they put forth their first act of faith in "The Souls Address to
Christ against these Assaults," despite the fact that two of the three ranks
of soul have not experienced the consolations of Mercy. In "The Souls
Address," the several ranks of soul recount their former evil ways in the
service of Satan, the mercy shown to them by their new master, and ask
Christ for protection from Satan's assaults on their loyalty to Him.

Most importantly, the several ranks of soul collectively recognize that
there is method to Satan's verbal assaults upon them—that Satan's

suggestions that they are only half-hearted in their service to Christ are in themselves designed to make the several ranks of soul waver in their loyalty to Christ. Aware that such are the "stratagems" ("The Souls Address," l. 22) of Satan, the several ranks of soul are able to assert collectively their trust in Christ and in fact challenge Christ to find fault in them that they are not prepared to amend:

> And if thou still suspect us come, and search:
>> Pluck out our hearts and search them narrowly.
> If Sin allow'd in any Corner learch,
>> We beg a Pardon, and a Remedy.
>
> (ll. 25–28)

If there were some question as to whether the assaults of Satan are in fact no more than stratagems (without any real substance) designed to make the souls waver in their loyalty to Christ, the next poem dispels that question.

In "Christs Reply" to "The Souls Address to Christ against these Assaults" of Satan, the several ranks of soul collectively experience the testimony of Christ in response to having put forward their first act of faith. In that testimony, Christ makes clear to the souls that so long as they persevere in His cause He will be their support:

> If that you stick unto my Cause
>> Opposing whom oppose my Laws
> I am your own, and you are mine.
>
> (ll. 4–6)

Also important for the development of the several ranks of soul that follows in *Gods Determinations* is Christ's advice here to the several ranks of soul that they must not credit Satan and believe what he says about their spiritual states. "Credit not your Enemy," says Christ to the several ranks of soul. Satan's "Chiefest daintie is a lie" (ll. 13–14).

> His murdering Canons which do roare
> And Engins though as many more
> Shoot onely aire: no Bullets fly.
>
> (ll. 19–21)

There is no substance to Satan's assaults upon the several ranks of soul, and this is an important point. The First Rank Soul will heed Christ's testimony here and, when further assaulted by Satan, will recognize Satan's stratagems for what they are. The First Rank Soul will experience a hope-fear dilemma but will immediately be able to turn once again to Christ for comfort, evidencing saving faith. This testimony of Christ will not be trusted, however, by the Second and Third Rank Souls; and when further assaulted by Satan later in *Gods Determinations*, the Second and Third Rank Souls will for a time credit Satan's lies and thus protract the hope-fear dilemma that they experience until such time as they receive the solacing and informative words of Saint. The Second and Third Rank Souls, like the First Rank Soul, eventually are brought up to such faith in Christ as fits them for participation in the Lord's Supper, and they too enter into full church membership.

In sum, *Gods Determinations* can be read as a carefully plotted verse-study in case divinity. The three ranks of soul do not appear suddenly, without preparation, in "Satans Rage at them in their Conversion," as one might think. Nor do the three ranks first appear, as Nathalia Wright suggests, in the previous poem, "The Frowardness of the Elect in the Work of Conversion." All three ranks are apparent in "A Dialogue," as are the general cases of conscience concerning conversion that these three ranks will experience—a fact revealed by comparison with Dickson's *Therapeutica Sacra* and that once more argues for the control that Taylor exercised in the creation of *Gods Determinations*. However, perhaps equally important are the particular types of elect soul that Taylor chose to single out in his verse study of case divinity and the paths of growth that he foresaw for these types of individuals. The excessively humble soul, who thinks himself not good enough for grace; the distracted soul who is so involved in the things of the world that he puts off his concern for God for another day; the distracted soul who is simply ignorant of all religion; the proud soul who thinks his wealth and works are such that he need not concern himself about salvation; and the proud soul who thinks his sin so small that he need not be concerned about salvation—these are the particular types of elect souls that Taylor selected to demonstrate the manner in which individuals stand in the way of their regeneration. Conversely, it is interesting to note that all of these individuals are converted—captured by Mercy and / or Justice; all collectively put forth a first act of faith ("The Souls Address to Christ against these Assaults"); and all collectively receive the testimony of Christ ("Christs Reply [I]"), although only the First Rank Soul—the soul that initially did not think itself good enough for Christ—has sufficiently heeded the initial testimony and has sufficient faith to call upon Christ when the need later arises. The other two ranks—all the other types of souls identified by Taylor—demonstrate what John Cotton and others called "weak faith," and when in need these individuals turn to Saint in order to bring them to faith sufficient to full church membership. That

Taylor chose to present the types of souls that he did and present the scenarios that he does might suggest that the dilemmas experienced and paths followed by the souls in *Gods Determinations* were those common to the parishioners of Westfield, although clearly additional research of another sort needs to be performed before such speculation might be confirmed.

Notes

1. It is necessary to point out, however, that Gatta continues to insist, as had Michael Colacurcio before him, that the several ranks of soul in the poem all experience substantially the same "disease": scrupulous melancholy (Gatta 119). While it might appear to be the case that there is very little difference between the voices of the several ranks of soul found in the poem, to suggest that these cases are all similar and therefore abandon the effort to distinguish the cases of what are, after all, *three ranks* of soul in the poem is necessarily to limit the significance of the poem in terms of what it might tell us about the different spiritual dilemmas confronted by seventeenth-century New Englanders and to underrate the learning and intelligence at work in *Gods Determinations*.

For a general review of the criticism on *Gods Determinations* see J. Daniel Patterson's article in this volume.

2. For another study of British literature and casuistry see Cathcart's *Doubting Conscience: Donne and the Poetry of Moral Argument* (1975). Also of interest are Thomas Wood's *English Casuistical Divinity During the Seventeenth Century* (1952), Elliot Rose's *Cases of Conscience* (1975), Jonsen and Toulmin's *The Abuse of Casuistry: A History of Moral Reasoning* (1988), and the collection of essays *Conscience and Casuistry in Early Modern Europe* (1988) edited by Leites.

3. But see John Gatta's "Edward Taylor and Thomas Hooker" where the point is made that Thomas Hooker's *The Poor Doubting Christian* contains dialogue between Satan and the soul that is similar to the dialogue in *Gods Determinations* (3–4). In all likelihood, Hooker, as well as Dickson, provided Taylor with model cases of spiritual distress.

4. For a discussion of the covenant of grace and the growth in faith presented in *Gods Determinations*, see Schuldiner's "The Doctrine of Spiritual Growth and Church Polity in Early America" and his *Gifts and Works*. See also J. Daniel Patterson's "*Gods Determinations*: The Occasion, the Audience, and Taylor's Hope for New England."

Works Cited

Ames, William. *Conscience with the Power and Cases Thereof*. London, 1641.

Cathcart, Dwight. *Doubting Conscience: Donne and the Poetry of Moral Argument*. Ann Arbor: University of Michigan Press, 1975.

Colacurcio, Michael J. "*Gods Determinations* Touching Half-Way Membership: Occasion and Audience in Edward Taylor." *American Literature* 39 (1967): 298–314.

Davis, Thomas M. *A Reading of Edward Taylor*. Newark: University of Delaware Press, 1992.

Dickson, David. *Therapeutica Sacra; or the method of healing the diseases of the Conscience concerning Regeneration*. Edinburgh, 1695 (Latin ed., 1656).

Gatta, John, Jr. "Edward Taylor and Thomas Hooker: Two Physicians of the Poore Doubting Soul." *Notre Dame English Journal* 12.1 (1979): 1–13.

———. *Gracious Laughter: The Meditative Wit of Edward Taylor*. Columbia: University of Missouri Press, 1989.

Grabo, Norman S. *Edward Taylor*. New York: Twayne, 1961. Rev. ed., Boston: Twayne, 1988.

Hall, David D., Comp. *The Antinomian Controversy, 1636–1638: A Documentary History*. Middletown, Conn.: Wesleyan University Press, 1968.

Johnson, Thomas H. "Taylor's Library." In *The Poetical Works of Edward Taylor*, 201–20. Princeton, N. J.: Princeton University Press, 1971.

Jonsen, Albert R. and Stephen Toulmin. *The Abuse of Casuistry: A History of Moral Reasoning*. Berkeley: University of California Press, 1988.

Leites, Edmund, ed. *Conscience and Casuistry in Early Modern Europe*. Cambridge: Cambridge University Press, 1988.

Miller, Perry, *Errand into the Wilderness*. New York: Harper & Row, 1964.

Norton, Arthur O. "Harvard Text-Books and Reference Books of the Seventeenth Century." *Publications of the Colonial Society of Massachusetts* 28 (1935): 361–438.

Patterson, J. Daniel. "*Gods Determinations*: The Occasion, the Audience, and Taylor's Hope for New England." *Early American Literature* 22 (Spring 1987): 63–81.

Perkins, William. *The Whole Treatise of the Cases of Conscience*. 3 bks. London, 1642.

Rose, Elliot. *Cases of Conscience: Alternatives open to Recusants and Puritans under Elizabeth I and James I*. New York: Cambridge University Press, 1975.

Schuldiner, Michael. "The Doctrine of Spiritual Growth and Church Polity in Early America." Diss., Kent State University, 1979.

———. *Gifts and Works: The Post-Conversion Paradigm and Spiritual Controversy in Seventeenth-Century Massachusetts*. Macon, Ga.: Mercer University Press, 1991.

Slights, Camille Wells. *The Casuistical Tradition in Shakespeare, Donne, Herbert, and Milton*. Princeton, N. J.: Princeton University Press, 1981.

Taylor, Edward. *Edward Taylor's "Church Records" and Related Sermons: Volume 1 of the Unpublished Writings of Edward Taylor*. Edited and with an introduction by Thomas M. and Virginia L. Davis. Boston: Twayne, 1981.

———. *Gods Determinations*. In Donald Stanford, ed., *The Poems of Edward Taylor*. New Haven: Yale University Press, 1960.

———. *Edward Taylor's Treatise Concerning the Lord's Supper*. Edited by Norman S. Grabo. Lansing: Michigan State University Press, 1966.

Wood, Thomas. *English Casuistical Divinity During the Seventeenth Century; with Special Reference to Jeremy Taylor*. London: S.P.C.K, 1952.

Wright, Nathalia. "The Morality Tradition in the Poetry of Edward Taylor." *American Literature* 18 (1946): 1–17.

The Homiletic Design of Edward Taylor's *Gods Determinations*

J. DANIEL PATTERSON

Gods Determinations is a strange poem. Ask anyone. And probably because it comprises so varied a mix of poetic types (e.g., epic, dramatic, lyric, in a dozen or more stanza forms), the range of critical approaches to this odd poem has been quite broad and remarkably diverse.[1] While each contribution to this rich array of published readings succeeds in illuminating one or more aspects of the poem, I find that analyzing the poem as a work that is deeply informed by the Puritan homiletic tradition more fully accounts for the work's structure, rhetoric, and artistic achievement[2] and helps us see *Gods Determinations* as indigenous rather than strange.

My argument, then, is that *Gods Determinations* can helpfully be described as a homiletic poem. In both structure and rhetoric the strategies of the standard Puritan sermon exert a pervasive and controlling influence on the poem. As a Puritan minister, Taylor regularly and frequently addressed his congregation, his audience, and he did so in what he believed was the divinely appointed mode that had become habitual with him—that of the Puritan sermon.

1

The Protestant sermon's long-established pattern was designed to reflect "the order of Nature" (Chappell 1); that is, it was designed to move the truth of Scripture from the head to the heart, from the memory and understanding to the will and affections. The Puritan view of human

131

psychology included an epistemology that accounted for humankind's fallen condition. Since any mortal's perception and understanding were confined to a state of corrupt nature, and since God wished neither to abandon nor to confound humans, he adapted the manner in which he revealed his truth and will to the capacity of his creatures. The outward and natural senses, usually sight and hearing, must first be acted upon. The senses conveyed information to the mind, where the power of memory was engaged. The understanding, the rational faculty, then analyzed the information and made it ready for the heart, the seat of the will and the affections. Any person's acquisition of knowledge conformed to this hierarchy of the powers of the soul (see Miller 239–79). Likewise, however, Puritans believed that God's grace acted on humankind in accordance with the same "order of Nature" and affected first the head and then the heart. For this reason, the Puritan sermon was designed to address, in order, the memory, the understanding, and, finally, the will and affections. The auditor's memory was engaged by the first part of the sermon, the reading of the biblical text. Next, the understanding or judgment was addressed by the explication, or opening, of the text and by the demonstration and proof of the doctrine derived from the text. Finally, the will and affections were stirred by the "uses" or "applications" of the doctrine, usually the longest section of the sermon.

William Perkins provides a convenient outline for the "sacred and onely methode of Preaching" in *The Arte of Prophecying*, a sermon manual known well among Puritans in the seventeenth century:

1. To reade the Text distinctly out of the Canonicall Scriptures.

2. To give the sense and understanding of it being read, by the scripture it selfe.

3. To collect a few and profitable points of doctrine out of the naturall sense.

4. To apply (if he have the gift) the doctrines rightly collected, to the life and manners of men, in a simple and plaine speech. (672)

Richard Bernard, author of another popular manual, *The Faithfull Shepherd*, clarifies the epistemological design of the sermon structure:

When the judgment is informed by Doctrine, the use must bee made to gaine the affection. These two cannot in nature bee severed, yet are they in themselves distinct. That precedes, this ever followes; the one is for the understanding, the other is for the will, both for the bettering of the soule, and to build us up in the way of life. (272)

This same epistemological pattern was apparent to Puritans even in the arrangement of the books of the Bible. As William Perkins demonstrates in *The Arte of Prophecying*, for example, the Old Testament opens with "Historicall" books (Genesis through Job), providing "stories of things done"; next are the "Dogmaticall" books (Psalms through Song of Solomon), "which teach and prescribe the Doctrine of Divinitie"; the last section of the Old Testament comprises the "Propheticall" books (Isaiah through Malachi), "Predictions, either of the judgements of God for the sinnes of the people, or of the deliverance of the Church, which is to bee perfitted at the comming of Christ." It is also significant that "with these predictions . . . they doe mingle the doctrine of repentance, and doe almost alwaies use consolation in Christ to them that doe repent." The New Testament also follows this pattern, moving from histories, through the Epistles, and finally to Revelation, "a propheticall history" (647–48). Thus, God had adapted to humankind's pattern of perception the manner in which he revealed his word and thereby had provided the instruments of his Word, the gospel ministers, with a structural model.

Working within this overall structure, Puritan ministers also designed their rhetorical strategies in accordance with human capacities and thus also in accordance with what Perry Miller terms their "doctrine of means" (234–35, 288–99, 358). A sermon's rhetorical or stylistic features that were intended for the senses and the understanding were so because that was the way to the affections in the heart. Again, the authority was Holy Writ, for the use of both plain and figurative language. On the use of plain language, John Downame supplies the Puritan rationale:

the Lord in the profunditie of wisdome could have written in such a loftie stile as would have filled even the most learned with admiration, yet he useth a simple easie stile fit for the capacity of all, because it was for the use of all, and necessarie to salvation to bee understood of all sorts and conditions. (341)

Puritan ministers typically were critical of their colleagues who did not use plain language and who thus became "like unskilful Archers; they shoot over the Heads, and much more over the Hearts of their Hearers, and miss their Mark, while they soar so high by handling deep Points; or by using of obscure and dark Expressions, or Phrases, in their Preaching" (Mather, Book 3:138). Puritans found biblical precedent also for the use of tropes and rhetorical figures. Because of the abundance of figurative

language in the Bible, anyone who wished to understand Scripture had
also to understand the use of rhetoric (Miller 310–11). Grammar alone
was not sufficient. Perkins addresses this issue by providing detailed
instructions for correctly interpreting the tropes and rhetorical figures
commonly used in the Bible (650–62). With the biblical precedent
clearly established, Richard Bernard lists and comments in each case on
the specific usefulness of eight figures of rhetoric which a minister "must
make use of " in his exhortation because they "have an incredible power
of attraction, & pulling to them the affections of hearers." Two of his
eight figures are remarkably dramaturgical and provide evidence of a
tradition continuing from the medieval pulpit: "Prosopopeia: the feigning
of a person; when we bring in dead men speaking, or our selves doe take
their persons upon us, or give voice unto senslesse things"; and
"Sermocinatio: or Dialogismus: which is, when a question is made, &
forthwith readily answered, as if two were talking together." This last
figure, Bernard explains, "stirres up attention, and makes the matter
manifest with delight; this our Savior used, speaking to the people of
John Baptist" (302–5). In her analysis of Benjamin Colman's homiletic
rhetoric, Teresa Toulouse also illuminates the basic premise of a Puritan
minister's use of rhetorical figures. Toulouse explains Colman's
argument: "Since our spirit is 'imbodyed' . . . people can best be
'worked' upon by 'Impressions' on our Sense and more particularly by
the Eye and Ear. Such belief in the necessity of 'Impressions' . . . offers a
rationale for the preacher's own use of dramatic language and dramatic
stories" (263). Or, as Taylor puts it, "Examples teach" (*Treatise* 195).

Taylor's extant sermons demonstrate that throughout his ministry he
practiced the structural and rhetorical principles of the Puritan homiletic
tradition. In the earliest of these, the "Foundation Day Sermon" of 1679,
Taylor first cites and then briefly "opens" his text; he then announces the
doctrine he derives from the text and goes on to explain and prove his
doctrine using both logical discourse and the standard device of questions
and answers (*"Church Records"* 118–58). In his later revision and
expansion of this sermon, Taylor enhances his proof of doctrine by
incorporating the similar strategy of a series of objections and solutions
(*"Church Records"* 283–373, especially 342–52). The third and final
section of this sermon comprises four applications of the doctrine, first
by way of "Information" and "Reprehention" for the use of the
understanding and judgment and then by way of "Exhortation" and
"Congratulation" for the use of the will and affections (*"Church
Records"* 143, 147). Taylor's *Treatise Concerning the Lord's Supper*
(which he dates from late 1693 to early 1694) is arranged according to
the same structure. From one text (Matt. 22:12) Taylor derives four

doctrines, or "truths," each of which he demonstrates and proves by means of queries and solutions. Each doctrinal section is followed by a series of "Uses," which begins by way of "information" and concludes by way of "exhortation" and "consolation." In addition, the *Christographia* sermons (dated 1701–3), each of which "Opened, Confirmed, and Practically improoved" scriptural material on the nature of Christ (1), show that Taylor continued to use the same homiletic structure, which he believed to be the most effective means for moving Scriptural truth from an auditor's head to his or her heart.

Just as Taylor's homiletic structure conformed to the "order of Nature," so too did his homiletic rhetoric. The sermon was his means of communicating God's Word to his auditors, and the rhetoric employed was designed to assist in the goal of making the divine intelligible to the human mind. Taylor praises Samuel Hooker's ability not only to help "Up Souls to Heaven" but also to bring "Heaven down to Souls" (*Minor Poetry* 117). One accomplishes this first of all by speaking in terms intelligible to all the congregation and then by making useful comparisons between the divine realm and the human. Christ, in his use of parables, Taylor writes, "took occasion to treate of Earthly things to demonstrate spirituall things by. . . . O! Earthly things do oft bravely illustrate spirituall things by. Hence the Ministers of the Word may warrantably illustrate divine Truth by earthly Comparisons" (*Harmony* 2:502). He illustrates his application of this rhetorical principle in a description of the body's physical torment in hell: since the punishment there is "beyond all conception," it is necessary that Taylor "indeavour to do something to help our thoughts about it." The description that follows takes up, in order, hell's effects on the senses of sight, hearing, smell, and touch (*"Church Records"* 85–86). Thus, Taylor saw homiletic rhetoric as a necessary means or medium by which his congregation could gain understanding of divine truth. This rhetoric supplied an initial impact on the outward senses in order to engage the understanding, the door to the will and affections.

In his discussion of the Puritan "doctrine of means" and of the accompanying theory of human psychology, Perry Miller points out that "By this doctrine were determined many aspects of the Puritan creed, and by it were ruled Puritan conceptions of the church, of the sermon, and of literary style" (289). Miller's judgment on this point reflects an important premise in Taylor's aesthetic: that is, the causal relationship that exists between Taylor's public purpose in *Gods Determinations* and the poem's homiletic structure and rhetoric. Whenever Taylor wants to move knowledge or an awareness of grace from the rational to the affective faculty, he addresses the powers of the soul in their "natural" sequence.

Since his purpose in *Gods Determinations* is public, he uses a public, homiletic structure and rhetoric. As Robert M. Benton explains, Puritan ministers in general reasoned that since the sermonic structure "was thought to be proper for that highest of all tests, the expounding of the Word of God, certainly it might also be considered proper for other works." Indeed, Benton suggests, "so strong a hold did traditional sermon structure have that it apparently dictated the form for other types of theological writing" (100, 98).

2

In its overall structure, *Gods Determinations* parallels the general plan of the standard Puritan sermon, the design of which, in Michael D. Reed's words, is "to move the theological truth from the head to the heart and impress upon the heart the beauties and glories of the divine" (307).[3] Within this general structural plan, the poem has five main divisions. The first begins with the opening "Preface" and ends with "Gods Selecting Love in the Decree" (ll. 1–418).[4] Taylor's primary concern in this section is to establish the basic doctrinal truths on which the remainder of the poem rests: that God created the world from nothing and gave it to humankind so that "Through nothing man all might him Glorify" (l. 38); that mortals by their own actions sinned; that they became thereby utterly undeserving and helpless; that God, while remaining both just and merciful, of his own sovereign will and love to humankind extended grace to some of the fallen creatures; and that many elect souls will face difficulty in their efforts to believe in their election since they will be caught between "Proud Humility, and Humble Pride" (l. 238). This division of *Gods Determinations* is analogous to the doctrinal section of a sermon: its chief concern is with describing, proving, and giving reasons for God's election of some for salvation. Taylor's use and arrangement of proofs and reasons is similar to Bernard's instruction to ministers to provide, in their treatment of doctrine, proofs of the doctrine first and then the reasons for it. "The proofe," he writes, "avoucheth the Doctrine to be true; the reason sheweth us also why that is so" (265). Taylor reflects this approach in his "Foundation Day Sermon": he first provides proofs (both "Inartificiall, & Artificiall") of his doctrine and then, as a final step in his demonstration of doctrine, provides three "Reasons" designed to answer specifically why his doctrine is true (*"Church Records"* 128–43). Similarly, in the opening section of *Gods Determinations*, Taylor simply states as true the facts of Creation, the

Fall, and God's decision to save some of humankind. This is the kind of "proof" that Taylor refers to as Inartificiall, meaning that it simply must be accepted on the basis of some authoritative testimony because the events themselves occurred beyond mortal perception (*"Church Records"* 458 n. 48). Through these first four poems, then, Taylor's "proof" consists of establishing these primordial events as facts, but he reserves any reasons that might explain why God decided to save some of humankind until near the conclusion of the first division. In "Gods Selecting Love in the Decree," Taylor provides his single "reason" for the doctrine of election:

> Almighty this [i.e., humankind's fall] foreseing, and withall
> That all this Stately worke of his would fall
> Tumble, and Dash to pieces Did in lay
> Before it was too late for it a Stay.
> Doth with his hands hold, and uphold the Same.
> Hence his Eternall Purpose doth proclaim.
> Whereby transcendently he makes to Shine
> Transplendent Glory in his Grace Divine.

(ll. 363–70)

Thus, the first homiletic division of *Gods Determinations* makes clear that God's selection of some for salvation has in fact occurred and that the only reasons why it has occurred are God's "Eternall Purpose" and his "Transplendent Glory."

The remainder of *Gods Determinations* comprises a series of—by this homiletic analogy—"uses" or "applications" of the fact, or doctrine, of election. The uses of a doctrine are designed to "gaine the affection" of the auditory after the proof of the doctrine has informed the understanding (Bernard 272). To show that a doctrine normally should be applied first generally and then more specifically, Bernard distinguishes "uses" from "applications." The use, he writes, is more general in its advice or admonition; the application, however,

> is a neerer bringing of the Use delivered, after a more general sort, in the third person . . . to the time, place, and persons of what sort soever then present: and uttered in the second person, or in the first, when the Minister, as the Apostle doth, will include himself with them. (327)

In addition, even though the uses or applications are generally aimed at the will and affections, Taylor consistently arranges the several standard types of uses in imitation of the overall sermonic structure, beginning usually with uses by way of instruction and reproof for the understanding, and concluding with uses by way of consolation and exhortation for the affections. Thus, even the section of the sermon whose primary function is to stir the affections addresses first the head and then the heart. The influence from the homiletic device of uses or applications is also apparent in the design and arrangement of the second, third, fourth, and fifth divisions of *Gods Determinations*.

The second division of the poem—beginning with "The Frowardness of the elect in the Work of Conversion" and ending with "The Effect of this Reply with a fresh Assault from Satan" (ll. 419–604)—represents the most general application of the doctrine to all of the elect. In this section the elect are drawn from Satan to Christ by Mercy and Justice. Christ, without assuring any particular group of grace, then makes a general statement of the condition of grace: "To him that smiteth hip, and thigh, / My foes as his: Walks warily, / I'le give him Grace: he'st give me praise" (ll. 565–67). The division then concludes with an encouraged First Rank and no suggestion that those souls will face serious difficulties in what follows, but with "Still Drooping" Second and Third Ranks and a strong intimation that Satan will effectively challenge them (ll. 571–92). Then, as if heeding William Perkins's instruction that a doctrine should be applied "according to the divers conditions of men and people" (665), in the third and fourth divisions Taylor addresses the elect according to his two main groups and more specifically applies the doctrine of election to the particular case of each, treating first those captured by Mercy, or the First Rank (ll. 605–1016), and then those captured by Justice, or the Second and Third Ranks (ll. 1017–1914). Finally, the poem's fifth division applies election again to all of the elect now in their ultimate mortal condition as "the Lambs espoused Wife," in a carefully detailed rhapsody of consolation (ll. 1915–2102). Within these four divisions, then, Taylor applies the doctrine of election first to the rational faculty and then to the will and affections. He treats first generally, by way of instruction, the effect of election on all of the elect, then in a more specific treatment demonstrates the effect of election on the diverse conditions of his audience. Finally, he addresses the affections directly in an attempt to present the consoling and "Comfortable Effects" of election. As the application of doctrine in any sermon was designed primarily to stir the will and affections, throughout these four divisions of *Gods Determinations* there runs an implicit exhortation to the poem's audience to find hope of their own election in the examples presented.

One convention of Puritan sermons that ministers used to assist in their proof of a sermon's doctrine or to obviate objections to an application of that doctrine was a series of questions, or objections, and answers to them, often also presented as problems and solutions. This technique is an appeal to reason amid a general effort to move the will and affections. Bernard, for example, lists as the first use to be made of a doctrine that "of Confutation," "because if the truth delivered have any adversaries, they must be confuted first: for, where the doctrine is gaine-said, there no other uses can be made; till it bee approved, and the errours or heresies be overthrown" (274). Similarly, Bernard advises ministers upon completion of the doctrine's applications to follow with "Prevention of Objections":

> for men are no sooner spoken unto, but if they dislike any thing they will speake against it. . . . If exhorted to good things, they have their excuses; all which must bee taken away. . . . It furthers much the matter, and cuts off the occasion of cavils. First, it is done either by propounding what might be said and answered. . . . Secondly, or else to answer an objection, which might bee made closely, without mentioning of it. . . . (343)

Taylor regularly employs this standard homiletic device in his sermons. At the end of his proof of doctrine in the "Foundation Day Sermon," for example, he sets up a series of three questions and answers. In his later revision of this sermon, he keeps these three questions and uses in addition a series of objections and solutions (*"Church Records"* 140–43, 342–54). Throughout both the *Treatise Concerning the Lord's Supper* and the *Christographia*, Taylor employs objections or questions and their solutions.[5]

Taylor's training and demonstrable skill in the use of this homiletic device manifest themselves in *Gods Determinations* in his abundant use of dialogue, in which his keen perception of the hopes and fears of those in his congregation emerges—a perception that grew out of his experience as a pastor counseling froward souls. In "A Dialogue between Justice and Mercy," for example, where Taylor revels in the Christian paradox that God remains just even when merciful, Taylor's pastoral interest in anticipating the various ways in which individuals might resist his exhortations is apparent in the companion stanzas of Mercy and Justice, both of whom "foresee" that "Proud man will me abuse" and that "the Humble Soul" will likewise resist the offer of grace (ll. 209–44). In the First Rank's direct confrontation with Satan ("First Satans Assault against those that first Came up to Mercy's terms"), Satan voices some of the persistent fears and doubts of Puritans. He begins by questioning the First Rank's very calling: "Why to an Empty Whistle did you goe?" (l. 606); the First Rank then makes an immediate answer as well as a nicely logical turn on Satan's own words: "It's not an Empty Whistle: yet withall, / And if it be a Whistle, then a Call" (ll. 609–10). First Rank Soul

consistently counters each of Satan's challenges with an effective
answer. In "A Threnodiall Dialogue between The Second and Third
Ranks," the two ranks sing in counterpoint what amount to objections
Puritans might raise against the proposition that they are saved. These
objections, however, in order to intensify the presently worsening
condition of the Second and Third Ranks, are not given solutions.
Finally, throughout the lengthy dialogues between Saint and Soul
(ll. 1347–1842), Taylor's skill with this standard homiletic strategy of
presenting real and often entangling objections to a proposition (in order
the more dramatically to demonstrate the clear and satisfying solutions to
them) is apparent in Saint's steady supply of answers to Soul's doubts. If
Soul's sins "Swim in Mercies boundless Ocean," then, says Saint, "they'l
. . . swim quite away / On Mercies main, if you Repenting Stay"
(ll. 1367, 1371–72). When Soul claims, "my Hopes do witherd
ly, / Before their buds break out, their blossoms dy," Saint counters,
"The Apple plainly prooves the blossom were. / Thy withred Hopes hold
out Desires as Cleare" (ll. 1485–86). And so on. In discussing Taylor's
use of dialogues, Michael Colacurcio praises as "a considerable literary
virtue" Taylor's "ability not only to anticipate the most worthy objections
from potential listeners but even to sympathize with their feelings" (300).
Taylor, of course, developed this ability in his training and experience as
a spiritual counselor and composer of sermons.[6]

The homiletic aesthetic of *Gods Determinations* shapes not only the
poem's overall structure but also its rhetoric. The diction, the use of
proverbs, the allegorical devices, and the imagery all contribute to the
general homiletic design, and they all are consistent with the Puritan
"plain style" of preaching; that is, they conform to the theory that words,
images, and tropes must be intelligible to the understanding of the "plain
man" before they can have the ultimate desired effect on his or her will
and affections. In Colacurcio's phrase, Taylor's concern is "to
domesticate the transcendent in the particular" (299).

The significance of the diction and use of proverbs in *Gods
Determinations* is best seen by contrast with the greater number of
difficult words and the relative lack of proverbial expressions in the
Preparatory Meditations. To support his view that Taylor's meditations
are private poems, Charles W. Mignon points out that Taylor uses "many
words" in them "which . . . would have been unfamiliar or archaic to
many of his contemporaries" (253). In *Gods Determinations*, however,
Taylor's homiletic purpose and accompanying awareness of audience
lead him to choose words his audience will be familiar with. All dialect
words in the poem, for example, are in general usage in the seventeenth
century, with the sole exception of "Squitchen" (l. 30), Taylor's

diminutive form of "squitch," which was then current in Leicestershire and three neighboring counties. Only two borrowings from Hebrew occur, and both would have been familiar from their use in the King James translation: "Shekel" (l. 216) and "Epha" (l. 1246). Only five specialized words from law and theology occur, and they represent simple, basic concepts: "Quittance" (l. 203), "surety" (l. 240), "Acquittance" (l. 314), "Amercement" (l. 635), and "distrain" (l. 638). Furthermore, none of the language in *Gods Determinations* was obsolete or archaic in the seventeenth century.[7] Robert Arner's study of Taylor's use of proverbs in *Gods Determinations* indicates a similar contrast with Taylor's private meditations, which, as Arner notes, contain almost no proverbs. Arner concludes that the abundance of folk proverbs in the poem results from Taylor's "ministerial training in the 'plain style'" ("Proverbs" 13). Yet Taylor goes beyond simply adopting known proverbs; he further acknowledges the usefulness of the proverb by occasionally using the form of the proverb for nonproverbial material. Mercy, for example, in her dialogue with Justice, laments: "Some will have Farms to farm, Some wives to wed: / Some beasts to buy; and I must waite their Will" (ll. 222–23). These lines demonstrate Taylor's artistry with the proverb, for they have the sound and imagery of an authentic folk proverb (with especially fine half-line alliteration). However, Taylor has based these lines on the following passage from Christ's parable of the "great supper":

> And they all with one consent began to make excuse. The first said unto him, I have bought a piece of ground, and I must needs go and see it: I pray thee have me excused. And another said, I have bought five yoke of oxen, and I go to prove them: I pray thee have me excused. And another said, I have married a wife, and therefore I cannot come. (Luke 14:18–20)

Later in the poem, Saint sums up a long speech to Soul with a proverb that does not appear in any of the standard collections of proverbs: "Give but a Child a Knife to Still his Din: / He'l Cut his Fingers with it ere he blin" (ll. 1555–56). Clearly, then, Taylor makes abundant use of proverbial expressions in *Gods Determinations*. This fact, taken together with the near absence of proverbs in the *Preparatory Meditations,* indicates that in *Gods Determinations* Taylor consciously keeps his rhetoric within the reach of even the least educated. It was, after all, the homilist, as Gerald R. Owst points out, who first clothed folk sayings "with a deep spiritual and social significance for the ordinary man, who linked them in his more polished speech with great religious themes and moral principles" (46).

Jean Thomas has shown that the allegorical figures and action in *Gods Determinations* are more likely influenced by the homiletic tradition than by the medieval morality tradition. Specifically, within the Puritan homiletic tradition, writers often cite examples of allegory that occur in the Bible, especially in the Epistles, as proper precedent for their own use of the device. William Perkins advises, however, the following "cautions" in the use of allegories:

> 1. Let them be used sparingly and soberly. 2. Let them not bee farre fetcht, but fitting to the matter in hand. 3. They must be quickly dispatcht. 4. They are to be used for instruction of the life, and not to proove any point of faith. (664)

Similarly, Richard Bernard advises that they "not be too far fetched, strained, obscure, or foolish" (244). With such prominent voices advocating pastoral restraint in the use of allegories, it is likely that Taylor would judge the sustained allegorical action of the morality plays to be inappropriate for a poem with a homiletic purpose and design. Thus, as Thomas for other reasons concludes, Taylor's allegorical models are more likely to have been products of the homiletic tradition. Furthermore, Taylor's use of allegorical figures in *Gods Determinations* is a logical extension of his own homiletic practice. In the "Foundation Day Sermon," for example, Taylor creates an extended analogy between a Congregational church and the construction of a physical building. This analogy results in an allegorical representation of Taylor's conception of a church of Christ. He begins the analogy as he opens the text by naming Christ as "both the foundation, & Corner Stone" of the structure. The Prophets and the Apostles are the "Wise Master builders, laying this foundation, under God" (here he cites St. Paul's use of this figure in 1 Cor. 3:10). As he completes the explication of the text and begins his treatment of the doctrine, he continues the analogy by explaining that the Bible, the ministry, and the ministers are "the tooles & Artists which God makes use of in raising this building," and that their building stones—the saints of a congregation—"are fetcht out of the Quarry, or Stone pit of Mankind, & hewen, & Squared by the Axe of the Spirit till they are rightly pollisht & fitted for this building" (*"Church Records"* 120–25). Taylor conceived this allegorical representation as a means of striking the senses and the understanding of his auditory, and for that reason he confines the allegory to the first section of the sermon, the treatment of doctrine.

Similarly, in *Gods Determinations,* Taylor employs allegorical action that works on the same principle; that is, it is designed to "Call / Upon the Understanding to draw neer, / By tabbering on the Drum within the eare" (ll. 334–36). Accordingly, Taylor limits the allegorical action in *Gods Determinations* to the two sections that address primarily the understanding: the first division (ll. 1–418) is analogous to the doctrinal section of a sermon; and the second division (ll. 419–604) is analogous to the first and most general "use" of a sermon's doctrine, which Taylor regularly intended for information—and hence for the understanding. The last allegorical action in *Gods Determinations* occurs in the final poem of this second division ("The Effect of this Reply with a fresh Assault from Satan"), where Satan, preparing to assault God's elect, drops his "glorious Angell" disguise and reveals his more familiar "Griping Paws, and Goggling Eyes" (ll. 580, 595). The remainder of the poem consists of dialogues and monologues, during which no dramatic action occurs. Even the closing, heavenward ascent of the narrator in "The Joy of Church Fellowship rightly attended" is a monologue describing a past event: "I dropt an Eare / On Earth" and "found it was the Saints who were / Encoacht for Heaven" (ll. 2073–76). Thus, Taylor's use of allegory in *Gods Determinations* is analogous to and generally influenced by the biblically sanctioned use of allegory in his sermons and in the homiletic tradition generally.

The homiletic impulse that imbues *Gods Determinations* is also apparent in the ordered arrangement of the three main categories of the poem's imagery. In his study of Taylor's imagery, Peter Nicolaisen finds that the poem has three main sections and that within each section the imagery has a different purpose. In the allegorical opening poems, the imagery is primarily sensuous and vivid in order to make imaginable for the audience the events of humankind's fall, God's judgment, and election. In the long middle section, the images are designed primarily for illustration and explanation. And in the closing "hymns," the imagery is very similar to that in the *Preparatory Meditations*, where the images serve primarily the function of amplification (138–57).[8] The vividness of God at his lathe turning the globe, of the predestined damned vomiting up their spleens, and of Satan's belling, roaring, rending, and tearing gives way to the illustrative comparisons of the middle section, where Satan explains: "Your Sins like motes in th' Sun do swim" (l. 653) and "hence as from a fountain Head there Streams / Through ev'ry part Pollution in the Veans" (ll. 1135–36). It is here also that the disheartened Soul compares himself to "a Frigot fully fraught / And Stoughed full with each Ath'istick thought" (ll. 1429–30). Finally, at the end of the work, a plain Congregational meetinghouse through amplification becomes "Christ's Curious Garden fenced in / With Solid Walls of Discipline" (ll. 1940–41), where "Flowers do grow: / Spanglde like gold: / Whence Wreaths of all Perfumes do flow" (ll. 2002–4).

Further evidence of the poem's homiletic design is apparent in the relative simplicity of its conceits. Most of the poetry Taylor wrote before *Gods Determinations* shows a clear, even central, interest and delight in complex poetic elements such as the pun, the acrostic, and the extended conceit.[9] Likewise, in the *Preparatory Meditations*, the involved, intricate conceit is a characteristic feature, as Karl Keller, for example, explains:

> the *conceit*, whether humorously brief or hyperbolically extended as a structure for a poem, is Taylor's way of reaching out again for God through "the faculty of enjoyment" throughout his sacramental poems. His yearning for salvation was so intense that it needed the most strained form of language he knew how to use. (185–86)

In *Gods Determinations*, however, Taylor very noticeably and significantly alters his usual handling of conceits. Relative to the rest of his poetry, the conceits in this poem are remarkably simple and thereby a further indication that Taylor here designs his imagery for the understanding of even the least sophisticated in his audience. Nowhere in the poem does a conceit become more complex, for example, than in the "mudwalld Lodge" passage in Taylor's debate between body and soul, where the soul accuses the body of staining both the body and the pure soul within it by soaking in the puddles of worldly sin. His conclusion to this conceit is an excellent proverbial verse that contains appropriately liquid imagery and effectively summarizes in a single image what the preceding nine lines establish: "A Musty Cask doth marre rich Malmsy Wine" (ll. 1309–18). Thus the pattern of imagery in *Gods Determinations* and the relative simplicity of the conceits reflect the poem's homiletic structure and purpose. Taylor has designed the imagery to affect first the outward senses, then the understanding, and finally the will and affections; and by curbing his usual poetic tendency to enhance and explore the implications of a conceit by elaborating it, he reflects the dominating influence of the homiletic aesthetic.

The design of *Gods Determinations*, then, is pervasively homiletic and reflects the artist's deliberate and adept pairing of form and meaning. Because the poem's basic concern is the elect's "Coming up to God in Christ," Taylor derives the structure from the standard sermon form, the divinely appointed means for communicating that meaning. Accordingly, the poem's rhetoric follows the same "order of Nature" that controls the sermon structure and conforms thereby to "plain style."

When seen as analogous to the structure of a sermon, the overall organization of *Gods Determinations* breaks down into a doctrine section followed by four "uses," or one "use" and three "applications":

Division 1 (ll. 1–418):   Doctrine of election.

Division 2 (ll. 419–604):   Use by way of information for all of the elect.

Division 3 (ll. 605–1016):   Application of election to those who come up to mercy with relative ease.

Division 4 (ll. 1017–1914):   Application of election to those who come up with greater difficulty.

Division 5 (ll. 1915–2102):   Application of election to all of the elect by way of consolation.

Division 1 addresses primarily the memory and the understanding. Division 2 addresses the will but also, as is common with the first use of doctrine in Taylor's sermons, the understanding. Divisions 3 and 4 are designed to affect the will, and division 5 is intended primarily to move the affections. Furthermore, in the first two divisions, where Taylor is concerned with the memory and the understanding, the epic and allegorical modes of presentation prevail. In divisions 3 and 4, where Taylor's intention is to alter the will of his audience, the dominant mode of presentation is dramatic dialogue. The final division, intended to stir the affections, operates chiefly in a symbolic mode. Thus, the poem moves from the epic and allegorical to the dramatic and finally to the lyric, as it parallels a sermon's movement from the head to the heart.

3

What makes this view of *Gods Determinations* compelling is that it illuminates so many of the poem's aspects at once. The poem's rhetorical features are consistent with the pastoral plain-style guidelines and, significantly, because of that "plainness," quite different from the rhetorical features of most of Taylor's other poetry. This characteristic strongly suggests that Taylor conceived of a public audience for this work—a public audience larger than but based on his Westfield congregation, those for whom the minister-poet had composed hundreds of sermons by the time he was working on *Gods Determinations*. The homiletic view of the poem also obviates the objection that the poem fails as drama; ministers had long made use of dramatic techniques in sermons that considered individually could not be described as dramas. Furthermore, the advantage of this approach over a reading of the poem as a formal, extended meditation is that it accounts for so many more of the poem's features. The view of the poem as an extended meditation partially explains the structure only. Thus, by viewing the structure of *Gods Determinations* as significantly influenced by Puritan sermon structure, we can see the epistemological basis for the arrangement and design of the poem. Likewise, the homiletic view explains the remarkable differences in rhetorical design that exist between *Gods Determinations* and Taylor's other poetry. And we ultimately see that the poet of *Gods Determinations* was in complete control of a complex and coherent work.

Finally, the aesthetic relationship between sermon and poem in *Gods Determinations* has deep meaning in its culture. As Harry S. Stout points out, by redistributing "power among many hands in local contexts," Congregationalism in New England marks an adaptation to the new environment, that is, to the "open spaces of the New World," an environment in which the sermon became more authoritative and influential than it was in England because of the near identity of civil and ecclesiastical authority in New England: "Sermons were authority incarnate" (20–26). Seen in this context, Taylor's most thoroughly homiletic poem becomes a significant cultural artifact because the aesthetic impulse, or the cultural need for its homiletic design, was caused by the new environment. Having come from England and then having lived just over three years in Boston, Taylor spent several years learning how to adapt to the strange, new conditions of frontier Westfield. But the time he decided to stay and gathered his church there in 1679, he was ready to compose a public poem that was—by design—indigenous to his new world's culture.

Notes

1. Briefly, the varying interpretations are the following: Wright describes the work's structure as dramatic and as influenced (if only indirectly) by the medieval morality plays. Thomas diverges from Wright by positing the sixteenth- and seventeenth-century "literature of religious instruction" and the medieval homiletic tradition behind this body of writing as the sources of Taylor's allegorical devices.

Grabo's analysis differs from both Wright's and Thomas's and within itself is somewhat diverse, if not ambiguous. The possible ambiguity results from his attempt to maintain a variety of viewpoints. On the one hand he states that *Gods Determinations* "is primarily lyric in structure rather than narrative or dramatic" ([1961] 161). He then, however, provides an extensive analysis of the poem as a "five-act drama," only to conclude that "a dramatic analysis—satisfying and informative though it may be—belies the basic fact that God's Determinations is not a play" (165). Grabo seems most interested in developing the influence of "formal Ignatian meditation" (166–67). In the revised edition of his book, he adds the possibility of musical influence on the poem; that is, the rhapsody, the cantata, or the chamber opera could be musical analogs for the "purposeful disunity" and "virtuosity" apparent in the poem (100–107).

Arner rejects any influence from a dramatic model on the structure of the poem, locating Taylor's plan rather in what he sees as the four thematic divisions indicated in the poem's full title ("Notes"). Gatta, in an analysis of the poem's rhetoric rather than its structure, demonstrates Taylor's use of wit and irony ("Comic"; Gracious 101–40). Scheick analyzes the poem's thematic concern with the hope / fear dilemma as an "underlying schema" that provides "an autonomous inner dynamic." Finally, Parker and Sebouhian discuss the degree to which the form of *Gods Determinations* is dependent on Taylor's understanding of spiritual growth.

2. Although several scholars have linked the poem to a homiletic tradition, the extent of that influence has not been exposed. Thomas, for example, even while describing the structure of the work as dramatic, points out that the homiletic tradition is a contemporaneous and likely source for Taylor's plot structure and allegorical devices. Lewalski illuminates the similarity between the overall structure of *Gods Determinations* and the structure of the formal meditation by explaining that the "structural model for deliberate meditation was the sermon" (152). One of the four ways Grabo suggests that the work may be profitably examined is "as a versified theological disquisition or sermon"; he further notes that the advice of Saint is similar to the application of doctrine in Taylor's sermons and that the final six lyrics, because of their affective nature, relate to the rest of the poem as the final, affective application of doctrine relates to the rest of a sermon (159, 166–67; rev. ed. 106–7). Arner indirectly acknowledges the influence of the homiletic tradition on Taylor's use of folk proverbs in the poem ("Proverbs" 13).

3. Reed's discussion supports the argument that homiletic form and rhetoric are important influences on Taylor's poetry. However, Reed limits his discussion to the *Preparatory Meditations* and Taylor's numbered occasional poems.

4. I am grateful to the Beinecke Rare Book and Manuscript Library of Yale University for permission to publish material from Taylor's "Poetical Works" manuscript. For convenience, since *Edward Taylor's Major Poetry* is not yet available, I give here the five divisions of *Gods Determinations* discussed in this essay together with the corresponding page numbers in Donald Stanford's edition, *The Poems of Edward Taylor*:

division 1 (ll. 1–418): pp. 387–401; division 2 (ll. 419–604): pp. 401–7; division 3 (ll. 605–1016): pp. 407–21; division 4 (ll. 1017–1914): pp. 421–53; division 5 (ll. 1915–2102): pp. 453–59.

5. In the *Treatise* (186–93), Taylor treats a series of six doubts that keep the froward elect from attending the Lord's Supper. These doubts and their solutions bear noteworthy similarities of tone and content to passages in "A Threnodiall Dialogue between The Second and Third Ranks" and the dialogues between Soul and Saint.

6. See Carlisle, who perceives as a "deep form" in the *Preparatory Meditations* the "Question-answer form," which he notes as "a rhetorical device from the sermons" (152). In addition, see Hammond, who shows that Wigglesworth adopts much of the rhetoric of *The Day of Doom* from homiletic practices. Hammond suggests that the arguments of Wigglesworth's sinners "function much like 'objections' inserted into a sermon as a means of refuting error or clarifying doctrine" (46) and that "Wigglesworth portrays the carnal perspective in a manner consistent with how a preacher would handle erroneous opinion within a sermon" (58). Throughout his study, Hammond maintains the "homiletic aims" of *The Day of Doom*. He concludes that, for Wigglesworth's readers, "such qualities as structure, characterization, and meter were inseparable from homiletic strategy" (61).

7. My authorities here are Murray and Joseph Wright.

8. See also Ball's discussion of Taylor's use of amplification in the *Meditations*.

9. See Hall on Taylor's early verse (1–134).

Works Cited

Arner, Robert D. "Notes on the Structure of Edward Taylor's *Gods Determinations*." *Studies in the Humanities* 3.2 (1973): 27–29.

———. "Proverbs in Edward Taylor's *Gods Determinations*." *Southern Folklore Quarterly* 37.1 (1973): 1–13.

Ball, Kenneth R. "Rhetoric in Edward Taylor's *Preparatory Meditations*." *Early American Literature* 4.3 (1969/70): 79–88.

Benton, Robert M. "The American Puritan Sermon before 1700." Diss., University of Colorado, 1967.

Bernard, Richard. *The Faithfull Shepherd*. Rev. ed. London, 1621.

Carlisle, E. F. "The Puritan Structure of Edward Taylor's Poetry." *American Quarterly* 20 (Summer 1968): 147–63.

Chappell, William. *The Preacher, Or the Art and Method of Preaching*. London, 1656.

Colacurcio, Michael J. "*Gods Determinations* Touching Half–Way Membership : Occasion and Audience in Edward Taylor." *American Literature* 39 (1967): 298–314.

Downame, John. *The Christian Warfare*. London, 1604.

Fulcher, J. Rodney. "Puritans and the Passions: The Faculty Psychology in American Puritanism." *Journal of the History of the Behavioral Sciences* 9.2 (1973): 123–39.

Gatta, John Jr. "The Comic Design of *Gods Determinations touching his elect*." *Early American Literature* 10.2 (1975): 121–43.

———. *Gracious Laughter: The Meditative Wit of Edward Taylor*. Columbia: University of Missouri Press, 1989.

Grabo, Norman S. *Edward Taylor*. New York: Twayne, 1961. Rev. ed., Boston: Twayne, 1988.

Habegger, Alfred. "Preparing the Soul for Christ: The Contrasting Sermon Forms of John Cotton and Thomas Hooker." *American Literature* 41 (1969): 342–54.

Hall, Dean G. "Edward Taylor: The Evolution of a Poet." Diss., Kent State University, 1977.

Hammond, Jeffrey A. "'Ladders of Your Own': The Day of Doom and the Repudiation of 'Carnal Reason.'" *Early American Literature* 19.1 (1984): 42–67.

Hudson, Roy Fred. "The Theory of Communication of Colonial New England Preachers, 1620–1670." Diss., Cornell University, 1953.

Keller, Karl. *The Example of Edward Taylor*. Amherst: University of Massachusetts Press, 1975.

Lewalski, Barbara Kiefer. *Protestant Poetics and the Seventeenth–Century Religious Lyric*. Princeton, N. J.: Princeton University Press, 1979.

Mather, Cotton. *Magnalia Christi Americana*. London, 1702.

Mignon, Charles W. "Diction in Edward Taylor's 'Preparatory Meditations.'" *American Speech* 41 (1966): 243–53.

Miller, Perry. *The New England Mind: The Seventeenth Century*. Cambridge: Harvard University Press, 1954.

Murray, James A. H., et al. *The Oxford English Dictionary*. London: Oxford, 1933.

Nicolaisen, Peter. *Die Bildlichkeit in der Dichtung Edward Taylors*. Neumünster: Karl Wachholtz, 1966.

Owst, Gerald R. *Literature and Pulpit in Medieval England*. Cambridge: Cambridge University Press, 1933.

Parker, David L. "Edward Taylor's Preparationism: A New Perspective on the Taylor-Stoddard Controversy." *Early American Literature* 11.3 (1976/77): 259–78.

Patterson, J. Daniel. *Edward Taylor's Major Poetry*. Unpublished manuscript, 1995.

Perkins, William. *The Arte of Prophecying*. In *The Workes of that Famous and Worthy Minister of Christ, in the Universitie of Cambridge*, 2:643–73. London, 1613.

Reed, Michael D. "Edward Taylor's Poetry: Puritan Structure and Form." *American Literature* 46.3 (1974): 304–12.

Scheick, William J. "The Jawbones Schema of Edward Taylor's *Gods Determinations*." In *Puritan Influences in American Literature,* edited by Emory Elliott, 38–54. Urbana: University of Illinois Press, 1979.

Sebouhian, George. "Conversion Morphology and the Structure of *Gods Determinations*." *Early American Literature* 16.3 (1981/82): 226–40.

Stanford, Donald E., ed. *The Poems of Edward Taylor*. New Haven: Yale University Press, 1960.

Stout, Harry S. *The New England Soul: Preaching and Religious Culture in Colonial New England*. New York: Oxford University Press, 1986.

Taylor, Edward. *Edward Taylor vs. Solomon Stoddard: The Nature of the Lord's Supper: Volume 2 of the Unpublished Writings of Edward Taylor*. Edited and with an introduction by Thomas M. and Virginia L. Davis. Boston: Twayne, 1981.

———. *Edward Taylor's "Christographia."* Edited by Norman S. Grabo. New Haven: Yale University Press, 1962.

———. *Edward Taylor's "Church Records" and Related Sermons: Volume 1 of the Unpublished Writings of Edward Taylor*. Edited and with an introduction by Thomas M. and Virginia L. Davis. Boston: Twayne, 1981.

————. *Edward Taylor's Harmony of the Gospels*. 4 vols. Edited by Thomas M. and Virginia L. Davis, with Betty L. Parks. Delmar, N.Y.: Scholar's Facsimiles and Reprints, 1983.

————. *Edward Taylor's Minor Poetry*. Edited by Thomas M. and Virginia L. Davis. Boston: Twayne, 1981.

————. *Edward Taylor's Treatise Concerning the Lord's Supper*. Edited by Norman S. Grabo. East Lansing: Michigan State University Press, 1966.

Thomas, Jean L. "Drama and Doctrine in *Gods Determinations*." *American Literature* 36 (1965): 452–62.

Toulouse, Teresa. "'Syllabical Idolatry': Benjamin Colman and the Rhetoric of Balance." *Early American Literature* 18.3 (1983/84): 257–74.

Wright, Joseph, ed. *English Dialect Dictionary*. 6 vols. London: Henry Frowde, 1898.

Wright, Nathalia. "The Morality Tradition in the Poetry of Edward Taylor." *American Literature* 18 (1946): 1–17.

Part 3
The Minor Poetry

"Diffusing All by Pattern":
Edward Taylor as Elegist

JEFFREY A. HAMMOND

Taylor scholarship, deep and varied as it is, has unwittingly created two Edward Taylors. The first, whom we know quite well, wrote *Gods Determinations* and the *Preparatory Meditations*, the drama and diary of redemption which have established him as our best poet before Whitman. The second Taylor, whom we scarcely know at all, was far more prolific. Nearly three-fourths of Taylor's poetic output consists of verse that has always seemed too conventional for comment: a 20,000-line epic of ecclesiastical history, extensive metrical paraphrases of Job and the Psalms, polemics against the Roman and English churches, a handful of poems dealing with natural events, and a small collection of elegies. Our propensity to ignore these varied poems has kept us from accounting for the "whole" Edward Taylor, or at least reconciling the strikingly original *Meditations* with a far larger body of verse disappointingly consistent in its adherence to the standard parameters of Puritan art. The usual critical response is to assert that when Taylor tried to write for readers, he wrote badly; these stiff, detached poems reveal that he could not successfully negotiate the demands of Puritan public art. Freed from such demands in the private meditations, he was able to write not just better poetry but poetry more deeply and directly expressive of his actual concerns.[1]

A close look at Taylor's elegies offers a useful test of this assumption as well as a valuable supplement to our nearly exclusive focus on *Gods Determinations* as his only noteworthy poem addressed to external readers. In these poems, Taylor does not eschew the formulaic literary codes of the ubiquitous New England funeral elegy. On the contrary, he exploits them fully, and in so doing articulates his lesser-known role as an accomplished public poet capable of working within the popular literary traditions of his time and place. The experiential vitality of these traditions has only recently begun to attract attention. For Word-centered Puritans, reading in the Bible and in devotional texts that mediated between self and Scripture was an ordinance vital to the believer's inner progress, whether preparatory to conversion or in the postconversion search for ever stronger assurances of salvation. Although all Puritan verse articulated and encouraged such an experience of self, the funeral elegy illustrates with special clarity the nature of Puritan reading as a ritual that pointed readers toward the redemptive paradigm that they sought to confirm within. So predictable were the forms effecting this ritual that by 1722 the young Benjamin Franklin could pen a satirical recipe for the elegy. But Franklin overlooked—as have more recent critics—the simple fact that Puritan elegies were formulaic because, for Puritan readers, the formula worked. The linking of the death with New England sin, the familiar imagery of fallen pillars and ravaged gardens, the speaker's professed inability to articulate loss, the idealized portrait of the deceased—all were indispensable to stimulating a vital individual experience of reading that made possible the communal appeal of these poems.[2]

If read in light of the Puritan experience of texts, Taylor's elegies emerge as powerfully evocative poems. Moreover, elegiac conventions enabled Taylor to generate within his audience a reading experience that echoed the meditative ritual central to the private poetry for which he is best known. Whether he eulogizes public figures, members of his immediate family, or himself, the gap between the public poet and the private contemplative is far narrower than the formal contrasts between his commemorative and meditative verse might lead us to believe. Experiential continuities that encompass elegy and meditation alike unify the two Taylors into one—a poet in whom the post-Romantic distinction between "conventional" and "expressive" is far more difficult to maintain than we commonly assume.[3]

* * *

Taylor's extant elegiac verse includes, in addition to private laments for his wife and two young daughters, nine "public" poems that make full use of the standard conventions of the New England elegy. While the meager attention generally paid to Taylor's public verse stems from our preference for his private poetry, these poems labor under an additional burden: the enormous and longstanding prestige of the pastoral elegy, a form of commemoration very different from those that came from his pen. While the *Meditations* at least partly satisfy modern expectations regarding private, reflective verse, Taylor's elegies do not even approach the ideal poem of mourning, as traditionally defined. The same is true of nearly all of the many elegies written in early New England. One critic writing in the late 1960s voiced an underlying cause of this judgment: "To remember that while Puritan Milton was writing 'Lycidas,' his American coreligionists were composing acrostic elegies is to recall how provincial American Puritanism quickly became" (Waggoner 13). Traditional expectations regarding the "literary" elegy—in practice, the pastoral elegy—have caused critics to divorce the Puritan commemorative poem from its ritual milieu, reading it instead within an aesthetic agenda shaped largely by a highly select canon of the great poems of mourning in English: Shelley's "Adonais," Tennyson's "In Memoriam," Whitman's "Lilacs," Arnold's "Thyrsis," Yeats's poem for Major Robert Gregory, Auden's poem for Yeats—all of which have roots in the pastoral tradition of "Lycidas."

Aesthetic expectations shaped by the pastoral elegy, seductive as they are, obscure the fact that New England elegies, including Taylor's, were written for reasons quite different from those imputed to Milton and his successors. These expectations promote an essentially ahistorical model of artistic assessment in which the privileging of formal beauty overlooks the cultural and psychological utility of texts in their own time. This conflict between formalist and functional approaches to the poetry of mourning is by no means new. Its roots lay in Renaissance England, where Protestantism initiated lively controversy surrounding the question of what constituted proper mourning. It was within this debate, with opinion ranging from disgust at pomp and ceremony as a relic of "Romish" practice to horror at Puritan-inspired funerary rites so plain that they seemed disrespectful, that the varieties of English elegy developed. The writing of elegies flourished during the Renaissance with the rise of humanistic individualism, printing, literacy, and a growing nationalism that prompted imitation of the great models of antiquity in the service of a literary Albion whose worthies deserved equal commemoration. Laments at Sidney's death in 1586 stimulated the elegy's popularity, and the raft of poems commemorating the 1612 death of Prince Henry, son of James I, solidified its status as the era's dominant public genre of verse. A relaxation of traditional strictures on grief and its expression during the later sixteenth century contributed to this popularity (Pigman 3, 126), as did the role played by elaborate funerary rites in shoring up the waning power of the aristocracy (Stone 572–81).

In order to understand the verse commemorations that Taylor and his New England contemporaries wrote, we need to remember that many options were available to seventeenth-century elegists. These options provide a historical basis for reconsidering the artistic rules that Taylor seems to have violated when he turned from meditative to commemorative verse.

Of the various types of Renaissance poems of mourning, only one was subsequently designated as "literary." This, of course, was the highly artificial and elaborate pastoral elegy, shaped chiefly by Spenser's lament for "Dido" in the "November" eclogue from *The Shepheardes Calendar* (1579) and his poems for Sidney, or "Astrophel" (1595). Ironically, especially given its longstanding place in the canon, the pastoral elegy remained relatively rare in the nearly sixty years between the "November" eclogue and the climax of the form in "Lycidas." Most elegists during this period took a more direct approach to verbal mourning, one that drew on Elizabethan patriotism and patronage and, later, Jacobean melancholy and popular devotional traditions. This type of poem, usually called the "funeral" elegy to distinguish it from the pastoral, was frequently incorporated into funerary rituals, with the poem recited at the service and pinned to the hearse during the procession. Many Tudor and Elizabethan funeral elegies were laments for nobility written for general distribution, as illustrated by the popular poems of Thomas Churchyard and George Whetstone. Initially, the funeral elegy reflected all religious persuasions and ranged from what John Draper in his classic study termed "Cavalier panegyric" to the more theologically oriented "Puritan lament" (*The Funeral Elegy* ix), the latter shaped by a turn to piety and introspection influenced by Donne's 1612 "Anniversaries" for Elizabeth Drury (Kay 91–123). Puritans gradually began to take over the more explicitly religious elegy, stylizing its forms, intensifying its millennial fervor during the Civil War, and using it to reinforce their political legitimacy during Cromwell's rule. By the early 1650s, the funeral elegy had become so closely associated with dissenters that the anonymous "J. C." equated "common formall Elegies" with the "Geneva Jig."[4]

The English Puritan funeral elegy could scarcely have posed a greater contrast to the classically based pastoral, in which the frank artifice of a timeless and placeless rural landscape helped transform mourning into a retreat from mortality toward the sanctuary of art. The death of a poet provided a special opportunity for the pastoral elegist to confirm his professional vocation and assert his virtuosity as a poet rising to the occasion of death. To elegize was both to acknowledge the void left by the deceased and to fill it as his rightful successor. The pastoral elegy thus came to play a special role in witnessing the poet's coming of age. In this, too, the ancients had shown the way: Virgil's pastoral verse witnessed the first stage in what came to be seen as the archetypal career of a poet. The vocational theme reached its culmination, of course, in "Lycidas": Milton's momentary questioning, in the face of Edward King's untimely death, of his own dedication to the "thankless muse" leads to a recommitment expressed by and embodied in the poem—a recommitment always seen, of course, with critical hindsight afforded by the achievement of *Paradise Lost*. To be sure, Milton confirms a Christian apotheosis for Lycidas, "sunk low but mounted high / Through the dear might of him that walkt the waves." What prevails, however, is the staged threat to—and recovery of—poetic vocation worked out through the key elements of the pastoral: the idealized landscape, the nostalgia for better times, the consoling power of nature, the commingling of grief with topical commentary, and the reassertion of continuity and purpose in response to rupture and anxiety. On one level, of course, such conventions effected a distancing from emotion that emulated classical restraint and made poems of mourning easier to write. Discursive indirection, however, enabled not just a muting of emotion but a deflection of function—a shift from mourning to other tasks that could be performed *through* mourning. The variety and interaction of those tasks permitted considerable thematic range, as the interwoven themes of "Lycidas" reveal.[5]

Puritans who did not share Milton's regard for the ancients took the "functional" side in the mourning controversy and either eschewed the pastoral surface altogether or deflected it back toward what they saw as its theological and soteriological core, as Milton briefly did in St. Peter's diatribe against the "Blind mouths" of the corrupt clergy. In contrast to the commemorations for "Astrophel" or "Lycidas," funeral elegies openly proclaimed their situational contexts by giving the real names of the deceased. Consistent with corresponding reforms in preaching, liturgy, and church polity, this more severe elegiac model attempted to reclaim for the mourning poem its most immediate use. Determined to adhere to what they saw as "real" rather than "fictive" discourse, funeral elegists refused to allow commemoration of the dead to stray from its theological significance, which was, in their view, a "literal" significance that transcended artistic representation. The counterpastoral impulse, however, was not solely religious in origin; the young author of "Lycidas" was certainly no less "Puritan" than his more rigorist contemporaries. As Draper first pointed out, an equally important factor was social: the rise of a largely Puritan merchant class to wealth, power, and artistic patronage (*The Funeral Elegy* 22). In contrast to the aristocratic and academic readers of the pastoral, this new audience made far more pragmatic demands on art. For them, the ideal commemorative poem was at once less worldly—that is, more directly concerned with salvation—and more practical in framing the grieving process in the explicitly religious terms familiar to most mourners.

Taking to heart Phoebus's lesson in "Lycidas" by shifting the elegiac concern with "fame" from the realm of poetry to the realm of piety, funeral elegists were far less indebted to Theocritus and Virgil than to the Bible, homiletic tradition, and the popular iconology of death fostered by broadsides and emblem books. These poets saw themselves as employing an Augustinian "high style" that eschewed ornamentation and was "created," as Ruth Wallerstein describes it, "by the ardor of the thought itself, by the ardent contemplation of truths seen as value, as a motive of the will." "In this style," Wallerstein adds, "the Bible abounds" (28). While the occasional image—the weeping willow, the funerary urn, the ministerial shepherds, and church-going flocks—afforded brief glimpses of a pastoral landscape, the urtexts for these poems were the great biblical expressions of loss, especially David's lament for Saul and Jonathan (2 Sam. 1:19–27). Funeral elegists took seriously Paul's admonition to "Rejoice with them that do rejoice, and weep with them that weep," taking care to "Mind not high things" and to "Be not wise in your own conceits" (Rom. 12:15–16). Unlike the pastoral elegist, usually a university-trained man of letters speaking as a professional "poet," the funeral elegist emulated Pauline humility by presenting the poem as an amateur performance that repudiated the vocational preoccupations of the pastoral. The funeral elegy succeeded only if it was *not* created as art. Indeed, its deeper message and aims, because divine, did not require a poet's skill so much as a prophet's vision.

At first, this kind of elegy assumed virtually identical form in both Englands. A poem written in 1636 by "I. L." for Rev. John Rogers of Dedham, Essex, whose grandson would become president of Harvard, features most of the hallmarks of the New England elegy. It celebrates the "happy change and blessed gain" of a generalized saint, "Our faithfull Moses" whose "graces" the reader is urged to "imitate": "So shalt thou live in happy state, / and pleasing in Gods sight" (Draper, *A Century,* 21). As the Rogers family illustrates, dissenting emigrants to the New World came chiefly from the principal English audience for such poems, and as a result, there was no significant demand in New England for the pastoral variety. The plainer style of elegy proliferated there, becoming increasingly codified after the Restoration forced a sharpening of New England's cultural distinctiveness and the elaboration of funerary customs as a means of reinforcing a community of believers. As William

Scheick points out, the New England elegy in this later form separated from its English precedents by laying greater stress on a "collective self" through which survivors could absorb the saintly traits of the deceased ("Tombless Virtue" 290–96). Replete with predictable forms and conventional structures appropriate to this increased ritualization of mourning, the New England elegy may also have compensated for the liturgical severity of the Puritan service and provided a communal supplement, similar to that offered by the jeremiad, to the lonely rigors of meditative self-scrutiny.[6]

Once established in New England, the funeral elegy achieved remarkable stability, resisting the shift toward neoclassicism and sentimentality, which began to mark the English elegy soon after the Restoration, until well into the eighteenth century. This conservatism points up the elegy's close fit with social as well as theological realities in early New England, where funeral elegies, circulated in manuscript or broadside among members of small, tight-knit communities, were written for a far more intimate circle of readers than those addressed in the published and more explicitly "literary" poems of London. Even more importantly, the New England elegy, like the English funeral elegy, was written for a very different *kind* of reader than that addressed by the pastoral. Unlike Milton, whose poem appeared in a commemorative volume produced by and for Christian humanists well acquainted with classical discourse, elegists in New England wrote for entire communities and thus did not risk undermining the devotional mandates of grief with pastoral conventions that presented a pagan surface if taken literally by the uninitiated. In keeping with this more democratic sense of audience, elegies in New England were not meant to be "appreciated" as art in anything like the modern sense, or even in the sense that Milton's Cambridge readers would have appreciated "Lycidas." Rather, they were written to be *used*—and those uses were linked to a process of grieving that was as valid for the illiterate farmer as for the university-trained minister. For the New England elegist, the redemptive significance of death was far too great to squander the moment in mere verbal display.

The homiletic directness of such poems in both Englands doomed them to subliterary status, especially in light of the subsequent prestige of the pastoral as the only "artistic" poem of mourning. "Lycidas" and its successors helped solidify powerful critical assumptions that arose within the specific development, during the eighteenth and nineteenth centuries, of an academic criticism whose preference for the self-contained, ideologically "neutral" work of art authorized a certain indirection in the commemorative act. In this view, the occasional poem achieved canonical status only if it transcended its specific occasion; failure to do so resulted in patent sentimentality, a view later reinforced by New Critics who identified such tendencies in poetry criticism as "fallacies," intentional and pathetic.[7] Attracted to the thematic swerve from death to art enacted by the pastoral elegy, critics considered the degree to which a poem may have brought real comfort to its initial readers irrelevant, and even harmful, to its artistic success. This view was nowhere more evident than in the quick and vehement rejoinders to Samuel Johnson's famous attack on the pastoral conventions of "Lycidas" as "trifling fictions" lacking in any "real passion." Thomas Wharton, in his 1791 edition of Milton's minor poetry, conceded that "Lycidas" contained "perhaps more poetry than sorrow. But let us read it for its poetry." In 1818, Hazlett cited with approval Milton's "tender gloom" in the poem, "a wayward abstraction, a forgetfulness of his subject in the serious reflections that arise out of it." In 1854, Henry Hallam responded to Johnson's charge by arguing that "many poems will yield an exquisite pleasure to the imagination that produce no emotion in the heart; or none at least except through associations independent of the subject" (Elledge 230–32, 236). We might add "independent of textual function": for all the outcry, Johnson was merely voicing functional rather than formalist standards for the poetic commemoration of loss.

Perhaps the chief factor, however, in our inability to read the Puritan elegy on its own terms is the tendency of traditional criticism to privilege an essentially secular response to death. Criticism grounded in the assumption of "pure" art naturally became increasingly uncomfortable with theological structures of grieving as experienced by most seventeenth-century mourners. In this view, the successful elegy seemed to have escaped history as an "enduring monument" by exchanging religious ideology for a more general framing of grief that proved attractive to later readers and critics who read for art, not solace. The attempts of later readers to isolate an "aesthetic" experience of texts made them largely indifferent, even hostile, to traditional religious expression. Wallerstein's comment that Milton "universalizes" his experience by putting it "not in a religious form but in an artistic form" (113) encapsulated this view. Seen as compelling support for an essentialist view of beauty and as a witness to art's supposed transcendence of history and ideology, the pastoral elegy became the supreme *monumentum aere perennius*. It defined an elegiac ideal that obscured the viability of *other* poems of mourning that stubbornly resisted the pastoral compulsion to aestheticize loss.[8]

It was this other kind of elegy that Edward Taylor wrote. Because his verbal gifts are clearly evident in other poems, we can safely assume that he *chose* to write it—that the fruits of that decision are deliberate rather than the result of some unexplained artistic deficiency, a charge routinely leveled at New England's other elegists. As the products of a gifted poet who willingly exploited this highly conventional form, Taylor's elegies provide an especially promising vehicle for probing the vitality of that form within Puritan literary culture. We can access that vitality not by reiterating the truism that these strange old poems disappoint us as verbal art, but by reconstructing, as specifically as possible, how they worked for their intended readers. While Taylor provides a useful basis for a functional analysis of this tradition, the tradition also tells us something about Taylor. Countering the usual image of an idiosyncratic, readerless poet, his elegies tell us, among other things, that the private visionary was also, as occasion and audience demanded, a craftsmanlike dealer in conventional structures. Such insights may also complicate how we read his private meditations, whose relation to other Puritan poetry has always been obscured by their apparently expressive and even confessional surface. If, as a result of these insights, Taylor seems to lose something of his originality, that loss is balanced by a clearer picture of a more historically situated poet, one who was artistically as well as theologically grounded in his own time and place.

* * *

Taylor's verse commemorations have met with a critical silence defined by our preferences for the pastoral elegy on one hand and for the *Preparatory Meditations* on the other. Yet his elegies have more in common with the *Meditations* than their surface suggests. The chief link between elegy and meditation emerges in an experiential dynamic that underlies the stylized forms of these most public of Taylor's poems. This dynamic, like that informing the meditative verse, reveals Taylor's consistent use of poetry to stimulate an experience of self consistent with the psychology of the redeemed soul charged with an ongoing quest for assurance of salvation. Such a soul, Puritans insisted, was defined by a constant battle against carnal tendencies, a battle mandated by theology and facilitated by rigorous self-scrutiny.[9] For Taylor, public elegy and private meditation shared equally in this struggle. As fulfillments of a duty adumbrated in David's lament for Jonathan and Saul, one of many Old Testament passages that Taylor paraphrased in verse, New England elegies were poems that *had* to be written, occasional counterparts to the process-oriented meditations in which "duty" repeatedly "raps" on the door of Taylor's "Muses garden" for "Verse" in praise of the Divine

(II.30). Increase Mather's passing demands "mourning poetry" (246), and as Taylor tells the deceased Samuel Hooker of Farmington, "It surely would / Be Sacraledge thy Worth back to withhold." When "brave Jon'than" dies, the poet asks, shall "David's place be empty? Sling ly by?" (116).

The mandate to commemorate the saintly deceased creates an artistic dilemma similar to that posed by the meditative command to praise Christ. Invoking in the elegies a situational parallel to the "Blunted Tongue" of the *Meditations* (I. 21), Taylor confesses to a sinful inability to lament the dead in the spirit of David as proto-elegist. In the Hooker poem, his "duty" to commemorate is blocked by natural grief, which "when Greate / And geteth vent" issues "Non-Sense sobs" (116). As in the *Meditations*, where Taylor repeatedly admits that he lacks "power, not will to honour" Christ (II.38), pious intent is subverted by fallen emotion. As he concedes in the poem for Mather, "Should silence now be hid our sorrows big / To get a vent would breake thy Coffin lid" (246). The speaker of the *Meditations*, similarly constricted by sin, is a "vessell" too small for his theme (I.12), a "pipkin" that cannot contain Christ's love (II.97) and a "pin box . . . too small / To hold praise meet for such praiseworthiness" (II.160). Mourning poetry, no less than meditative verse, could easily collapse into stunned silence: sorrow at the death of Pastor Zecharia Sims of Charlestown threatens to "tie our ton[gue]" (22). At the passing of sister-in-law Mehetabel Woodbridge, Taylor complains of being "Choakt with the Rising of the Lungs thro' Griefe" (124). Indeed, the poem must issue from his eyes—from the "Pearles" of his tears—rather than his voice.

In the nine elegies, the conventional structures that force the poet's silence also permit him to move himself and his readers beyond that silence. Seizing upon the saint's death as an opportunity to push his audience toward the same inner struggle he pursues in the private verse, Taylor makes accessible to others the intense spiritual work that he undertakes in the *Meditations*. At the death of Francis Willoughby, deputy governor of Massachusetts, Taylor enlists his readers as pious "Volunteers" in "Sorrows Regimentall plot" (22) by universalizing his dilemma as poet, thereby linking his artistic difficulty with deeper problems inseparable from grieving. The speaker's professed verbal inadequacy showed readers, first of all, how *not* to mourn. Not to weep— or to write—would expose a horrifying indifference to the passing of God's people. At Sims's death, Taylor complains that "We Senseless at their Hearse / Do hardly mourn halfe halfe an houre in verse" (21). Because all the weeping in the world was insufficient to the loss, too many tears were just as shameful as too few. As the Hooker elegy affirms, "Tears are a Dress / Becoming us, come they not to excess" (122). Survivors must strive to "keep due measure," Taylor warns: "Your too much is too little far for him." The difficulty of striking the proper balance echoes Taylor's confessions in the *Meditations* that "I can, yet cannot tell this Glory just, / In Silence bury't, must not, yet I must" (I.17). Mere "Non-Sense sobs" could no more produce a fitting elegy than a "Lisp of Non-sense" (I.17), "blottings" (I.10), or "ragged Rhimes" (I.32) could produce a successful meditation. If "Griefe" alone could "make a Poet," Taylor declares when Sims dies, "[Su]rge after Surge of Sorrow sure would do it" (20). Clearly, however, mere grief would never do; as a result, death generates a situational confirmation of the sin-consciousness that pervades the *Meditations*. Taylor forces the reader to see that a shoddy commemoration is as inevitable as the "Bubs hatcht in natures nest" (I.39) that he repeatedly confesses in the *Meditations* . As Taylor confirms, natural grief is sinful precisely because it *is* natural—a sad reminder of the sharp difference between the human and the divine perspectives on dying. To grieve is to stand convicted in a response to death that reflects, however normal and human it may be, an imperfect grasp of the redemptive significance of the loss.

The deceased's apotheosis as a self who, like Increase Mather, "chose not the World to seeke" (247) only makes verbal and spiritual matters worse by underscoring the survivor's still-fallen nature. Like the Christ of the *Meditations*, represented as an "Almightiness" that constantly exposes the speaker's insignificant "Mite" (II.48), the dead saint has achieved a peace that throws earthly turmoil into high relief. As Taylor proclaims at Willoughby's death, "Unworthy We, oh Worthy he!" (22). At the death of Increase's father, Richard, he concedes that "whilst we drown in griefe he swims in Joy" (20). In addition to convicting survivors in self-centered panic over their own fate, the saint's death challenged their humility by demanding a celebration of someone *else's* joy. As Taylor confirms at the death of the elder Mather, "our losse, its grea[t]; whilst we are thus / Above with him" in our thoughts, "he's not below with us." Separation from the holy dead replicates the agonizing distance from Christ frequently lamented in the *Meditations.* As Taylor exclaims at the memory of a particularly vivid experience of the Lord's Supper, "Oh! that thou Wast on Earth below with mee / Or that I was in Heaven above with thee" ("The Return"). The "reader" of the *Meditations* is a Christ whose ascent provokes, in Taylor's darker moments, an ongoing complaint: "must I be without thee here below?" (I.20). To find oneself similarly abandoned and outstripped in glory by the departed saint was equally humbling, as Taylor's final words to President Charles Chauncy of Harvard suggest:

Well, Chauncey, well, thou, where thou wouldst be, art.
We Sink in Sorrow, judgment, & the Darke.
  In middst of all the Combat pray do we
  Inable us, oh Lord, to Shine as Hee.

(35)

Taylor's thinly veiled envy of the dead highlights the deceased's homiletic role as chastiser of the living. Deacon David Dewey's escape from a world of "Sorrows, Sighings, Tears, and Sin" (84) makes poignantly clear the fallen realm in which Taylor and his readers must remain. The eulogized deceased in fact takes up Christ's role in the *Meditations*, functioning as a sacred Other who points up the carnal sluggishness of all earthly believers. Like Christ, the holy dead can be depicted only in contrast to a fallen speaker who has lost an indispensable spiritual guide. Death has made Hooker into nothing less than "a bit of Christ" (123) who has become, like the Christ of the *Meditations*, a "Wealthy Theam" too rich for Taylor's "Feeble Phancy" (I.27).

Taylor leads himself and his readers beyond convicting grief by shifting his focus from the wounded self to this christic Other. Willoughby's death forces him to move beyond self-pity at the "Hide bound" (I.22) state that he repeatedly laments in the *Meditations* in order to "count" how the deceased's "great Gain, doth our great loss Surmount" (24). Envy, fear, and heartbreak force Taylor's speaker—and readers following his lead—to abandon the "Non-Sense" of pathos in order to decode the divine meaning concealed in the death. Reconsidering precisely what it is about Dewey, Chauncy, Woodbridge, and the others that makes them worth commemorating, Taylor, like other Puritan elegists, finds that his real theme is not the saint but sanctity itself—the dimension of the deceased's personality that has made the poem necessary in the first place. As Samuel Willard insisted in a funeral sermon on mintmaster John Hull, "There is no greater Argument to be found that we should excite our selves to mourne by, then the remembrance that they were *Saints*." Of all the deceased's traits, Willard states, "this, this outshines them all; that he was a Saint upon Earth" (371, 373). Taylor accordingly redirects the poem toward a focus defined not by those personal characteristics that marked the deceased as an individual, but by those qualities that he or she shared with all saved souls. Rewriting the dead into paradigms of redemption, Taylor consistently absorbs the details of their lives into broad portraits of a saintly metaself that emerges as the actual subject of the poem. Faith "in each believer individually," William Ames confirms, assumed one form, "the form of those that are called" (176). Because the central purpose of the elegy was to celebrate this "form" in just such a self, spiritual accuracy demanded a clearly legible portrait drawn in accordance with a hagiography that applied equally to all redeemed souls.[10]

By representing the deceased in the most edifying form possible, Taylor recovers his voice as an elegist. Urging his readers to move from grieving for the letter of the deceased as a fallen individual to celebrating the spirit of the deceased as a glorified saint, he describes not Samuel Hooker but "God in him" (121), not Zecharia Sims but the "aged Nazarite" that faith made him into (22). While Taylor idealizes the external form of sister-in-law Woodbridge as a "Gentlewoman neate, accomplish't, true," he encourages the reader's deeper interest in "Her Inward man" as "a Storehouse of rich ware. / Of Sanctifying Grace, that made all fair" (125). Such portraits were intended to reconfirm Christ's ability, proclaimed throughout the *Meditations*, "To spiritualize the life in every part" (II.98). Like other Puritan elegists, Taylor suppressed external detail by "spiritualizing" the worldly particularity of the dead into inspiring icons of sanctity. The generalized pattern of the saintly parent, for example, is embodied in Dewey, whose "sweetest Breathings" and "Dewy Rhymes" fell "In Admonitions, on thy Offspring all: / To bring them up to Christ" (82); in Woodbridge, the saintly "Loving Wife" and "Tender Mother Sweet" (125); and in Hooker, "A Loving Husband; tender Father" who gave "Pious, Rich Discourse" to his children (119). Like other elegists, however, Taylor gives fullest play to a ministerial ideal embodied in departed clergy—to what Urian Oakes called in his elegy on Thomas Shepard II the "Scripture-Bishops-Character" (Meserole 217). Increase Mather's "Learning & thy pious life so vext / A fowle crew when Sin played rex" (246); Hooker was "an Angell Choice" who "Preacht Zions Grace with Sinai's thundering voice" (117). Even Taylor's physical description of the diminutive Hooker, "in Person neat, of lesser Sise, / With Ruddy Looks, & with quick rowling eyes," quickly defers to a spiritual portrait of the godly minister, "His Head a Magazeen of Wisdom rich" and "a Fine Spun Fancy . . . Producing Notions brave, & Rhetorick" (117–18).

The deceased, celebrated as a "bit of Christ" (123) in each poem, has been transformed by grace and death—and now by language—into a figure who is no longer merely human. Dewey's "noble Soul" is now "refin'd, all bright," swimming "In fulgent Glory, fill'd with Bliss to th' brim" (83); Richard Mather is now "out of Satan gain Shot, freed from Sin" (20); Chauncy "doth Swim in Bliss / Where he in Glorys Throne inCrowned is" (34). Hooker's essence, as Taylor distills it, is a *via media* of faith: he was "Grave, not Morose. Courteous, yet did Comand / A Distance due; & by a gentle hand." He was a "steady" saint, "Not on, &

Off" (118). Consistent with such hagiographic portraiture, the saint's death is represented as a localized reenactment of Christ's. The Crucifixion is celebrated in the *Meditations* as a "Brave Pious Fraud" (I.19), an apparent death that actually proclaims eternal life. Taylor reacts to the similarly transformed deceased with a pious awe that echoes his response to the celestial Christ in the *Meditations*. Taylor's Hooker, whose "Shining Beams did fly to lighten all" (117), has achieved such a thorough "Chrystallizing" (123) that saint and Savior have become virtually indistinguishable:

> An Orb of Heavenly Sunshine: a bright Star
> That never glimmerd: ever shining fare,
> A Paradise bespangled all with Grace:
> A Curious Web o'relaid with holy lace
> A Magazeen of Prudence: Golden Pot
> Of Gracious Flowers never to be forgot
> Farmingtons Glory, & its Pulpits Grace. . . .

(123)

Omit the last line and the images could describe the Christ of the *Preparatory Meditations*. Convinced with Ames that the elect soul received "the bestowal of total perfection" at death (174), Taylor deliberately presents his readers with a Hooker who has been completely refashioned by the divine operations of grace.

* * *

The contrast between iconic dead and stung survivor stimulates a humility that informs elegy and meditation alike. Shifting from fallen self to gracious subject, from how this death affects him to what he can read in the deceased as the embodied Word, Taylor enacts the antithesis of mere self-expression. As Ruth Wallerstein once remarked in reference to "Lycidas," "There were two griefs, the personal grief which kills, [and] the grief of repentance leading to God" (110–11). By confessing the former in order to move himself and his readers toward the latter, Taylor, like other Puritan elegists, reshaped survivors from passive victims into active celebrants of yet another victory for God's people. In this lay the Puritan poet's true calling, whether as elegist or as contemplative: Taylor writes not as an inventor of what Herbert denounced as "fictions only and false hair," but as a seer who ratifies eternal truths authored by God Himself.

The legible piety of the dead allows Taylor to escape the performative burden of writing by shifting the elegy's success from his skill as poet to the deceased's virtues as saint. As he asks Hooker, "Shall thy Choice Name here not embalmed ly / In those Sweet Spices whose perfumes do fly / From thy greate Excellence?" (116). He similarly studs Woodbridge's coffin with "Wealthy Vertues decking thee before" (124), and he tells Increase Mather that "When many left Christ's holy word thou stoodst fixt to 't / Which makes my gray goose quill commence thy poet" (248). Taylor becomes not a mere writer of elegies but a fluent *reader* of human texts already written by God, found poems of grace that needed only to be explicated for the faithful. Ames insisted that the redeemed "are transformed" into the "form and pattern" of Scripture (256). As explicator of biblical "form and pattern" in the deceased, Taylor enacts Willard's advice to "embalm the memory of the Saints with the sweet smelling Spices that grew in their own Gardens" (373). Because the deceased had already been embalmed with grace, all that remained was to seal with words what God had already accomplished in gracious reality. As embodiments of faith, the holy dead animate Taylor's elegies in precisely the same manner in which Christ animates the *Meditations*, where the poet repeatedly concedes that "My Theme is rich: my Skill is poore untill / Thy Spirit makes my hand its holy quill" (II.6). In terms of an ongoing trope in the *Meditations*, the saint commemorated in each elegy becomes the "Musician," and Taylor becomes his or her "well tun'de Instrument" of redemptive celebration ("The Return").[11]

Taylor's role as a conduit for the deceased's piety permits an escape from the stasis of grief into a meditative reconsideration of the redemptive miracle. As catalysts of this reconsideration, the now-christic dead achieve identity only within the Word. Dewey is "David by Name, David by Nature" (82); Chauncy recapitulates "Peters Faith, Pauls Preaching, Johns Love Strong" (34); Hooker exemplifies a virtual compendium of biblical heroes, including John the Baptist, Paul, and Samuel (118–19). Such souls are honored by survivors who are rehabilitated—through the very act of honoring them—as neobiblical citizens of the new "Israel" (119). Just as the "Golden Bosses" of Scripture seal the poet to Christ in the *Meditations* (II.154), the Bible reconciles the living with the dead in the elegies. As in the *Meditations*, where each poem enacts Taylor's declaration that "In Sacred Text I write" (II.58), the embalmed saint becomes another scriptural pointer— another "golden Key" (II.115)—to the survivor's hope for redemption.

Taylor presents the deceased as a neobiblical link to glory by stressing inner patterns shared by all true believers, living and dead. The dead saint manifests, if readers prove faithful, their future selves—a completed version of an inchoate identity that they are constantly seeking for themselves. As Scheick observes, the New England elegy "transfers its text to the soul, the reason and will, of each member of its audience. Its final emphasis, then, falls upon this text of the self, this tombstone or elegy to be read within each person" ("Tombless Virtue" 296). By celebrating the dead as embodied fulfillments of a salvific process that readers hoped to discover in their own inner lives, Taylor presents the difference between living self and dead saint as a parallel to what Ames called the "double form—that of sin and that of grace" crucial to gracious self-experience (170). The inner dichotomy toward which Taylor leads his reader is identical to that which he pursues throughout the *Meditations*, in which he begs Christ to "force my Will, and Reason to thee so / And stifle pleas made for the other part" (II.36). His acute consciousness of that "other part," of the carnal "Bubs" that he tries to "Conquour" "but cannot them destroy" (I.39), results in a dichotomized meditative speaker, a paradoxical identity who repeatedly describes himself as "Dry Dust" eating "Living Bread" (I.9), "A Dirt ball dresst in milk white Lawn" (I.46), "An Angell bright" dwelling "in a Swine Sty" (II.75). Taylor's commemoration of the dead virtually forces this salvific duality upon survivors: one dimension of the self stands convicted in sin by death and sorrow, while another finds consolation in the deceased's redemptive victory.[12]

Like the Bible from which they derive their fixed, celestial identities, Taylor's dead both chasten and encourage. As human sermons they serve, like Samuel Hooker's preaching, to "dart / Christs firy Shafts into the flinty heart" as well as to "dress with Gilliads Balm to make it Sound" (119). Making certain that each of his subjects wields, like Hooker, both "Gospell Bow & balsom" to the reader, Taylor presents the dead as legal texts that convict by the radical otherness of their celestial perfection and by their payment of sin's wages. But while each saint's death reasserts God's Justice, each saint's glory reconfirms God's Mercy as Taylor shifts his elegiac explication of the deceased from exemplum of the consequences of the Law to proof of the rewards of the Gospel.[13] Mediating between the human sin that caused the saint's death and the divine grace that animated the saint's life, Taylor reshapes his subjects into consolatory guides to heaven. As Taylor's Hooker assures the reader, "In Faith, Obedience, Patience, walk a while / And thou shalt soon leape o're the parting Stile, / And come to God, Christ, Angells, Saints, & Mee" (122).

Such encouraging words from beyond the grave articulate the balance of fear and confidence that Taylor voices throughout the *Meditations*:

"Hold up this hope. Lord, then this hope shall sing / Thy praises sweetly, spite of feares Sad Sting" (II.46). Extending salvific experience as the tie that binds glorious dead to sorrowful living, Taylor assures his readers that the deceased once underwent the same struggles now plaguing them. Like his grieving survivors, the living Hooker had once been "A Stage of War, Whereon the Spirits Sword / Hewd down the Hellish foes that did disturb" (117). Dewey's earthly self was "a Seat of Sin, Corruption's nest"—a self by definition "True only to Untruth" (83). In addition, the deceased is finally liberated from the same natural corruption that grief has exposed in the survivors. Dewey (83) and Allen (31) escape their corporeal "Tabernacle," Richard Mather "his Reeling, Mudwald Tent" (20), Woodbridge her "Tent of Clay" (126). In spiritual reality as in rhetorical fact, Taylor affirms, the dead saint has been emptied of worldly particularity, "Stript," like Hooker's "dust," "of all that Wealth, & Station" that defines the earthly self (117). However numinous the dead have become, they promise a final defeat of the carnality exposed by the reader's grief. Having performed his duties as deacon "Untill thy Person was dichotomiz'd / By death's sharp Sword," Dewey is both "parted and departed": his body and soul now "standeth part from part" "As doth the *Zenith* from the *Nadir* stand" (83). The conflict of bitterness and piety set in motion by the elegy is resolved not only in the immediate peace of the dead but in the projected reunion of their bodies and souls in the fullness of time, a reward that Taylor underscores in the final "repair" of Dewey, whose "Person spoild while 'ts parts asunder are" will be made whole by grace (84). Taylor thus confirms a peace that is at once eschatological and current: the deceased's final reward not only models the resignation toward which the poem guides its readers but strengthens their own anticipation of celestial rest as assured believers capable of commemorating God's people. [14]

Like other Puritan elegists, Taylor invokes communal pride to encourage the reader's hopeful identification with the holy dead. With the repeated claim that one of us is now in heaven, the reader's time and place become starting points to celestial glory. By urging a personified New England, Connecticut, and Farmington to grieve for Hooker, Taylor transforms physical residence into spiritual orientation. His call to "Let Harvard mourn" underscores Chauncy's earthly place as a link to heaven (34); had Willoughby not died, "[H]e yet had stood within our garden, pal'd" (24). With Dewey's sudden call from "our Deaconry laid void," the reader's here and now similarly become the glorified saint's there and then (83). By reconnecting the dead and the living within the experience of grace, Taylor rewrites death from earthly defeat to celestial victory. After lamenting that Sims's passing reveals how "Death Supplants our

Plants & Planters," he interrupts himself: "Supplants said I? Soft, fie, the
better Style / Is, it Transplants them to a richer Soile" (21). Absorbed by
elegiac convention into a meditative ritual that bolsters the performer's
salvific hope, death is transformed from a sad disruption of New
England's mission into its glorious goal.

Taylor's transplanted saints confirm Karen Rowe's observation that in
"histories and elegies, the elimination of Christ from the typological
equation allows the contemporary Christian to emulate the *exemplum
fidei* without feeling self-defeated by the *exemplum exemplorum* of
Christ Himself" (*Saint and Singer* 87). The holy dead mediate between
earth and heaven by providing accessible copies of the Divine: as Taylor
urges Hooker's survivors, "Strive for his Spirit; rather Christ's, than His"
(123). Particularly crucial to the elegiac ritual is the exhortation to imitate
the holy dead in the very act of mourning. Taylor insists that weeping for
Hooker "is honour due from you. / Yet let your Sorrows run in godly
wise / As if his Spirits tears fell from your eyes" (123). Don't simply
grieve *for* Hooker, Taylor insists: you must grieve *like* him—like
someone who has already achieved the perspective on death and dying
that the celestial Hooker now enjoys.

Taylor's readers found themselves imitating not just the christic dead
but Christ Himself, who wept at Lazarus's death but then effected his
resurrection—the direct biblical antecedent of the verbal and spiritual
ritual that the Puritan elegy enacted. "*When the Saints die*," Willard
warned, "*beware of irregular Mourning*: though we are to lament their
Death, yet we must beware that it be after the right manner . . . after the
same Language that Christ did to those weeping Women" (372). The text
to which Willard refers, Christ's admonition to "weep not for me, but
weep for yourselves, and for your children" (Luke 23:28), underlies
Taylor's efforts to redefine his readers' tears from natural heartbreak to
salvific remorse.[15] Holy deaths, Taylor confirms at the passing of
Increase Mather, are "stings" designed to make "Sinners" accept divine
correction: "repent then e're it be too late / Less thou eternally smart in
the horrid Lake" (247). Hooker's death, like the convicting moments
confessed in the *Meditations*, offers similar opportunity to "weep thy
Sins away, lest woe be nigh": "Watch, Watch thou then: Reform thy life:
Refine / Thyselfe from thy Declentions. Tend thy line" (120). Taylor
draws his readers into salvific repentance by testing their desire to
emulate the deceased's escape from the dark glass of sin and self. The
celestial Chauncy issues this challenge when he asks, "Who'de feare the
Grave? Death's but the golden Doore / Wherein we must unto bright
Glories Shore" (35). Like each meditation, each pious death provided yet
another "Gospell Glass" (119), as Taylor declares in the Hooker elegy, in

which earthly believers could glimpse not only the horror of their sin but the promise of their salvation.

Repeatedly transforming death into a mirror of redemptive hope, Taylor offers his elegies not as literal biographies but as neogospels in which he speaks as an apostle proclaiming the *kerygma* of the saint's life. Just as the deceased Chauncy had devoted himself to "Diffusing all by Pattern," the poet diffuses the redemptive message of Chauncy's life (33). Similarly asserting that Increase Mather's "pen hast playd Christ's intrest Dear: / And hast recorded his blesst doings here" for "future ages to behold" (248), the poet becomes a latter-day apostle to the now-christic Mather. Taylor's miniature gospels reenact evangelical proclamations of the Resurrection by means of the formulaic "good death," a convention adapted from the English elegy and indispensable to presenting the saint's death as a victory within reach of the living. The dying Dewey, noting that *"The Wind is high,"* asserts that *"by to Morrow I'st above it be!"* (83). In her last breath, Woodbridge exclaims, "Come, one more Pray're, & Then" (126). Hooker, observing his cold limbs, exclaims that "They are Dead, you see, and I / Have done with them" (119). And Taylor presents Sims's final words—"my Head! me head!" (22)—as an ambiguous conflation of current and biblical realities. Those words, the same uttered by the stricken son of the "Shuhemite" or Shunammite, whose faith in Elisha's power made possible his resurrection (2 Kings 4:18–37), reinforce Taylor's assertion that Sims now awaits a bodily resurrection of his own.

Taylor shared these victories with readers by invoking the pious balance of fear and hope that was the experiential goal of all Puritan meditation, including his own. John Allen's death provokes a roll call of the "Spirituall Gamesters" who have "slipt away," leaving survivors in need of a "Fencing Schoole" to keep up the good fight. Taylor's sense of abandonment prompts him to ask "Shall none / Be left behinde to tell's the Quondam Glory / Of this Plantation?" (31). Like other Puritan elegists, however, he implicitly answers his own question: *he* is still here—and the plantation's ultimate glory increases with each saint that he embalms. This is New England's answer to Milton's rededication to song in "Lycidas": encouraging a shift in the traditional elegiac concern with vocation from that of a poet to that of a saint, Taylor's elegies reshape speaker and reader alike into still imperfect versions of the glorious selves whom they jointly commemorate. Like the *Meditations*, these poems offered hope that the real barrier separating earthly sinner from celestial saint was not death or even sin, but time.

* * *

The elegiac conventions that Taylor exploits, as the poem on
Mehetabel Woodbridge suggests, were equally adaptable to public and
private loss; Taylor's mourning ritual is the same whether he writes to
commemorate the well-known Chauncy, Hooker, and the Mathers or to
absorb the more private loss of his sister-in-law. The application of
communal ritual to private grief is most striking, however, in Taylor's
most poignant elegiac pieces, "Upon Wedlock, & Death of Children" and
the "Funerall Poem" for first wife, Elizabeth Fitch. These poems, apparently written chiefly for the poet and his immediate family despite Cotton
Mather's reprinting of two stanzas from "Upon Wedlock" in a sermon on
the proper handling of grief, manifest an underlying textual experience
identical to that fostered by the public elegies: the redemptive struggle of
a self who is, like the speaker of the *Meditations*, "for thy sake out with
my heart" (I.26).[16] When faced with intense personal loss, Taylor does
not abandon the stylized forms and underlying ritual of the Puritan elegy.
On the contrary, he seizes upon these structures as reliable sources of
comfort for himself and his family in their time of greatest need.

"Upon Wedlock, & Death of Children," a lament for two infant
daughters, reconfirms a theme shared by elegy and meditation alike:
mortality's sad reminder that "Earth is not heaven: Faith not Vision"
(II.96). In "Upon Wedlock," Taylor attributes his grief to a confessed
blurring of the two realms. His family, a product of divine decree, is
initially represented as an institution as much of heaven as of earth:

A Curious Knot God made in Paradise,
    And drew it out inamled neatly Fresh.
It was the True-Love Knot, more Sweet than spice
    And Set with all the flowres of Graces dress.

(106)

By celebrating the biblical origin of his family in Eden, Taylor sets
himself up for his own fall. While wedded love indeed began in the
Garden, family tragedy started there as well, in the sin by which
"Wedlock" and "Death" became inseparably bound. Even in Taylor's
post-Edenic family "an Hellish breath" can intrude (107), and in order to
come to terms with the loss of children in the New Eden, he must return
to the Old and relearn the full legacy of the first parents. That legacy, like
the occasional ritual of mourning and the ongoing experience of
salvation, is dual: his family mirrors not just primordial happiness but
postlapsarian suffering. As in the formal elegies, grief exposes a

convicting gap between Taylor's will and God's, a gap underscored by his confession that the death of "this flowre" Elizabeth at one year of age "almost tore the root up" of her father (107). The heartbreak comes because the hour of grief was "unlookt for" in a human forgetting of that other, darker legacy of the first marriage.

Like the public elegies, the poem presents immoderate grief as an inevitable result of human sin. In an epicyclic structure necessitated by the poem's function as a double elegy, each of two sections—one for each daughter—reenacts the ritual embedded in all of Taylor's elegiac verse. At Elizabeth's death, Taylor articulates the pious response to loss: "Lord take't. I thanke thee, thou takst ought of mine, / It is my pledg in glory, part of mee / Is now in it, Lord, glorifi'de with thee" (107). Voicing a clear resignation to God's will resulting from his meditative "pausing on't," he has made sense of the tragedy. However, the death of Abigail five years later finds him once again unprepared, as dramatized by the graphic depiction of "the tortures, Vomit, Screechings, groans, / And Six weeks Fever" that "would pierce hearts like Stones" (107). The mere fact of grief reveals that "nature fault would finde" with God's dealings, and in a renewed conviction that leads to a second resignation, Taylor again moves from the bitterness expressive of his carnal "nature" to a gracious attempt to accept what God has wrought:

> Griefe o're doth flow: & nature fault would finde
>   Were not thy Will, my Spell Charm, Joy, & Gem:
> That as I said, I say, take, Lord, they're thine.
>   I piecemeale pass to Glory bright in them.
>   I joy, may I sweet Flowers for Glory breed,
>   Whether thou getst them green, or lets them Seed.

(107)

Confessing his need to trust in a Providence that he cannot yet fully understand, Taylor embraces God's will as his "Spell Charm, Joy, & Gem," images recalling the talismanic use of redemptive language in the stylized public elegies. Like Anne Bradstreet, who urges herself at the death of grandson Simon to "say He's merciful as well as just" (237), Taylor asserts such language as a means of striving for the perspective that it articulates. At the second death, he repeats the pious words that had allowed him to sustain the first: "as I said, I say" (107).

The invocation of the mourning ritual in "Upon Wedlock" parallels Taylor's characterization of the *Meditations* as "each day's atoning Sacrifice" (II.25). Reversing the usual elegiac transfer of divine glory from older to younger generations, Taylor recasts his now-sainted daughters, idealized as "sweet Flowers," as "part of mee" and "my pledg

in glory" (107). They become, like the poem itself, ritual offerings—
"take, Lord, they're thine"—that demonstrate his ability to relinquish
what the natural self loves. Offering no reason for the deaths other than
God's will, Taylor turns the irrationality of the loss into a sharp reminder
that divine decree must be accepted even when it cannot be explained.
Only such acceptance could transform the survivor's perception of death
from a "Hellish breath" into the act of "a glorious hand." As if to remind
himself that the Lord gives as well as takes away, Taylor is careful to
record the births of sons Samuel and James, who have not died. Here, as
in the other elegies and in the *Meditations*, where redemptive language
also helps assure the poet that "now I'm sure that I prize naught above
thee" as he struggles to reject the "world with all her dimples" (I.48),
verbal ritual offers the means of generating the consolation that the poet
seeks.

At the death of his wife seven years later, Taylor once again turned
grief at the loss of a beloved saint into a ritual celebration of sainthood
itself. Charles Hambrick-Stowe has called the result "a private occasional
poem since it is not a public elegy" (Introduction to *Poetry* 47). Yet "A
Funerall Poem upon the Death of my ever Endeared, & tender Wife Mrs.
Elizabeth Taylor" manifests the ritual of conviction and consolation
central to all Puritan elegies, including Taylor's other, more public
exercises in the genre. Before Taylor can begin part 3, which examines
what made Elizabeth "a reall, Israelite indeed" (113), he pursues in parts
1 and 2 the humility necessary for absorbing the redemptive lessons of
her life. He dutifully seeks not only Christ's permission to create "this
little Vent hole for reliefe" (110) but also the now-christic Elizabeth's,
that she might "Spare me thus to drop a blubber'd Verse / Out of my
Weeping Eyes Upon thy Herse" (111). Although Taylor does not wish to
"repine" (110), he must face the convicting consequences of his grief if
the poem and the ritual that it embodies are to succeed. Confirming that
his "heart" is in danger of being "Squeez'd . . . To pieces" in the "True
Love Knot" of his marriage, he once again speaks as an all-too-human
vessel that must be vented or it will "burst." That it is the carnal
dimension of his identity which *needs* the poem is clear from the forced
supplication that he voices. Although he sorely misses his "bosom
Friend" and "Comfort," "Yet my Lord, I kiss thy hand."

In part 2, Taylor continues his movement toward the elegiac transcendence of raw emotion. Denigrating the poem itself as a conventionally
"mournfull Song," "a blubber'd Verse" that testifies to fallen need, he is
especially anxious to assert his right to write, and bases his claims not
only on David's "Poetick gusts" but on secular precedent: "Do Emper-
ours interr'd in Verses lie? / And mayn't Such Feet run from my

Weeping Eye?" As in the public elegies, the "Dutie" that he admits "lies upon mee much" is to break through his own sinful grief in order to celebrate Elizabeth's sanctity. If he were to "naile" her virtues "in thy Coffin" by not writing, "How shall thy Babes, & theirs, thy Vertuous shine / Know, or Persue unless I them define"? He must "define" her life, like those of his more public subjects, as a legible paradigm of sanctity in order to move beyond the self-indulgence that he sees reflected in his grief. Like the public elegies, too, the poem is validated not by the poet's "blubbering" performance but by the deceased's piety. "Thy Grace," he assures Elizabeth, "will Grace unto a Poem bee / Altho' a Poem be no grace to thee" (111).

Despite Taylor's claim that "in Salt Tears I would Embalm her Clay," what he must actually embalm is the generalized identity repeatedly commemorated in the public poems: Elizabeth's "Noble part" as a saintly model who guides him from purgative venting to redemptive celebration (110). Convinced that she has mastered a redeemed view of death not yet fully available to him, he has her gently chide his human need "at my Grave to Sing" (111). In accordance with Puritan elegiac ritual, hagiography must replace particularity, and with part 3 Taylor begins a more impersonal description of Elizabeth's saintly identity. Vowing not to "abuse" the ears of "Bright Saints, & Angells" with empty "Hyperboles," he dramatizes the Puritan assumption that no praise of a demonstrable saint could possibly be hyperbolic. Back-reading Elizabeth's life in light of her final glory, he produces what Norman Grabo aptly calls "an idealized portrait of the Puritan wife—one to be emulated rather than known" (77). Like Mehetabel Woodbridge, Elizabeth was "Her Husbands Joy, Her Childrens Chiefe Content. / Her Servants Eyes, Her Houses Ornament," emanating a "Shine as Child: as Neighbour . . . As Mistriss, Mother, Wife" (112). Elizabeth becomes, no less than the public figures, a saintly icon diffusing redemptive lessons to all—a transformation effected, in Taylor's view, by her faith rather than his words. Underscoring his reverence for what she has become, he keeps his distance by referring to himself in the third person. Seeking to embalm her in the most edifying form possible, he speaks part 3 less as a widower grieving for his wife than as an apostle proclaiming the good news of all saintly lives.

The apostolic role enables Taylor to focus on Elizabeth's "Walke With God" as the central fact of her life. From her childhood as "a Tender, Pious Bud / Of Pious Parents" (112), the "Obedient, Tender, Meek" Elizabeth has taken the pilgrimage of all elect souls. As a neighbor, she was "ever good," enacting a compassion suggestive of the Canticles Bride, whose "fingers" drip "sweet smelling myrrh" (Cant. 5:5): "Her

Fingers dropt with Myrrh, oft, to her power." As mistress, she replicated the divine balance of justice and mercy: she "Remiss was not, nor yet severe unto / Her Servants: but i' th' golden mean did goe." As mother, she embraced the chief responsibility of a Puritan parent, teaching her children "The Law of Life" and giving "Correction wisely, that their Soules might Live" (113). Like Woodbridge, Dewey, and Hooker, Elizabeth as spouse is inseparable from Elizabeth as saint: "As Wife, a Tender, Tender, Loving, Meet, / Meeke, Patient, Humble, Modest, Faithfull, Sweet / Endearing Help, she was." Taylor's catalogue of virtues results in a portrait not so much of his wife as of the presumed effects of grace upon her.

Reordering the sequence of Elizabeth's life to emphasize redemptive rather than worldly chronology, Taylor saves his most explicit treatment of her "Noble part" for last. Because the climax of her inner life was her conversion, he ends the poem with an account of her struggle as "a Reall, Israelite indeed" (113), the same struggle embodied in the subjects of the public elegies and voiced by the speaker of the *Meditations*. Returning to her gracious beginnings, when "She did inherit / The very Spirits of her Parents Spirit," Taylor recounts the classic story of doubt, turmoil, and triumph central to all Puritan life-narratives. Her conviction in sin was both harsh and genuine: "that Smart, / She then was under very, few did know: / Whereof she somewhat to the Church did Show." Describing her preparation for conversion in a present tense that equates her progress toward faith with the reader's experience of the poem, Taylor attests that "Repentance now's her Work"; "Faith, carries her Christ as one of his." Her preparation, in which "She's much in Reading, Pray're, Selfe-Application," witnesses a balance of hope and fear by which she "Holds humbly up, a pious Conversation." When she finally "makes profess[ion]" to the Westfield Church, the event culminates a spiritual process embodied equally in her life and in his text. After a brief recounting of the fruits of her faith, especially her "gracious Speech," Taylor abruptly concludes by reporting her love of Wigglesworth's best-selling manifesto of the redeemed perspective: "The Doomsday Verses much perfum'de her Breath, / Much in her thoughts, & yet she fear'd not Death" (114). By commemorating Elizabeth as an iconic soul convinced by faith that "Justice can do no wrong," Taylor embalms his wife as a guide to his own and his family's salvation. Like all the Puritan dead, she is textualized as a compelling model for the survivor's best self.

On the most immediate level, of course, Taylor's confidence that Elizabeth now "Swims in bliss" (110) must have brought him incalculable comfort. Moreover, his desire to commemorate her glorification was doubtless reinforced by his parental responsibility to teach his children the salvific meaning of their mother's life. Like the broader readership addressed in the public elegies, Taylor and his family needed a perpetuation of the deceased's most edifying and comforting identity as a true "Israelite." By making certain that his wife's role as guide to her "Babes, & theirs" would continue (111), Taylor enhanced his own sense—and his children's—of a "Noble part" that would follow her to glory. Death had made her into a faithful copy of all redeemed souls: commemorating her death helped Taylor recast himself into an imperfect copy of her. Like the contemplative episodes recorded in the *Meditations*, Elizabeth's death posed a test of the poet's gracious identity. And as in the *Meditations*, where Taylor constantly tries "if I be in the Faith, / For Christ's in me if I bee'nt Reprobate" (II.155), redemptive self-experience stimulated by verbal ritual helped him feel that even this most painful loss presented a test that he could pass.

* * *

Taylor's elegies, like those of his less famous contemporaries, support Hambrick-Stowe's observation that "Devotional acts sparked by grief became for Puritans the means of a deeper satisfaction" (Introduction to *Poetry* 20)—a satisfaction that could be communicated to others only through predictable verbal structures. Moreover, the poems on his wife and daughters demonstrate Taylor's determination to administer to himself the same comfort that he gave others in his more public commemorations. He consistently absorbs all grief, personal as well as public, into his attempts to seek and promote the faith that "cleares" the sight of "reasons Eye," as he attested in the *Meditations*, "to see things quite above its Sphere" (II.108). A merely carnal reading of death, like fleeting glimpses of Christ through the "bodies Eyes," could not satisfy sincere believers. Mourning, whether public or private, stimulated the struggle from worldly blindness to "the internall Eye Sight" (II.147) that was the goal of meditation and commemoration alike. Just as the elegies echo Taylor's private meditative responses, the *Preparatory Meditations* manifest the elegiac ritual whenever death intrudes upon his private search for assurance. In Meditation I.33, written on the day Elizabeth died, Taylor blames himself for placing so much affection on a "Toy" and a "mite," thereby reconfirming the elegiac lesson that when "Hells Inkfac'de Elfe" strikes, it is inevitable that "Nature's amaz'de." A little over ten years later, he brought his grief for his son James into his private devotions by squarely facing divine "Preheminence," pledging to "kiss

the Rod, and shun / To quarrell at the Stroake. Thy Will be done" (II.40).
His next meditation, written on the twelfth anniversary of the death of
James's mother, repeats his plea to learn "Obedience" in "Sorrows
Schoole" (II.42).[17]

The fundamental unity of Taylor's meditative and elegiac modes is
clearest, however, when the poet contemplates his own death, a theme
that pervades the *Meditations*, especially the late poems based on the
Song of Songs, in which he complains that "My Muses Hermetage is
grown so old": "Old age indeed hath finde her, that she's grown Num'd"
(II.122). Increasingly yearning, as the Second Series progresses, to sing
"at that bright Doore . . . untill thou'st take me in" (II.142), Taylor
records his growing interest in an eschatological self "whose form
transformd shall bee / To be shap'te like thy glorious body, Lord" (II.76).
This interest culminates in his final identification with the Canticles
Bride as the fullest biblical allegory of the celestial self. Taylor's
obsession with personal eschatology is also evident in three "occasional"
poems written toward the end of his life. In these anticipatory self-
elegies, he appropriates a redeemed identity with a bold assurance that
echoes the confidence with which he embalms others.[18] In "Upon my
recovery out of a threatening Sickness in December Ano Dmi 1720," he
immediately complains that "the golden Gate of Paradise" is "Lockt up
'gain that yet I may not enter" (218). Although he tries to "center" his
heart "In thy Will" and to rejoice "heartily" at his recovery, he admits to
the irony of resisting a deliverance: "Thy Will be done, I say, do ask me
to do the same; / I'de rather dy than cast upon it blame" (218). As in the
elegies, Taylor speaks as a humbled survivor. Here, however, he has
survived his *own* death, and he interprets his exclusion from heaven's
"Sweet house" as evidence of his need for further purification. If he were
"a Silken Plock & full of Seems," he concedes, "'Twould be onely like to
be a webbed Strainery" (218). Accepting the check on his pride, he
settles for "Some bits" of Christ's glory "while I'm quartering" on earth:
"Times Jurisdiction I here to thee bring / Entreating thy acceptance untill
I / My Quarters moove into Eternity" (219). "Entreating" is a far cry
from the near-outburst with which the poem opens. While "Upon my
recovery" ostensibly records a shift from illness to health, its deeper
focus is Taylor's "recovery" from immoderate grief at his own survival
to an acceptance of God's decision to let him live. As when he
commemorates others, the poet writes his own movement from
opposition to accord with the Divine Will.

Two other self-elegies written during this period, "A Valediction to
the Whole World" and "A Fig for thee Oh! Death," exhibit Taylor's
search for an eschatological self identical to the saintly personality

commemorated in his elegies. Begun some two months after "Upon my recovery," the "Valediction" corrects the unreadiness for death discovered and confessed in the earlier poem through a full-scale farewell to the world and its charms. Yet the final version, so sweeping and systematic in such renunciation that it reads like a cosmological poem, is by no means a *contemptus mundi*. As John Gatta points out, Taylor's leave-taking conveys "more of a frolicsome and affectionate farewell to nature than a repudiation of all its gifts" (*Gracious Laughter* 203). The first three cantos, which bid farewell to "the Celestiall Bodies" (232), "the Aire" (233), and "the Terraqueous Globe" (235), depict a perceptual reversal of Genesis, an uncreating of the world by a self who no longer needs it. For Taylor, as for the eulogized dead, the natural world has already ended: the celestial bodies are already extinguished and "now no light can borrow" (233). Playfully anticipating God's final putting out of the light, Taylor links his private apocalypse with the dissolution of the world. Hoping to dance "far above" the shine of stars whose "Sparkling glory shines too dim" (232) and to travel "Into a purer air by far" (234), he portrays the physical universe as a transitory "realm of Sense & Sensualities / Enveagling our Senses by shadow verities" (235), an illusory world that faith has already permitted him, like the saints he has embalmed, to overcome. Like them, Taylor no longer draws comfort from the "mocking Crew" of created things (237): "I bid you all farewell both good & bad / You never elevated mee" (235). Not even earthly love can satisfy the identity that religious assurance helps him imagine. "All could not keep me Sweet," he tells his family, "my vessell soon / Would Taint, tho' all your Love, & skill should bloom" (236). Determined to achieve eschatological unity with the holy dead, Taylor defines his identity solely in relation to Christ. His impatience with carnal selfhood assumes especially vivid form when he internalizes the division of "part from part" undergone by Deacon Dewey (83) by verbally dismantling his body and its parts. God has "lent mee them," Taylor asserts, "to tend me to the banks, / Of thy all glorious Eternall Throne, / And here I leave them now altho' mine own" (237). Once he transfers all worth from a corporeal self as a "Sorry Crumb of dust" (239) to a Savior who offers "t' bleed for me & dy" (239), his body, a tenuous network of "Nerves" and "Vitall Spirits" (236), unravels as swiftly and inexorably as the rest of creation.

Taylor's chant-like assertion that God has "graciously with grace thus graced mee" is tempered by an echo of the elegist's dilemma: the confession of "Churlish Clownish" thoughts that accuse him of "gross Presumptions." How can he sing "Heavens songs," he asks, while "iniquity" still abides in his "skirts" (239–40)? Yet, as the elegies and the

Meditations also attest, poetry intensifies his ability to glimpse a saved self despite his sin-consciousness. Although he cautions himself not to sing "tryumphant joy before / Thou hast past thro' Christs blessed Palace doore" (240), the "Humble Selfe abasement" that he voices revives his confidence that "Faith never holds whats promisd in suspense" (240). Declaring that God "decreedst & 'lect me to / Enjoy thy Gospell Grace which now I know" (238), he celebrates his election "from Eternity" (237): "That lott thou then didst cast I now do See, / In Gospell times & places, Seated me" (238). "Tush! Im resolvde," he declares, "my Faith shall never Crinkle / It on Christs Truth & Promises relies" (240). Justifying such boldness by proclaiming his commitment to "Gospell Obedience" and his vehement rejection of "Unbelief," Taylor appropriates the last words of the eulogized deceased as a means of intensifying his "hope to take a trip" (234) to the far better place where his celestial identity will enjoy "higher tunes & melodie" (237). By internalizing the conventional "good" death of the eulogized saint, Taylor pierces through "these foggy Vailes" (240) to imagine a self in whom sanctification is nearly complete: "I am within Gods Paradise's View, / Where my best life is; & no Physick there / Is ever needed" (236). Articulating the escape from carnality enjoyed by those souls whom he has embalmed, Taylor asserts a final separation from the sinful element against which he has struggled all his life. Confident that death and the final reunion of body and soul will complete the refashioned identity that he desires, he declares that "Our bodies" must "Be laid a mellowing within the grave. / And so be purged of these stains & disease, / And then be set together as God please" (237).[19]

Nowhere, perhaps, is Taylor's longing for a postmortem self "set together" by God more evident than in "A Fig for thee Oh! Death." Like *Meditations* I.34 and II.112, the poem contrasts the saint's desire for death with a sinner's fear of the death's head as a terrifying reminder of depravity and guilt, a "King of Terrours with thy Gastly Eyes / With Butter teeth, bare bones Grim looks likewise / And Grizzly Hide, & clawing Tallons" (263). Having voiced the convicting fear of an elegiac survivor, Taylor appropriates the gracious joy of the eulogized dead by declaring that the skull is "not so dreadfull unto mee thro' Grace." Once again internalizing the self-division into dust and glory projected onto the subjects of his elegies, souls for whom death *was* dead, he turns the skull into proof that the grave has no "victory" and death no "sting" (1 Cor. 15:55). By destroying the carnality that hinders the perfection of faith, death will liberate Taylor's soul from its "Cask," a corporeal "shell" in which his "Heavenly kernells box / Abides most safe" (263). The strength of his imagined share in Christ's victory permits him to crow over death as a conqueror with a final taunt that echoes Christ's command to "Get thee hence, Satan" (Matt. 4:10): "Altho' thy terrours rise to th' highst degree, / [I] still am where I was, a Fig for thee" (264).[20]

The actual focus of the poem is not physical death but the death of sin within the saved soul—the same inner transformation pursued throughout the *Meditations* and celebrated in the elegies. Christ's destruction of death's "venom" links the skull with the serpent of Eden and the sin that constitutes the truly dangerous "grave" into which partakers of "evill joyes" fall (263). Like the elegies, "A Fig for Thee" defines Taylor's real foe not as death itself but as an unregenerate perspective on dying—not the death's head but the sinner's terror of it. Vowing to let death take his captured body to its "dungeon Cave," the poet instead fights death's experiential counterpart, the "vile harlot" of carnality who labors "to drown me into Sin's disguise / By Eating & by drinking such evill joyes." Defining himself in opposition to a dying body, Taylor anticipates a final resolution of redemptive turmoil when his soul will be reunited with a purified body that is no longer his sworn enemy. At that time, the struggling polarities of experience extolled and dramatized in the elegies and meditations would be reconciled "as two true Lovers": "[E]ry night how do they hug & kiss each other. / [A]nd going hand in hand thus thro' the Skies / [U]p to Eternall glory glorious rise" (264). As in "Upon my recovery" and the "Valediction," Taylor looks toward a final cessation of turmoil when he, like the commemorated dead, would be "raised up anew & made all bright / And Christalized" (264).

While death undergoes a dramatic transformation in "A Fig for thee," Taylor does not: "[I] still am where I was" (264). Once again taking up the elegist's role in confident self-embalming, he reconfirms within himself the "New Creature" repeatedly exercised in the *Meditations*, an identity revitalized by grace with "New Heart, New thoughts, New Words, New wayes likewise" (I.30). This was a self capable of speaking assurance with a "new set of Words and thoughts" borrowed from "beyond the line" in the "other Realms" of the sanctified dead (II.106). Elect souls, Taylor insisted in the *Meditations*, speak with "Tongues tipt with Zion Languague" (II.109), speech that "Brightens its Superstructure where it builds / A Lofty Tower of Holy Life Divine" (II.89). For Taylor, the "Superstructure" encompassing meditative as well as commemorative poetry was the paradigm of gracious experience that writing enabled him to honor in the dead, encourage in his readers, and activate in himself. His ongoing verbal construction of a "Tower of Holy Life," equivalent to the "Ebenezer" of victory erected by Samuel and confirmed by Bradstreet (243) and Wigglesworth (93) in their self-examinations, unifies all of his verse, whether he invites others to honor the completed

monument of a saint in glory or builds his own monument, poem by
poem, as a saint in the making.

* * *

   As points of access to the "other," little-known Taylor, the elegies
confirm the poet's ability to respond to situational and conventional
mandates when occasion required. Like *Gods Determinations*, long
recognized as a text written to comfort troubled readers, these poems
reveal Taylor's acute sensitivity to the spiritual needs of an audience. The
elegiac verse supports Thomas M. Davis's suggestion that, given the
frequent distribution of such poems in manuscript, Taylor may well have
considered himself both a "public" and a "published" poet, despite our
usual tendency to think of him as almost exclusively readerless ("Edward
Taylor's Elegy" 81). In addition, the elegies show that even the most
stylized Puritan poetry directed its intended audience toward a rich and
complex experience of reading. What we identify as literary or spiritual
convention was internalized by Puritan writers and readers as felt
experience, fully as "real" to them as its verbal traces seem constructed
and artificial to us. For Taylor and his contemporaries, the very
predictability of the elegiac formula brought comfort by strengthening a
sense of membership in a community of the faithful. As texts of
belonging, all Puritan elegies—indeed, all Puritan poetry—offered the
consolation that Taylor extends to Hooker's widow, who can "spend
fewer tears of sorrow" because she "dost so many borrow" from the
saintly community and from the speaker as an apostle of the saint's life
(122). Finally, the identical sources of consolation that the poet
administered to others and to himself suggest a closer bond of the
conventional and the expressive in Taylor than we commonly assume.
While his elegies illuminate the experiential vitality of Puritan public
verse, they also expose a stylized, ritualistic element in the private poetry
for which he is best known. Taylor saw the *Meditations* as a kind of
spiritual workbook; each poem existed not as an end in itself but as the
record of a regulated process by which he could generate a deeper
experience of the faith. The deaths of saints offered similar opportunities
for strengthening redeemed identity. The chief difference between the
meditative and elegiac dimensions of this ongoing process was that the
latter posed the additional challenge of diffusing the glory of such a self
to a reading community that shared this spiritual goal. The deceased
saint, as Taylor said of President Chauncy, had gained glory by

"Diffusing All by Pattern" (33). The saint's embalmer, faced with the duty to transform affliction into blessing, could hardly do better than to follow that lead.

This inner dynamic underlies the formal, generic, and situational choices reflected in the diversity of the poetry. It unifies the two Edward Taylors of the criticism into one: a poet who consistently celebrates the redemptive struggle from sin to glory, whether through the ages, as in the *Metrical History of Christianity*, through an archetypal conversion, as in *Gods Determinations*, through the lives and deaths of pious contemporaries, as in the elegies, or through private devotional acts in which he strains to see beyond his own "Mudwall tent" (II.75) in order to glimpse his identity as a true Israelite destined to follow Dewey, Hooker, the Mathers, and Elizabeth Fitch Taylor down the glorious path that they had blazed. Taylor's consistent use of verse to internalize and promote this identity, whether he writes solely for himself and Christ or for other believers, confirms Davis's observation that "the poetry is the one concern which brings together and unites the major interests of his life" (Introduction to *Poetry* xi). It also unites the seemingly diverse speakers projected in Taylor's work. While Karl Keller correctly points to a "self-mythologizing process" in the verse, it is not true that the poet deliberately forged poetic personas that he considered to be in any way fictive (*Example* 75, 131; "Acting Poet"). Whether in private meditation or in public commemoration, Taylor wrote to intensify what he hoped would be his real and eternal identity, always seeking an inner congruence with gracious patterns that convinced him that he, like Paul, had "fought a good fight" and was "now ready to be offered" (2 Tim. 4:6–7). The later meditations especially record his confidence that the most miraculous "Sacred Text" (II.58) which God had written could be read within his own heart. It was the same text, after all, that Taylor repeatedly explicated in the holy dead, those perfected versions of the nascent self that the private verse helped him to imagine within.

Notes

Quotations from Taylor's elegies, with one exception, refer by page number to *Minor Poetry*; the David Dewey elegy is in Davis, "Edward Taylor's Elegy." Quotations from the *Preparatory Meditations,* by Series and poem number, and from "The Return" refer to texts in *Poems*.

1. Keller, for instance, remarked that the *Metrical History of Christianity* was "written by a different Taylor from the Taylor of the Meditations," which makes the poem "all the

less interesting" (*Example* 143). Taylor's view of public verse, Keller suggested in reference to *Gods Determinations*, was "too low, too issues-oriented, quite provincial" (137). Among the few critics who comment at all on Taylor's elegies, Grabo (71, 77) and Keller (*Example* 71) agree on their artistic inferiority to the *Preparatory Meditations*. While this assessment is consistent with post-Romantic and New Critical definitions of good poetry (textual unity, direct feeling, vivid imagery, original expression), the elegies appear in a different light when read as ritual scripts designed to provoke specific patterns of grieving among a wide range of readers. As Draper long ago observed, their public role makes elegies "an admirable medium for the study of social ideals" (*The Funeral Elegy* viii). Elegies also reveal psychological and, in the case of the Puritans, theological ideals. In his discussion of the English elegy, Sacks argues that because the conventions of elegiac verse reveal "the actual project of mourning" in an anthropological and psychological sense, the elegy demands attention "not so much to the figures of language as to the workings of the mind that uses them" (22). For a brief discussion of Taylor's elegies as psychological scripts, see Hammond (*Sinful Self, Saintly Self* 175–82).

2. Studies of the American Puritan funeral elegy include Bowden, Daly (113–17, 147–51, 162–76), Draper (*The Funeral Elegy* 155–77), Elliott, Hahn, Hammond ("The Puritan Elegiac Ritual"), Henson, Pearce (24–41), Scheick ("Standing in the Gap"; "Tombless Virtue"; *Design in Puritan American Literature* 80–88), Schmitt-v. Muhlenfels, Schweitzer (41–74), Silverman (121–32), and the Tashjians (39–44).

On the role of reading in helping New England Puritans achieve and maintain a sense of self consistent with theological expectation, see Hall ("The World of Print" 166–80; *Worlds of Wonder* 21–70), Hammond (*Sinful Self, Saintly Self* 3–36), and King (13–82). Pious texts—sermons, histories, biographies, journals, professions of faith, and public poems such as elegies—were important vehicles for disseminating ideal patterns of Puritan self-experience. Watkins notes that for Puritans the "inner landscape had already been mapped by experts. A man knew what he ought to find, because everyone was alike" (231). King, asserting a similar relation between individual experience and cultural paradigm, argues that patterns of self-perception set forth in spiritual autobiographies helped Puritan readers "build experience out of the innate confusion of sensation" (43). Cohen agrees that "cultural systems teach people how to perceive, and theology among Puritans had a major impact in shaping experience": consequently, the individual experience of the faith "acquiesced in the ministry's paradigm of grace" and "ratified the cultural definition of conversion experience" (21, 147).

3. Critics have recently begun to heal the rift between the public and private poet. Davis links them by invoking Taylor's sense of readership; even the private meditations, Davis argues, were "completed" poems reflecting not only Taylor's sense of a "general audience" but his attempts at creating a poetic "artifact" as he recopied blocks of poems (*A Reading of Edward Taylor* 15, 17, 50). For an audience-centered reading of the *Preparatory Meditations* based on Taylor's conception of Christ as his "reader," see Hammond ("Who Is Edward Taylor?"; *Sinful Self, Saintly Self* 186–212). Additional work on Taylor and audience will likely be stimulated by Craig's concordance to the Davis and Davis edition of the *Minor Poetry*. Surveys of Taylor scholarship include Scheick and Doggett, Rainwater and Scheick, and Hammond (*Edward Taylor*).

4. Quoted in Draper (*The Funeral Elegy* 57). Studies of the English funeral elegy, in addition to Draper, include Wallerstein, Bennett, Hardison, Pigman, and Kay. The popularity of the form is suggested by the fact that Draper identified almost three hundred seventeenth-century funeral elegies published as broadsides; this does not include the

poems published in commemorative volumes or circulated in manuscript. For a selection of English broadside elegies, see Draper, *A Century*.

5. The scholarship on the English pastoral elegy is enormous. Excellent studies representative of recent work include Sacks, Pigman, and Schenck. Sacks and Pigman relate the form to psychological models of grieving; Pigman, who discusses nonpastoral as well as pastoral elegies, stresses Renaissance attitudes toward mourning, while Sacks stresses transhistorical patterns of loss and recovery. Schenck traces the panegyric impulse through the "ceremonial" genres of epithalamium and elegy. The pastoral elegy, a decidedly learned genre, was directly indebted to classical models that encouraged its thematic versatility. In classical verse, "elegiac" referred simply to a particular metrical form—alternating dactylic hexameters and pentameters—that proved adaptable to a wide variety of reflective or satirical themes. Although those themes included the lament, classical elegies also contained topical commentary as well as more general philosophical or moral reflection. The *loci classici* for the elegy of mourning included Theocritus's first idyll, Bion's poem for the dying Adonis, a lament for Bion attributed to Moschus, and Virgil's fifth and tenth eclogues, the former a poem for Daphnis and the latter a dirge for the lovesick Gallus, famous for its claim that "omnia vincit Amor."

One of the most moving classical expressions of loss, Catullus's famous "ave atque vale" to his brother, epitomized an emotional restraint that proved congenial to Christian mourning, in which excessive grief was further checked by the ascetic ideal and the compensatory stress on eternal life and heavenly glory. During the Middle Ages, poetic laments usually blended stoic decorum with Christian edification either by invoking the homiletic tradition of the *ubi sunt*, as in Geoffrey de Vinsauf's poem for Richard I, or by taking a more allegorical turn in confirming earthly transience and vanity, as in *The Pearl*. The Christian lament offered a more direct literary precedent for the Renaissance funeral elegy than did the classical pastoral.

6. Scheick warns against overstating the uniqueness of the New England elegy prior to the Restoration ("Tombless Virtue" 287–88). On the increasing elaboration of funerary customs in late seventeenth-century New England, see Stannard (122–26).

7. Strickland notes a long-standing New Critical aesthetic bias in the historical scholarship on the elegy, which he claims accounts for a consistent inability to deal with its noncanonical or popular forms. In her stress on poetic professionalism in the elegy, for instance, Schenck downplays the poem's role as a facilitator of actual mourning, arguing that Milton's Latin poem on Charles Diodati fails as a "literary gesture" in part because of its narrowly "contemporary horizon" (102–3). On the general critical bias against the occasional poem, see Hardison (107–8).

8. Classic studies of the funeral elegy, English as well as American, were often marred by condescension, as if these poems were direct precursors of the "Ode to Stephen Dowling Bots, Dec'd," a "tribute" so formulaic, Huck Finn solemnly reports, that Emmeline Grangerford "didn't ever have to stop to think." "If half the elegists who unhappily found a printer had only been content to waste their sorrows on the desert air," Draper remarked, "the present study had been much mitigated, and the general average of English poetry much advanced" (*The Funeral Elegy* vii). Wallerstein began her study by claiming that, of the elegies under examination, "almost all are literary in the sense of being formal literary celebrations and not merely of that class of admonitory consolation which Mr. Draper describes among his mortuary elegies" (5). Tyler, writing in 1878, praised Urian Oakes's elegy on Thomas Shepard II as a product of "true imaginative vision," but he noted that the poem was "blurred also by some patches of the prevailing

theological jargon" (270). Finally, although Murdock noted in 1927 that it would be "worse than foolish" to read New England elegies "unmindful of their spirit," he conceded that "the bulk of the world's great poetry is no whit increased" by their publication (xxi, lxii).

9. Discussions of the ongoing Puritan psychomachia include Bercovitch (15–25), Cohen (104–8), King (15, 41–42), McGiffert (4, 19–26), and Watkins (12–14, 19, 228). As Cohen observes, "Saints accumulate a measure of comfort from discerning this 'self-combat,' which demonstrates that 'sin hath no quiet possession in thee'" (105). Because sin had to be faced before it could be fought, a primary function of all Puritan autobiographical texts was to expose the writer's corrupt nature. As Shea notes in his discussion of the diary of Thomas Shepard I, "the diary would fail in its purpose if the writer could not bring himself to view his most abhorrent self" (142). McGiffert, commenting on Puritan diaries, similarly observes that an "ability to sustain this methodical, painful discipline could be regarded as a mark of a gracious soul, and the regulating of the exercise may itself have contributed to the diarist's composure" (18). On the postconversion search for assurance, see Hambrick-Stowe (*Practice of Piety* 198–203) and Schuldiner (*Gifts and Works*). For an excellent early study of redemptive self-deprecation in Taylor's *Meditations*, see Mignon ("Decorum"). Davis posits that Taylor's search for humility prompted him to restrict his artistic ambitions as the *Meditations* progressed (*A Reading of Edward Taylor* 202).

10. Given the indispensable role of the iconic dead in Puritan mourning, it is somewhat beside the point to complain that Taylor's elegies are "elaborately ingenious, but not personally involved" (Grabo 75). Silverman, relating the radical distancing of the deceased from the reader to the elegy's function as a jeremiad, calls such generalized depictions "portraits of the Saved Soul" and the "idealized great man" (123, 126–27), while Scheick argues that the elegist's emphasis on "the broad configuration of saintliness" enhanced the deceased's function as a communal self with whom each mourner could identify ("Tombless Virtue" 290–94, 296). In her reading of John Fiske's elegy on John Cotton, Schweitzer similarly notes that the facts of Cotton's life are "suppressed by the standard formula" (47). Bosco discusses a similar invocation of the generalized saint in funeral sermons (xxvi–xxviii), while Breitwieser relates this sermonic technique to "exemplification" as the central trope of Puritan mourning (53–70).

11. Hammond ("The Puritan Elegiac Ritual" 87–90), Scheick ("Tombless Virtue" 297), and Schweitzer (63, 68–70) comment on the deceased's objectification as a text of piety, while the Tashjians note that "in a transcendent yet concrete bisecting dimension, the deceased *becomes* the poem, chanted by the elegist, reenacting the interpenetration of word and flesh" (44). The Tashjians similarly observe that the anagrams frequently accompanying Puritan elegies produce "a verbal correlative to the spiritual metamorphosis" of the saint: "In his discovery of the anagram the poet was simply recreating that which had already occurred spiritually, by demonstrating the iconic power perceived in words" (44).

12. Taylor's suspension between opposing modes in the *Meditations* has often been noted. Mignon, for example, observes his balance between "certitude and doubt" ("A Principle of Order" 116); Reed places him between "pride and hypocrisy" (311); Scheick locates him between "presumption and despair" ("Order and Disorder" 8) and between "the temporal and the eternal realms" (*Will and the Word* 131); Rowe finds a polarity of "rationality" and "heightened affections" (*Saint and Singer* 275–76); and Hammond cites an ongoing dichotomy of the "sinful" and "saintly" dimensions of Puritan selfhood

("Who Is Edward Taylor?"; *Sinful Self, Saintly Self* 164–85, 186–212). On the role played by a similarly dichotomized self in *Gods Determinations*, see Bush, Gatta ("Comic Design" 134), and Scheick ("Jawbones Schema").

13. On the homiletic and psychological applications of the Law and the Gospel in Puritan thought, see Cohen (47–74), Hall (*Faithful Shepherd* 18–19, 63–66, 163–65), Knott (11, 133, 142–44), Levy (25–27), Pettit (17–18), and Watkins (8–9).

14. The split portrayals of the deceased in Puritan elegies support Clark's discussion of the importance of liminality in Puritan discourse. As Clark points out, Christ and the Bible served to bridge "the ontological gap between the visible and invisible worlds" ("The Honeyed Knot" 70). The newly dead saint, having recently passed from this world to the next, bridged this gap as well.

15. Sacks comments that to write an elegy is to adapt to the change posed by death, to perform a concessive act in which "the mourner must prevent a congealing of his own impulses" by bringing "his loss into language, testing how it feels to speak *and hear* of it in words" (22, 25). For Puritans, this meant that one could not remain silently convicted in the face of God's will but had to "Shake off," in John Saffin's words, "the Shackles of thy Contemplation" in order to celebrate the saint's final victory (Meserole 199).

16. Taylor sent "Upon Wedlock" to Samuel Sewall, who probably gave it to Mather. On the printing of stanzas 5 and 7 in Mather's *Right Thoughts in Sad Hours* (London, 1689), see Johnson.

17. Davis ("Occasional Meditations" 21–25) and Hambrick-Stowe (Introduction to *Poetry* 44) suggest that the increasingly ritualistic cast of the *Preparatory Meditations* reflects Taylor's devotional response to family sorrows. On Taylor's treatment of his wife's death in the *Meditations*, see Keller (*Example* 47), Hambrick-Stowe (Introduction to *Poetry* 46–48), and Davis (*A Reading of Edward Taylor* 113–19).

18. The increasingly eschatological thrust of the later meditations is discussed in Hammond ("*Ars Moriendi*"; "Approaching the Garden"; *Sinful Self, Saintly Self* 228–35), Lewalski (416–25), Lowance (91–96), and Rowe ("Sacred or Profane?"; *Saint and Singer* 257–60). On the importance of the *ars moriendi* tradition in Protestant culture, see Beaty (108–56), Geddes, Martz (135–44), and Stannard.

The self-elegy was extremely popular in early New England; better-known examples include several passages in Philip Pain's *Daily Meditations* (Cambridge, 1668), Bradstreet's "Upon a Fit of Sickness" and "As Weary Pilgrim," and poems attributed to Bradstreet's father, Thomas Dudley, and to William Bradford. As Draper notes, the self-elegy was also common among English Puritans (*The Funeral Elegy* 157–58). A poem attributed to an English dissenter probably encouraged its popularity in New England. The *New-England Primer* contained an "Exhortation to his Children" supposedly authored by Marian martyr John Rogers shortly before he died. Referring to himself as already dead, as he would actually *be* in the reader's present, the speaker leaves behind "a little Book" in verse, "That you may see your Fathers face, / when he is dead and gone" (Ford 31). Watters discusses this poem in terms of a theme central to the Puritan elegy: the transfer of sacred authority from older to younger generations (206–7).

19. The apparent strength of Taylor's religious assurance, especially in the later poetry, supports Cohen's argument that Puritans could be more certain of their salvation than is commonly thought: "God encourages the believer with hope of mercy, and hope, looking toward His 'unspeakable compassions,' makes it 'clear and certain' that the regenerate already possess His glory." Maintaining that conversion gave the saint a power "to cooperate with grace in combating the flesh," Cohen discusses the postconversion

identity of the believer as a new creature whose will has been transformed by grace (101, 210, 95–98). Keller, raising a rhetorical parallel to Cohen's "potency" of conversion, suggests that poetry may have been "a *liberating* art in Puritan culture" and for Taylor in particular (*Example* 236), a view elaborated in Gatta's study of Taylor's meditative and verbal wit as an antidote to religious melancholy (*Gracious Laughter* 33–62).

Discussions of biblical and theological influences on Taylor's "self-fashioning," to use Greenblatt's phrase, include Clark ("The Subject of the Text" 125, 129), Fithian, Gatta (*Gracious Laughter* 76), Hammond ("Who Is Edward Taylor?"; *Sinful Self, Saintly Self* 213–35), Keller (*Example* 74–75; "Acting Poet"), Rowe (*Saint and Singer* 22, 148, 163, 223), Scheick (*Will and the Word* 161–62; "Typology and Allegory" 85), and Schuldiner ("Christian Hero").

20. As Gatta notes, "Death, like Satan in *Gods Determinations*, will unwittingly play his part in the divine scheme by . . . refining . . . the poet's bodily essence" (*Gracious Laughter* 202). On the iconographic sources of Taylor's emblem of the skull, see Hammond and Davis.

Works Cited

Ames, William. *The Marrow of Theology*. Translated by John Eusden. Boston: The Pilgrim Press, 1968.

Beaty, Nancy Lee. *The Craft of Dying: A Study in the Literary Tradition of the Ars Moriendi*. New Haven: Yale University Press, 1970.

Bennett, A. L. "The Principal Rhetorical Conventions in the Renaissance Personal Elegy." *Studies in Philology* 51 (1954): 107–26.

Bercovitch, Sacvan. *The Puritan Origins of the American Self*. New Haven: Yale University Press, 1975.

Bosco, Ronald A. Introduction to *New England Funeral Sermons*, edited by Ronald A. Bosco, ix–xxviii. Delmar, N. Y.: Scholars' Facsimiles and Reprints, 1978.

Bowden, Edwin T. "Urian Oakes' Elegy: Colonial Literature and History." *Forum* 10 (1972): 2–8.

Bradstreet, Anne. *The Works of Anne Bradstreet*. Edited by Jeannine Hensley. Cambridge: Belknap-Harvard University Press, 1967.

Breitwieser, Mitchell Robert. *American Puritanism and the Defense of Mourning: Religion, Grief, and Ethnology in Mary White Rowlandson's Captivity Narrative*. Madison: University of Wisconsin Press, 1990.

Bush, Sargent, Jr. "Paradox, Puritanism, and Taylor's *Gods Determinations*." *Early American Literature* 4 (1969/70): 89–96.

Clark, Michael. "The Honeyed Knot of Puritan Aesthetics." In *Puritan Poets and Poetics: Seventeenth-Century American Poetry in Theory and Practice,* edited by Peter White., 67–83. University Park: Pennsylvania State University Press, 1985.

———. "The Subject of the Text in Early American Literature." *Early American Literature* 20 (1985): 120–30.

Cohen, Charles Lloyd. *God's Caress: The Psychology of Puritan Religious Experience*. New York: Oxford University Press, 1986.

Craig, Raymond A. *A Concordance to the Minor Poetry of Edward Taylor (1642?-1729): American Colonial Poet*. 2 vols. Lewiston, N.Y.: Edwin Mellen, 1992.

Daly, Robert. *God's Altar: The World and the Flesh in Puritan Poetry.* Berkeley: University of California Press, 1978.

Davis, Thomas M. "Edward Taylor's 'Occasional Meditations.'" *Early American Literature* 5 (1970/71): 17–29.

———. Introduction to *Edward Taylor's Minor Poetry*, edited by Thomas M. Davis and Virginia L. Davis, xi-xxiv. Boston: Twayne, 1981.

———. "Edward Taylor's Elegy on Deacon David Dewey." *Proceedings of the American Antiquarian Society* 96, part 1 (1986): 75–84.

———. *A Reading of Edward Taylor.* Newark: University of Delaware Press, 1992.

Draper, John W. *The Funeral Elegy and the Rise of English Romanticism.* New York: New York University Press, 1929.

———, ed. *A Century of Broadside Elegies.* London: Ingpen and Grant, 1928.

Elledge, Scott, ed. *Milton's Lycidas.* New York: Harper and Row, 1966.

Elliott, Emory. "The Development of the Puritan Funeral Sermon and Elegy: 1660–1750." *Early American Literature* 15 (1980): 151–64.

Fithian, Rosemary. "'Words of My Mouth, Meditations of My Heart': Edward Taylor's *Preparatory Meditations* and the Book of Psalms." *Early American Literature* 20 (1985): 89–119.

Ford, Paul Leicester, ed. *The New-England Primer.* 1897. New York: Teachers College, Columbia University, 1962.

Gatta, John, Jr. "The Comic Design of *Gods Determinations* touching his Elect." *Early American Literature* 10 (1975): 121–43.

———. *Gracious Laughter: The Meditative Wit of Edward Taylor.* Columbia: University of Missouri Press, 1989.

Geddes, Gordon E. *Welcome Joy: Death in Puritan New England.* Ann Arbor, Mich.: UMI Research Press, 1981.

Grabo, Norman S. *Edward Taylor.* Rev. ed. Boston: Twayne, 1988.

Greenblatt, Stephen. *Renaissance Self-Fashioning: From More to Shakespeare.* Chicago: University of Chicago Press, 1980.

Hahn, T. G. "Urian Oakes's *Elegie* on Thomas Shepard and Puritan Poetics." *American Literature* 45 (1973): 163–81.

Hall, David D. *The Faithful Shepherd: A History of the New England Ministry in the Seventeenth Century.* Chapel Hill: University of North Carolina Press, 1972.

———. "The World of Print and Collective Mentality in Seventeenth-Century New England." In *New Directions in American Intellectual History,* edited by John Higham and Paul Conklin, 166–80. Baltimore, Md.: Johns Hopkins University Press, 1979.

———. *Worlds of Wonder, Days of Judgment: Popular Religious Belief in Early New England.* New York: Knopf, 1989.

Hambrick-Stowe, Charles E. *The Practice of Piety: Puritan Devotional Disciplines in Seventeenth-Century New England.* Chapel Hill: University of North Carolina Press, 1982.

———. Introduction to *Early New England Meditative Poetry: Anne Bradstreet and Edward Taylor,* edited by Charles E. Hambrick-Stowe, 7–62. New York: Paulist Press, 1988.

Hammond, Jeffrey A. "A Puritan *Ars Moriendi*: Edward Taylor's Late Meditations on the Song of Songs." *Early American Literature* 17 (1982/83): 191–214.

———. "Who Is Edward Taylor?: Voice and Reader in the *Preparatory Meditations.*" *American Poetry* 7.2 (Spring 1990): 2–19.

———. "Approaching the Garden: Edward Taylor's Progress Toward the Song of Songs." *Studies in Puritan American Spirituality* 1 (1990): 65–87.

————. "The Puritan Elegiac Ritual: From Sinful Silence to Apostolic Voice." *Studies in Puritan American Spirituality* 2 (1991): 77–106.

————. *Edward Taylor: Fifty Years of Scholarship and Criticism*. Columbia, S.C.: Camden House, 1993.

————. *Sinful Self, Saintly Self: The Puritan Experience of Poetry*. Athens: University of Georgia Press, 1993.

Hammond, Jeff, and Thomas M. Davis. "Edward Taylor: A Note on Visual Imagery." *Early American Literature* 8 (1973): 126–31.

Hardison, O. B., Jr. *The Enduring Monument: A Study of the Idea of Praise in Renaissance Literary Theory*. Chapel Hill: University of North Carolina Press, 1962.

Henson, Robert. "Form and Content of the Puritan Funeral Elegy." *American Literature* 32 (1960): 11–27.

Johnson, Thomas H. "A Seventeenth-Century Printing of Some Verses of Edward Taylor." *New England Quarterly* 14 (1941): 139–41.

Kay, Dennis. *Melodious Tears: The English Funeral Elegy from Spenser to Milton*. Oxford: Clarendon, 1990.

Keller, Karl. *The Example of Edward Taylor*. Amherst: University of Massachusetts Press, 1975.

————. "Edward Taylor, The Acting Poet." In *Puritan Poets and Poetics: Seventeenth-Century American Poetry in Theory and Practice,* edited by Peter White, 185–97. University Park: Pennsylvania State University Press, 1985.

King, John Owen III. *The Iron of Melancholy: Structures of Spiritual Conversion in America from the Puritan Conscience to Victorian Neurosis*. Middletown, Conn.: Wesleyan University Press, 1983.

Knott, John R., Jr. *The Sword of the Spirit: Puritan Responses to the Bible*. Chicago: University of Chicago Press, 1980.

Levy, Babette May. *Preaching in the First Half Century of New England History*. 1945. New York: Russell and Russell, 1967.

Lewalski, Barbara Kiefer. *Protestant Poetics and the Seventeenth-Century Religious Lyric*. Princeton, N. J.: Princeton University Press, 1979.

Lowance, Mason I., Jr. *The Language of Canaan: Metaphor and Symbol in New England from the Puritans to the Transcendentalists*. Cambridge: Harvard University Press, 1980.

Martz, Louis. *The Poetry of Meditation: A Study in English Religious Literature of the Seventeenth Century*. Rev. ed. New Haven: Yale University Press, 1962.

McGiffert, Michael. Introduction to *God's Plot: The Paradoxes of Puritan Piety,* edited by Michael McGiffert, 3–32. Amherst: University of Massachusetts Press, 1972.

Meserole, Harrison T., ed. *American Poetry of the Seventeenth Century*. 1968. University Park: Pennsylvania State University Press, 1985.

Mignon, Charles W. "Edward Taylor's *Preparatory Meditations*: A Decorum of Imperfection." *PMLA* 83 (1968): 1423–28.

————. "A Principle of Order in Edward Taylor's *Preparatory Meditations*." *Early American Literature* 4 (1969/70): 110–16.

Murdock, Kenneth B. Introduction to *Handkerchiefs from Paul,* edited by Kenneth B. Murdock, xv–lxxiii. Cambridge: Harvard University Press, 1927.

Pearce, Roy Harvey. *The Continuity of American Poetry*. Princeton, N. J.: Princeton University Press, 1961.

Pettit, Norman. *The Heart Prepared: Grace and Conversion in Puritan Spiritual Life*. New Haven: Yale University Press, 1966.

Pigman, G. W., III. *Grief and English Renaissance Elegy*. Cambridge: Cambridge University Press, 1985.

Rainwater, Catherine, and William J. Scheick. "Seventeenth-Century American Poetry: A Reference Guide Updated." *Resources for American Literary Study* 10 (1980): 121–45.

Reed, Michael. "Edward Taylor's Poetry: Puritan Structure and Form." *American Literature* 46.3 (1974): 304–12.

Rowe, Karen E. "Sacred or Profane? Edward Taylor's Meditations on Canticles." *Modern Philology* 72 (1974): 123–38.

———. *Saint and Singer: Edward Taylor's Typology and the Poetics of Meditation*. Cambridge: Cambridge University Press, 1986.

Sacks, Peter. *The English Elegy: Studies in the Genre from Spenser to Yeats*. Baltimore, Md.: Johns Hopkins University Press, 1985.

Scheick, William J. *The Will and the Word: The Poetry of Edward Taylor*. Athens: University of Georgia Press, 1974.

———. "Typology and Allegory: A Comparative Study of George Herbert and Edward Taylor." *Essays in Literature* 2 (1975): 76–86.

———. "Standing in the Gap: Urian Oakes' Elegy on Thomas Shepard." *Early American Literature* 9 (1975): 301–6.

———. "The Jawbones Schema of Edward Taylor's *Gods Determinations*." In *Puritan Influences in American Literature,* edited by Emory Elliott, 38–54. Urbana: University of Illinois Press, 1979.

———. "Tombless Virtue and Hidden Text: New England Puritan Funeral Elegies." In *Puritan Poets and Poetics: Seventeenth-Century American Poetry in Theory and Practice,* edited by Peter White, 286–302. University Park: Pennsylvania State University Press, 1985.

———. "Order and Disorder in Taylor's Poetry: Meditation 1.8." *American Poetry* 5 (1988): 2–11.

———. *Design in Puritan American Literature*. Lexington: University Press of Kentucky, 1992.

Scheick, William J., and JoElla Doggett. *Seventeenth-Century American Poetry: A Reference Guide*. Boston: G. K. Hall, 1977.

Schenck, Celeste Marguerite. *Mourning and Panegyric: The Poetics of Pastoral Ceremony*. University Park: Pennsylvania State University Press, 1988.

Schmitt-v. Muhlenfels, Astrid. "John Fiske's Funeral Elegy on John Cotton." *Early American Literature* 12 (1977): 49–62.

Schuldiner, Michael. "The Christian Hero and the Classical Journey in Edward Taylor's 'Preparatory Meditations. First Series.'" *Huntington Library Quarterly* 49 (1986): 113–32.

———. *Gifts and Works: The Post-Conversion Paradigm and Spiritual Controversy in Seventeenth-Century Massachusetts*. Macon, Ga.: Mercer University Press, 1991.

Schweitzer, Ivy. *The Work of Self-Representation: Lyric Poetry in Colonial New England*. Chapel Hill: University of North Carolina Press, 1991.

Shea, Daniel. *Spiritual Autobiography in Early America*. Princeton, N. J.: Princeton University Press, 1968.

Silverman, Kenneth, ed. *Colonial American Poetry*. New York: Hafner, 1968.

Stannard, David E. *The Puritan Way of Death: A Study in Religion, Culture, and Social Change*. New York: Oxford University Press, 1977.

Stone, Lawrence. *The Crisis of the Aristocracy, 1558–1641*. Oxford: Clarendon, 1965.

Strickland, Ronald. "Not So Idle Tears: Re-Reading the Renaissance Elegy." *Review* 14 (1992): 57–72.

Tashjian, Dickran, and Ann Tashjian. *Memorials for Children of Change*. Middletown, Conn.: Wesleyan University Press, 1974.

Taylor, Edward. *The Poems of Edward Taylor*. Edited by Donald E. Stanford. New Haven: Yale University Press, 1960.

———. *Edward Taylor's Minor Poetry: Volume 3 of the Unpublished Writings of Edward Taylor*. Edited and with an introduction by Thomas M. Davis and Virginia L. Davis. Boston: Twayne, 1981.

Tyler, Moses Coit. *A History of American Literature 1607–1765*. 1878. Ithaca: Cornell University Press, 1949.

Waggoner, Hyatt H. *American Poets: From the Puritans to the Present*. Boston: Houghton Mifflin, 1968.

Wallerstein, Ruth. *Studies in Seventeenth-Century Poetic*. Madison: University of Wisconsin Press, 1950.

Watkins, Owen C. *The Puritan Experience*. London: Routledge and Kegan Paul, 1972.

Watters, David H. "'I Spake as a Child': Authority, Metaphor, and *The New-England Primer*." *Early American Literature* 20 (1985/86): 193–213.

Wigglesworth, Michael. *The Diary of Michael Wigglesworth 1653–1657: The Conscience of a Puritan*. Edited by Edmund S. Morgan. New York: Harper and Row, 1965.

Willard, Samuel. *The High Esteem Which God hath of the Death of his Saints*. Boston, 1683. In *The Puritans*, edited by Perry Miller and Thomas H. Johnson, 1:371–74. New York: Harper and Row, 1963.

A Farewell to David:
Edward Taylor's Valediction and Psalm 19

ROSEMARY FITHIAN GURUSWAMY

The Puritans of New England were a textual people. Etta Madden has suggested, in response to their funeral elegies, that they viewed "life as a text," finding it easier to live by the word than by human encounter (232– 33). They established their theocracy upon laws already written in the Bible, particularly the Old Testament and, because they wished to promote literacy in the colony, gave priority to educational institutions, at least for the males in the community. As David Hall has said, New England Puritans often conflated the consumption of the written word with the growth of their spirituality (18). The Puritans lived by the Word in more ways than one.

Of all the biblical texts that occupied Puritan attention, the Book of Psalms was perhaps the foremost, if only because its applicability to verbal situations is so diverse. Meditation and other devotional practices, singing in worship and in private, writing poetry and prose, translating and paraphrasing—all these linguistic activities can find root and model in the Psalms. Most Reformation and post-Reformation exegetes support David's text as a pattern for generating devotional language. As a pious artist or the speaking subject of text, David becomes for many Christians in the sixteenth and seventeenth centuries the voice of a person struggling to find assurance, grappling with doubt, and always hoping for heaven. For the New England Puritans, through the process of christological interpretation of the Old Testament, David takes on the particular identity of the regenerate soul and, after 1680, the saint privileged to receive the Supper (Guruswamy 294–97).[1] His conversion,

usually placed in Psalm 51, and the subsequent strong expression of his
faith become the central focus of many Puritan allusions to David.

It is no wonder, then, that Edward Taylor—a textually oriented Puritan
and a generator of literary text—was attracted to the Book of Psalms. His
use of the psalter as a model for his poetry and psalm paraphrases[2]
indicates his love for biblical tradition and the necessity he felt to have a
prototype for his writing that had scriptural sanction—both textual
impulses that he shared with his culture. But his use of the psalter more
precisely reflects a Puritan desire to approach textually the administration
and reception of the Lord's Supper in the way God would wish.
According to psalmic exegesis, in the old Israel, David had known the
formula for doing so. Living in the new Israel, Taylor attempted to
incorporate his knowledge of the New England psalm tradition to make
his verse acceptable to its audience—his God. Apparently this impulse
remained with Taylor his entire life, because in the composition of his
final poetic attempt, the "Valedictory Poems," Taylor turns to Psalm 19
as a working model.

In the New England colonies, the popular practices and exegetical
attitudes concerning psalmody which affected Taylor remained generally
the same as those that had been developing among Protestants in England
and on the Continent since the Reformation. Singing psalms in worship
and in private homes and using David's verses as a framework for
meditation informed the faith of the Puritans in the wilderness as it had in
the Old World. In addition, since most Protestant interpreters saw the
psalter chiefly as a prophecy of the New Testament—"The Gospels
Index; in one word, The Register, Enchiridion, Summarie, pith, and (as it
were) Briefe of the whole Bible" (Boys 1:n.p.)—it became even more
central to a people seeking to establish the perfect Christian community.

The Christology that had been associated with the Psalms since
patristic times increased its usefulness as a locus for expression of
Christian experience. This usage dovetailed nicely with the colonists'
perception of themselves as the New Israelites, which Sacvan Bercovitch
connects to the psychological repercussions of John Winthrop's
declaration that the Massachusetts Bay colony was to be "a Citty upon a
Hill," the New Jerusalem that would finally fulfill the covenant the
Israelites had not accomplished (Bercovitch *passim*; Lowance 27).
Because the psalter is a historical as well as a poetic book and the people
it chronicles lived for a time in the wilderness, the colonists saw parallels
with their experiences in the verses of the psalter. They viewed the Book
of Psalms as a prototypical account of God's treatment of wilderness
peoples, and consequently as a guidebook for them. Because several
psalms focus on a wilderness wandering, either historically in relation to

the Exodus (for example, Psalms 44, 68, 74, 78, 105–7, and 136) or personally concerning David's experiences of hardship (Psalms 55, 63, 69, and 102), the psalter became as applicable to the New Englanders' experience as the Book of Exodus was to the Israelites. In such psalms, the colonists saw their own lives reflected both privately and publicly, and so they adopted the psalter as a handbook for both the wilderness soul and those people cast into a "dry and thirsty land" (Psalm 63:1), a drama analogous to their own condition as well as a biblical precedent.[3]

The New Israelite perception involving the psalter also occurs in colonial histories and elegiac poetry through the association of certain founding fathers with David. The practice of paralleling New England leaders with those of the Old Testament is a common rhetorical device in elegies on the departed founders; Bercovitch suggests that sometimes such identifications attain the status of hagiography (27, 56). David's public, private, and literary roles encourage a broad range of correspondances with different New England personages; the majority of "new Davids" are men who show spiritual leadership worthy of a David. John Wilson, John Eliot, and Sir William Phips are all described as Davids in their own particular ministerial or magisterial roles.[4] In *Wonder-Working Providence*, Edward Johnson refers to the writers of the Cambridge Platform as "God's Davids" because of their translation into human language of doctrine from God (104). Whether such elegiac identifications constitute hyperbole or an actual attempt to grant saintly status to the New England experiment, surely they served as one impetus for the similar connection Edward Taylor made between David as God's poet and himself.

Another way the Psalms became particularly important in the colony was through their association with the Lord's Supper. Several traditional attitudes, such as the conjunction of the Word and the sacrament and the relationship between meditation and being prepared to take the Supper, persist in American Puritan thought from British tradition. The translators of the *Bay Psalm Book* and John Cotton,[5] the only writers in the seventeenth century to consider extensively the practice of psalmody in the colonies, specify psalm-singing as an ordinance because of its use of scriptural language. The writers of the *Bay* "Preface" allude to the authority of the psalmic words even when they are translated metrically: "[David's words] . . . are of morall, universall, and perpetuall authority in all nations and ages" (Haraszti, *Bay Psalm Book*, n.p.).[6] Cotton also states in *Singing of Psalmes a Gospel Ordinance* that the words, when read or sung, have the power of an ordinance: "[Psalms are] Gods own Ordinance to convey, and quicken, and enlarge the Spirit" (30); he reinforces this view by insisting that the "Singing of Psalmes holdeth forth as much of Christ externally, as reading of the Word, or as the hearing of it read or preached, or as the falling downe upon our knees in prayer" (4). In sermons preached between 1680 and 1700, Samuel Willard supports Cotton's definition, citing the establishment of psalm-singing as an institution in the Hebrew church, its continuance in the prescribed worship of the New Testament, and its public and private practice in the early Christian era (898). In his *Treatise Concerning the Lord's Supper*, Edward Taylor stresses the power of this ordinance to convert: "[Praying and singing psalms] are both vocal and auditory, and so suitable instruments to convey converting grace into the soul" (70–71). Thus, the use of psalms could work—as ordinances did in the colony—to betoken sanctification or, for the unconverted, to provide a channel for God's grace to enter, if it would, and thus serve as a prelude to the Supper, available only to the regenerate. Later in the 1680s and 1690s, as the controversy concerning whether the Supper was meant only for the elect or whether it could serve as a converting ordinance itself developed, the psalter assumed a more clearly defined position as a useful part of the Word to prepare one for the converting experience necessary for receiving the Supper. [7]

The insistence in New England on the converting potential of psalm usage is no doubt the reason why the colonists emphasized the literalness of the translation they used for singing. Shortly after the Puritans arrived in the Bay Colony, they replaced the Ravenscroft edition of the Sternhold-Hopkins psalter, used in England since 1621, with the more literally translated *Whole Booke of Psalmes Faithfully Translated into English Metre*, or the *Bay Psalm Book* (1640), the first book published by an American press. The need to replace Sternhold-Hopkins because of the colonists' belief in linguistic exactness within the walls of a meeting house is evidenced in the *Bay Psalm Book* "Preface": "It is not unknowne to the godly learned that they [Sternhold and Hopkins] have rather presented a paraphrase than the words of David translated according to the rule" (Haraszti, *Bay Psalm Book*, n.p.). [8] However, such linguistic activity was apparently not looked upon as a grammatical chore. In their close work with the words, the *Bay* translators attempted to reach "the very spirit of the Psalms" (Foote 27) by concentrating on the vivid connotations of the Hebrew. Although the *Bay Psalm Book* was virtually the only metrical psalter produced in the colony, [9] it went through nine editions in the seventeenth century, the third of which (1651) sustained major revisions. [10] It served the colony, for the Psalms were sung in worship, before and after sermons and the celebration of the Lord's Supper, at the declaration of the covenant among the fellowship, and before the dismissal of church assemblies. [11]

Certain colonial leaders also recommended that private, spontaneous, and individual prayers for personal devotion be modeled on the Psalms. John Cotton notes in *Singing of Psalmes a Gospel Ordinance* that a person with poetic talent might pray in private song: "He may both frame [a spiritual song], and sing it privately, for his own private comfort, and remembrance of some special benefit, or deliverance"; such songs might be compiled out of the words of the Psalms, while not being literal translations of the Psalms themselves.[12] The next step is obvious, and several New England poets took it, most notably Edward Taylor: the adoption of the Psalms as a guidebook for private poetic responses to religious life in the colony. Although evidence exists that Anne Bradstreet and Michael Wigglesworth also used the Book of Psalms as a scriptural model for their verse, Taylor's employment of it seems to be more comprehensive.[13]

This conscious use of textual inspiration and pattern continued for Taylor to the end of his poetic (and earthly) life, when he turned to Psalm 19—in the Protestant exegetical tradition one of the most christological psalms[14]—as a model for his "Valedictory Poems." These three poems exist as separate, similar drafts, the first two of which Taylor copied into his "Poetical Works" and the third into his "Manuscript Book" (Taylor, *Minor Poetry,* 315).[15] Thomas and Virginia Davis surmise that Taylor worked on a poem and, when he was satisfied, copied it into the "Poetical Works" (Taylor, *Minor Poetry,* 217; Thomas Davis, "Valedictory," 38); nevertheless, version 3 of the "Valedictory Poems" seems the most polished, especially syntactically, which has caused those who have written about these final Taylor poems to assume the third to be the finished version.[16] Also, the substantial amount of repetition that occurs in the final canticles of version 1 suggests that this version must be a working copy of the poem, perhaps containing two separate endings bound together. At any rate, the three versions—none of which seems really polished or complete—do at least indicate that, even as he reached an age few of his contemporaries attained, Taylor continued to be an active craftsman. As Thomas Davis suggests, the aged Taylor was well aware that most of what he had lived for had fallen to the ravages of time and change. His art remained one constant in this world of "mutability and decay" (Taylor, *Minor Poetry,* xx), even though the "Valedictory" versions show the failing Taylor still fascinated with the energy of linguistic change. A comparison of the three drafts with Psalm 19, also keeping in mind what Taylor knew about psalmic prosody and had previously employed in his *Preparatory Meditations*, indicates that, until the end of his earthly life, the Psalms remained an anchor to Taylor that secured his art in the "spiritual equilibrium" Davis perceives (ibid. xx).

Psalm 19 begins with a declaration of created nature as testimony of God's work; verses 2, 3, and 4 contain allusions to the logocentric power of the Creation:

> The heavens declare the glory of God;
> And the firmament showeth his handiwork.
> Day unto day uttereth speech,
> And night unto night showeth knowledge.
> There is no speech nor language;
> Their voice is not heard.
> Their line is gone out through all the earth,
> And their words to the end of the world. [17]

The psalmist then enters into the christological metaphor of the sun as bridegroom:

> In them hath he set a tabernacle for the sun,
> Which is as a bridegroom coming out of his chamber,
> And rejoiceth as a strong man to run his course.
> His going forth is from the end of the heavens,
> And his circuit unto the ends of it;
> And there is nothing hid from the heat thereof.

Verse 7 begins with a digression on Jehovah's attributes, including his ordinances, followed by several verses meditating on the avoidance of sin:

> The law of Jehovah is perfect, restoring the soul:
> The testimony of Jehovah is sure, making wise the simple.
> The precepts of Jehovah are right, rejoicing the heart:
> The commandment of Jehovah is pure, enlightening the eyes.
> The fear of Jehovah is clean, enduring for ever:
> The ordinances of Jehovah are true, and righteous altogether.
> More to be desired are they than gold, yea, than much fine gold;
> Sweeter also than honey and the droppings of the honeycomb.
> Moreover by them is thy servant warned:
> In keeping them there is great reward.
> Who can discern his errors?
> Clear thou me from hidden faults.
> Keep back thy servant also from presumptuous sins;
> Let them not have dominion over me:
> Then shall I be upright,
> And I shall be clear from great transgression.

Finally, the psalm ends with another allusion to language:

> Let the words of my mouth and the meditation of my heart
> Be acceptable in thy sight,
> O Jehovah, my rock, and my redeemer.

Even a cursory reading of the psalm reveals what might have attracted Taylor to it at this point in his life. Besides its importance in the commentary tradition, verse 11 about the keeping of the ordinances would have spoken to Taylor's concern for the legitimate place of the Lord's Supper in the Puritan tradition; the psalmist appears to state the conservative position which Taylor maintained throughout his life. The psalm's bridegroom image also accords with the image clusters Taylor had been creating in the *Preparatory Meditations* for several years while working with the imagery of the Canticles and anticipating his own glorification.[18] Also, Taylor would have been drawn to this psalm, as he was to so many, because of its allusions to language and its clear picture of David as a writer-meditator. The "Valedictory Poems," when considered together as an unfinished work, attempt to imitate this psalm, yet the arch way in which Taylor adapts the psalmist's imagery and ideas allows him to acknowledge his closeness to glorification.

All three versions begin with a consideration of the firmament—"the Stars & Sun & Moon & Aire" and "the Terrqueous Globe" in version 1, "all the world" and "the Aire" in version 2, and "the Whole World," "the Celestiall Bodies," "the Aire," and "the Terraqueous Globe" in version 3. However, despite the similarity in subject matter to the beginning of Psalm 19, Taylor immediately departs from the tone and purpose of the psalmist. The Puritan Taylor, rather than viewing creation as evidence of God's presence in the universe, instead denigrates the nature he portrays, even denying that the common uplifting technique of "meditation on the creatures," espoused by Protestant exegetes such as John Calvin, Thomas Taylor, John Preston, and Richard Baxter and alluded to in this very psalm, would ever work for him:

> Your golden Beams, your Silver Tressell shall
> In no wise be my ladders rounds to soare mee
> To Christ's bright Mantion house, his glorious Hall
> Nor to carry mee up to Gods house of Glorie.
>   I never purposed on these Stares t' ascend
>   Up to Christs brightest Hall, deckt for his Friend.
>
>   (3:26–31)[19]

Taylor's lack of trust in the cosmos arises from his perception of its transience. The day and night of Psalm 19, which to the psalmist contain portentous knowledge, for Taylor are a "golden Clew of light" and a "silver Tenis Ball" who chase "each other out at Barly breaks" in a "Chrystall Play house" (3:19–24). While not disavowing the psalmist's declaration of God's involvement in the cosmos (the playhouse is, after all, "Chrystall"—modified by the pun Taylor has been using for decades to insinuate Christ's involvement with material reality),[20] he still conveys the cynical perspective of a converted soul quite a bit closer to death than the exuberant writer of Psalm 19.[21] In version 3, he implies that only "bound" people find sustenance in the heavenly bodies (3:5), evidencing his own imminent freedom from his earthly existence.

Later in each version, however, Taylor becomes more affirmative of nature to balance the whimsical negativity of his opening picture and accord more closely to the tone of Psalm 19. Despite the absence in most of his poetic canon of an active picture of the wilderness that surrounded him or his temporal life, here Taylor says a detailed farewell to the heavenly bodies, the air, sensual phenomena, his clothes,[22] his bed, the food he eats and the liquid he drinks, his own faculties, his study and the tools of his trade, and the fellow human beings who have been close to him, finally ending with:

> But yet my Lord I give thee hearty thanks
> Thou'st let me these to tend me to the banks
> Of thy high & Eternall glorious Throne
> And now do leave them here tho' calld mine Own.

(1:176–79)

In versions 1 and 3, he follows these lines with a hopeful wish that God will return these components of nature to him, properly cleansed, after the Last Judgment (1:180–91, 3:174–203). Taylor, in this part of the poem, seems to value natural objects not only as symbols but also as actual aids from God to assist his search for salvation.[23] Though his orthodox Puritanism resounded the equation between carnality and sinfulness most emphatically, Taylor still had many exegetical and biblically sanctioned sources—including Psalm 19—to support the more conciliatory side of his view of nature.[24]

This double view of nature in the poem reflects what Jeffrey Hammond calls the "saintly doubleness" that informs all of Taylor's poetry, particularly that written late in his life (*Approach* 66).[25] An assured Puritan could not escape this knowledge of being a creature of both carnality and grace, in a world created to contain both at once.

Additionally, the dimensions of the search for salvation, even after one's conversion experience was confirmed but one was still living on earth, required a hope-doubt dilemma that preoccupied so many of the New Englanders throughout their lives, making them uncertain about how to deal with the created world. One clear model of a man who continued to be plagued with doubt after his assurance and to be preoccupied with earthly matters as well as heavenly was David in the Psalms. [26] So, even when Taylor departed from the tone of the psalm on which he was modeling his own verse, he still adapted this recognized persona of the psalmist to do so.

Taylor's double view of nature informs his use of the next image of Psalm 19, the "voice" of creation. In the psalm, the firmament's "speech" is not heard even though it has "gone out through all the earth" (verse 4), implying a failure in the hearts and minds of the people to understand God's testimony through creation. Again Taylor rings changes on the psalm. Pivoting his consideration on the psalmic word "line" in verse 4 ("Their [the creation's] line is gone out through all the earth, / And their words to the end of the world"), in the first version Taylor implies that any witness that the creation is able to give of God—whether it be nature, humans made in His image, or the songs those humans are able to offer as praise—must be necessarily inferior to what can occur in heaven. [27] He writes:

I in the Angell upper Chamber Spread
Pav'd ore with Sparkling Saphires do design
With these bright Spirits t' dance over your Head
An Holy Gulls aire soon above *your line*
   Of Well tun'd Praises to my Glorious King
   For whom your Sparkling Light is shine too dim.

(1:7–12; emphasis mine)

Although the psalmic word "line" does not appear in either version 2 or 3, Taylor maintains the idea and clarifies the language by making the spirits "blesst" (3:10) rather than merely bright and by changing the obscure "Gulls aire" to the more familiar "Galliard" (2:10, 3:11). In all versions, his intention remains the same: to contrast earthly praises such as those depicted in Psalm 19 with a superior picture of the afterlife. The "line" that covers the earth with language may indeed contain "Well tun'd Praises to [Taylor's] Glorious King," but those praises—whether or not they are heard and understood by humans—are essentially nothing when compared to what Taylor will soon be singing in heaven.

What follows in all three versions reinforces this psalmic twist. Taylor acknowledges that, while he still clings to his earthly existence, he—even though one of the elect—can perceive the voice of creation only in terms of "Non-Sense" or "a riddle." As he perfects the image in version 3:

> You [the sun and moon] never more Shall Hemisphere my nose,
> For my dim glasses t' reade your Letony
> Or gather up the non-Sense some expose
> In witty or unwitty riddles.
>
> (3:44–47)

Here, Taylor seems to say to the psalmist that even when the voice of creation is heard, its interpretation is spurious—but the incomprehensibility of the speech stems from the inferiority of all material reality.

Thus Taylor continues by blaming the air, not the people, for these earthly problems with sound and language. While acknowledging that some meaningful sounds do surface in this "Metall & minthouse" of "Sounds & Words" (3:56–57), Taylor intends to convey the mixture of good and bad language that characterizes the air of earth:

> Thou dost as readily hoist up thy Saile
>   To Cuckews notes, & Carrion Crows that Qwake
> As to the Whistling Thrushs, & Nighting gaile
> As to a praying Saint, or Wretcheds Rope.
> Thou chearest dost the putrid Lungs of Sinners
> That in their Feasts took up the Divells Dinners.
>
> (2:60–65)[28]

He emphasizes the negative, creating a cacophony of images to contrast with his picture of what exists above earth's "Rich Canopy" (2:77).

An obscure image that Taylor maintains throughout all three versions, the "syllabicableness" of the air, becomes clearer when one considers Taylor's writing in light of Psalm 19. In versions 2 and 3, he relates this quality of sound not solely to the air in general, as he does in version 1, but specifically to the evil sounds it contains. In version 2, he specifically employs the psalmic word "line" to clarify the image, producing the best of the three versions:

> Hark, thou Cerulian Air, blew Bonnets shine
>   That fills up heavens Vast profundity
> Thou thorough fare of Angell & brave Divine
>   Sent out from heavens Hall in Sanctity,
>   And hold of Evill Spirits wretched line
> Syllabuckle all from the top to th' toe.
>
> (2:39–44)

Clearly, this tendency of earthly evil's "wretched line" of sound to be broken down into syllables contrasts with the continuous "line" of sound that goes out "through all the earth" and "to the end of the world" in Psalm 19. Taylor's suggestion of the fragmentation caused by evil discourse parallels his complaint about the transience of heavenly bodies in the earlier part of the poem—both are problems endemic to earthly life that he is soon to escape. In both cases, his voice contrasts the psalmist's attitude about the glory of the carnal creation to which Taylor is about to bid adieu.

Another psalmic allusion in the "Aire" section of the poem consists of the "Circles" which provide a path for the mixture of sounds that travel across the globe. In version 2, Taylor adds the adjective "Curld" to describe these circles:

Thy Nasty Speech & harsh Scurrility,
   The * * * horrid Oaths & Curses
Belcht out on thee with hellish blasphemy
   Do make thy self their * * * purses;
   These all as well as gracious language tride
   A pick pack forth on thy Curld Circles ride.

(2: 54–59)

The circles that support the good and bad speech parallel the "Curled Locks" (2:13) of the heavenly bodies, whose influence he is denying.[29] This use of imagery gives further unity to the way in which Taylor contrasts the psalmist's attitude in the first two sections of his valediction.

Earthly sounds, like carnal nature, do bode well for Taylor in one part of the poem, again manifesting his double view of nature. As he grapples with his lifelong problem of finding the proper words with which to praise God, Taylor lights upon some creatures of the natural world who can help him in this endeavor:

I hence do crave thy leave to borrow
What Melody I meet with in my Sorrow.

And first I'de borrow of all birds within
The Woods where they their bagpipes blow make sing.

(1:226–29; see also 1:293–96)

These are obviously the good birds, the thrushes and nightingales cited above (from 2:60–65) or the dove in version 3. Even they, of course, will not touch God "with a fresh new joy," but Taylor still seems positive about their effect:

> But yet my Tunes enlinde with holy praise
> Keep table to thee in richest phrase
> And will thy Saints & Angells bright make to Sing
> And with Sweet Melody thy palace t' ring,
>
> (1:238–41)

and its even more positive alternate version:

> But yet my Songs well lines [sic] with thy praise
> Are unto thee acceptable alwayes.
> And will make Saints & Angells sing
> And with sweet melody thy Heavens ring.
>
> (1:307–10)

God's acceptance of earthly birdsong as a model is, of course, unusual for Taylor to profess; he may have in mind the birds protected by Jehovah who sing in Psalm 104 (a psalm whose allusions appear in several meditations), although a more apt reference may be Canticles 2.12: "The time of the singing of birds is come" which juxtaposes with the "voice of the turtle" image Taylor uses in version 3 (220) while writing about the surety of his election.[30] All these allusions point, of course, to Taylor's time of life; his softening toward nature is indeed psalmic, but it also accords symbolically (and somewhat ironically) with other images and biblical sources that betoken a man near his time of glorification.

Moving on through Psalm 19, the psalmist next considers the image of the bridegroom in his chamber. In Taylor's allusion to this section of the psalm, doubleness appears again: there are two suns, the earthly ruler of the cosmos and the christologized image of the "Angell upper Chamber" from which the bridegroom / sun in the psalm emerges and where Taylor hopes soon to be dancing over the head of the earthly sun. Although Taylor appears to have reserved the appearance of the bridegroom for his later meditations, in the "Valedictory Poems" we do see Psalm 19's "chamber."[31] In both versions 1:7 and 3:8, as noted above, Taylor uses the "Angell upper Chamber" as the place above the cosmos where he intends to reside after his glorification. In other passages in version 1, it becomes "Christs Chamber joy" (1:243) and the "dining Chamber" (1:30, 3:36) where Christ eats "in flaming Glories Joy" (1:31). The adjective "flaming" accords with the sun image in the psalm; the specification of the chamber as Christ's place to dine corresponds to Taylor's concern about the Supper and its apotheosis in the heavenly banquet, which, as mentioned earlier, was considerable toward the end of his life. At first glance, it may seem odd that Taylor drops the psalmic image of the chamber in version 2 to picture instead an "Angell play house" (2:7). Yet he still may have had Psalm 19 in front of him as he revised, for the sun's actions in that psalm do seem playful: "a bridegroom coming out of his chamber, / And rejoiceth as a strong man to run his course" (verse 5). The playfulness is even more evident in the words of Taylor's own paraphrase of this psalm:

Which as a Bridesgroom coming forth
   Out of his Chamber ('s place)
Rejoyceth as a Strong man doth
   (Swiftly) to run a race.

(Minor Poetry 70)[32]

Finally, the technique of antithesis—common to Taylor's poetry and borrowed from psalmic style—surfaces in version 1, where Taylor depicts his own mortal "leantoe Tent Affections" (193) to contrast with Christ's more glorious chamber.[33]

Taylor thus far seems to be using Psalm 19 largely as a basis for contrast. As Hammond has explained, a great deal of Taylor's motivation to use Canticles as a model for the late meditations consisted in its exegetical framework as a biblical model of the timeless Christ, an allegory of eschatology (*"Ars Moriendi"* 192–96). The persona of Psalm 19, on the other hand, though he employs the image of the bridegroom, still speaks from the confines of the finite. What Taylor does with the imagery and attitude of Psalm 19 seems to suggest that he views the psalmist as caught much more tightly than he in "saintly doubleness," with one eye on the beauty of nature and the other on his spiritual life. Although the pattern of this dilemma had made an excellent model for the *Preparatory Meditations* and Taylor has not totally escaped from it even as he writes his last poetry, in the "Valedictory Poems" Taylor operates basically to "age" the psalmist's point of view by employing psalmic antithesis. In doing so, he contrasts within the lines of the poem the two ladders by which men gain heaven, even though the one Taylor employs is not precisely defined (Daly 174),[34] the good and evil sounds on earth, his bed and his coffin, earthly food and the tree of life, good and bad liquors, his earthly and spiritual senses, and earth and heaven as places to reside. Most striking, however, is the use of antithesis to define the two languages with which Taylor may praise God: the one he is using to write this poem, limited and frustrating even while based on a biblical text and techniques, and the one he anticipates being able to use in heaven in just a short time—purified and perfect. Of course, Taylor has employed this particular antithetical subject from the beginning of his *Meditations*;[35] the difference in the "Valedictory Poems" consists of his confidence that both sides of the antithesis surely exist for him:

> And as I enter do Christs Palace Hall
> He to the Angells Cry, help me to Sing
> Sweet praise to Christ my King that rules ore all,
> Who brought me hither to, & took me in.

(3:299–302)

Thus Taylor uses the psalmic technique of contrast or antithesis not only to restructure the images and allusions of Psalm 19 to suit his purpose in his valediction but also within the poem itself to create poetic tension and to aptly illuminate his theme. In version 1, Taylor next attempts a parallel passage to the psalmist's on God's attributes. In lines 255–72 and again in lines 323–58, Taylor discusses God's properties, most particularly noting how they are infinite absolutes:

> In thee they named are thy Properties.
> But as we unto thee describe the same
> We do & rightly Absolutes them name.
> Which are distinctive terms & always are
> When rightly taken do their Limits ware.
> Where as Infinity thy rightfull property
> Admits no limits nor Distinctive tie.

(1:256–62)

Taylor's creation here of another antithesis—between man's ability to perceive absolutes in finite terms and God's ability to embody those absolutes infinitely—again points out his intention to contrast the psalmist. Whereas the idea of absoluteness accords with the language of the psalm (David calls the attributes of Jehovah "perfect," "sure," "right," "pure," "clean," and "true"), Taylor's insistence on God's unlimited representation of these attributes contrasts with how David in Psalm 19 relates them specifically to what God can do for man while he is on earth. Taylor seems more concerned with how these attributes will appear to him once he is in eternity with God.

The next psalmic passage, verses 12 and 13, is a digression on sin:

> Who can discern his errors?
> Clear thou me from hidden faults.

Keep back thy servant also from presumptuous sins;
Let them not have dominion over me:
Then shall I be upright,
And I shall be clear from great transgression.

Taylor touches briefly on the idea of his acquittal from sin at the Last
Judgment in version 1 (186–87), but he explores this issue in greater
depth and closer to the psalmic intention in version 3. Lines 178–98
stand as revisions of this Last Judgment passage in version 1. In them, he
concentrates on the inherence of sin, giving the psalmic word "hidden" a
Calvinistic dimension:

The Stain doth remain that they by Sin attaind,
Is sunke so deep, that it can't be nitred out
The Leprosy hath wrought its mischief is so stoute
It having took the Worse it can't be washed thence
By any humane Art nor purged thence.

                                                              (3:179–83)

He concludes that only death can truly rid man of his sin. However, later
in the poem, Taylor considers another dimension of the forgiveness of
sin: "th' Gospell Golden Trumpet loud 'gainst Sin / In Gospell Sermons
Gospell Preachers make" (3:221–22). Here, Taylor seems to be alluding
to the ordinances in verses 9 and 10 of the psalm as a way, short of death,
to absolve sin.

In the last sections of version 3, Taylor debates the certainty of his
own election and, in doing so, also alludes to the psalmic lines about
"presumptuous sins." In canticle 6 of version 3, Taylor applies the
certainty of election to himself, as he pictures his afterlife experience "in
that glorious Room" praising God with "My Golden Michtem" (3:278–
79). Canticle 7, however, follows with:

Doth any Churlish Clownish thought begin
To Chide my Faith & at it cry Fy Fy?
What gross Presumptions here? Heavens songs to sing
While in thy skirts abides iniquity?
Oh! Sing thou, not tryumphant joy before
Thou hast past thro' Christs blessed Palace doore.

                                                              (3:282–87)

Taylor here expresses the psalmic fear of the sin of presumption, so
tempting to a Puritan who knows he has had the conversion experience.[36]
However, in the spirit of one whom God has already made "upright" and

"pure," Taylor calls this suspicion a "Churlish Clownish thought" and, at the beginning of Canticle 8, finally accepts the fact of his own salvation. Thus, at the end of his life, he can abandon the "hypothetical mode" that has characterized his statements of praise throughout the *Meditations*— and which seems to be implicit in the tone of this psalm—because his glorification is imminent.[37]

Hammond has offered evidence that another reason Taylor turned to the Canticles as he approached the end of Series 2 of the Meditations was his wish to explore the allegory's "mysteries as keys to another realm for which he yearned" ("Approaching" 65). The poetry of Taylor's final years, then, becomes truly "preparatory'" to the final union with Christ that Taylor anticipates for his glorified soul after death (*Approach* 67).[38] His choice of biblical headnotes and sources for imagery denotes a pronounced assurance. The tone of the later meditations is also confident, despite Taylor's continuing concern about the limitations of his poetic language. This confidence continues in the "Valedictory Poems," especially version 3, which alone contains the self-conscious debate about the expression of assurance which ends with Taylor's declaration of certainty.

What kept Taylor's poetic talents ripe to the end of his life was what he had come to realize through the writing of his *Preparatory Meditations*: that, in the typological fulfillment of Israel which was New England, he was the New David, their official (though private) psalmist in the wilderness. Although Taylor's major impetus to model his work on the Book of Psalms was largely traditional, a result of his pressing orthodox need to find scriptural sanction for his craftsmanship, his constant involvement with psalmic technique over the last forty-plus years of his life constituted a private reactionary act to the interminable theological turmoil that surrounded him in his public career. Regardless of what was happening in the outside world, in his private preparation to administer the Supper, Taylor was still deliberately involving himself with the ordinance of the psalter because he knew the Eucharist should be offered to the regenerate alone, and that he should engage in sanctified behavior to be worthy to do so.

The beauty of the "Valedictory" versions thus exists in Taylor's choice of Psalm 19 and what he does with its literal and exegetical significance as he stands so close to his glorification. The "bound" psalmist meditates on the creatures and extols God's earthly creation; Taylor counters with reminders of the frivolity and sinfulness incarnate in earthly matter, even as we appreciate it, and of the gulf that exists between God's greatness and the nature He formed. The psalmist admires God's attributes and how they relate to man in his Christian walk; Taylor reminds us and him that those attributes are, above all, infinite and will thus be much more appreciated by man once he is glorified. David begs God for protection from presumption; Taylor admits that he has been reticent too long, because of fear of impertinence, about acknowledging the truth of what God has done for him. After all, "Faith never holds whats promisd in suspense" (3:298). Finally, while the psalmist asks that his language be acceptable to God, Taylor voices his realization that, when all is nearly said and done, his is:

> But when I entred am in that bright Glory
> Of thy most Shining Habitation,
> My praise shall be raisd to the highest story.
> Praise can ascend up too; & here upon
>   Refind most bright & raised up most high
>   And to thee Sung my me Eternally.

(3:329–34)

In the final analysis, Taylor uses Psalm 19 as the model for his valediction to demonstrate that he has transcended his need for the earthly persona of the psalmist now that he has accepted the truth of his impending glorification.

Notes

All quotations from the "Valedictory Poems" are from the Davises' edition of *Minor Poetry* and will be cited by version and line numbers. I also cite what, to me, is the clearest version of each set of lines I refer to.

1. For typical examples of David's role in New England writing, see Francis Cornwel's "Epistle Dedicatorie" to Cotton, *Gospel,* n.p.; Cotton, *Treatise,* 77–78, 80–81; Danforth 4; Samuel Hooker 12, 20; Thomas Hooker 1:201–2; Increase Mather 29–31, 34, 56; and Edward Taylor, *Treatise,* 153, 219.

2. The extent of Taylor's knowledge and employment of the aesthetics of psalmody in his *Preparatory Meditations* is explored in Fithian, "The Influence of the Psalm Tradition," and "'Words of My Mouth.'" Taylor's psalm paraphrases are collected in Taylor, *Minor Poetry,* 44–101.

3. Bradford 130; Samuel Mather 154. See also Gosselin 5; Reid 43–44; and Roston 46.

4. Murdock xli, xliii; Cotton Mather, *Magnalia* 3:186.

5. Haraszti suggests that Cotton was the author of the *Bay Psalm Book* "Preface" as well as of his own treatise (*Enigma* 20–25).

6. See also "The Draft of the Preface" (*Enigma* 108). Thomas Welde, whom Haraszti considers to be one of the translators of the 1640 edition of the *Bay Psalm Book*, reinforces the "Preface" statement:

> And because we desire to sing, (as well as to reade) the pure word of God, it being an Ordinance of God, as sacred as the other, wee have endeavoured, according to our light and time, to retranslate the Psalmes as neer the originall as wee could, into meeter, because the former translation was very defective, and sing them in the Churches according thereunto. (7)

See also Hambrick-Stowe 93–94, 113.

7. For a detailed account of how the psalter was used in this controversy, see Guruswamy passim.

8. Haraszti suggests that American Puritans disliked the word "paraphrase" (*Enigma* 37). See also Thomas Clark: "God wrote out the Book of Psalms, that with them the generations to come into life, even in the New-Testament times, should praise the Lord with these very words" (14–15). Clark's reaction to Isaac Watts's eighteenth-century poetic hymnal, loosely translated from the Psalms, is typical of the more conservative Puritans of his century and harkens back to the attitude expressed in the *Bay Psalm Book*.

9. The only evidence of other metrical psalters are John Eliot's translations of Sternhold-Hopkins for the Massachusetts Indians (1658; 1663) and Edward Taylor's unpublished partial paraphrases (*Minor Poetry* 44–101). An advertisement at the end of his *Compleat Body of Divinity* lists Samuel Willard's forthcoming, complete psalm book, but an extant version does not exist, nor is it again mentioned, as far as I can tell. *The Psalter for Children* is also advertised in 1682, and listed in Evans's *American Bibliography*, but no copy has been located. The only two metrical psalters composed in the eighteenth-century colony are Cotton Mather's *Psalterium Americanum* (1718) and Matthew Henry's *The Psalms of David in Metre . . .* (1783).

10. All editions were translated from the Hebrew, but the 1651 edition is substantially different. Virginia L. Davis notes that 24 percent of the 1651 *New England Psalm Book* was considerably rewritten (19), mostly for purposes of easier singing. Revisions occur, according to Davis, in stanza unity, line unity, accent, and rhyme (21).

11. Cotton, *The Way*, 9, 67, 69–70; Lechford 16–17. See also Hambrick-Stowe 111.

12. Cotton, *Singing*, 15, 28–29; *Modest* 9, 37. Such private compositions based on the Psalms is also encouraged by Samuel Mather (4–5) and Cotton Mather (*Psalterium* iv-v; *Proposals for Printing* 4). In *Magnalia*, Cotton Mather cites John Eliot as one who constructs private prayers in the manner of the psalmist (3:186). See also the "Preface" to the *Bay Psalm Book*: "Every good minister hath not a gift of spiritual poetry to compose extemporary psalmes as he hath of prayer" (Haraszti n.p.). Psalmody intended for public worship is thus clearly differentiated from private composures that might be based on the Psalms. See also Thomas Clark 7; Cotton, *Gospel Conversion, 50;* and Haraszti, *Enigma* 109, for strictures against singing these privately composed hymns in the meeting house.

One Old World precedent for private psalm-inspired composition is Martin Luther (Lewalski 32–33). See also Keller 16.

13. For relations of Puritan poets to the psalter, see Craig passim; Fithian ("Influence") passim; and Hammond, *Sinful Self, Saintly Self,* passim. See also Lewalski's section on Psalms as "the compendium *par excellence* of lyric poetry" for the British devotional poet (39–53).

14. Dickson 1:255; Luther 12:259; Boys 1:8.

15. In *Reading*, Davis suggests that there may have been more versions of the poem (48).

16. Davis, "'Valedictory,'" 40 n. 4; Daly 243 n. 6. Internal evidence also suggests that Taylor had versions 1 and 2 in hand while working on version 3. For example, in the section on air, line 46 of version 1 states: "Thou thorrow Fair of Angells Bright that shine." In version 2, the similar line 41 reads: "Thou thorough fare of Angell & brave Divine." In version 3, line 52 says: "Thou thorrow fare of Angells bright divine." While version 1 is fine metrically, it repeats the end word of line 44 rather than creating a rhyme. Version 2 remedies the rhyme problem but breaks the metrical pattern with an extra syllable. Version 3 remedies both flaws.

17. All quotations from Psalm 19 are from the King James version of the Bible, Standard Edition.

18. See Hammond's various works on the *Meditations* and the Song of Songs.

19. The earlier versions have similar, although less clear, statements about the unfit ladder of ascension.

Daly discusses some meditative writers who advocate meditation on the creatures and Taylor's denial of this in the "Valedictory Poems" (22–23, 72–74, 174). Lewalski cites Psalm 19 as a common model for meditations on the creatures (162). See also Michael Clark 68; Gatta 192.

Hammond notes Taylor's negative attitude about attachment to earthly things in the late meditations (*"Ars Moriendi"* 198). Yet, in earlier writing, Taylor posits the standard Puritan line of the "sweet harmony of reason" that exists in natural creation and thus allows men to use "natural things . . . to illustrate supernaturals" as Christ does in His parables (*Treatise* 43; see also Scheick 17; Grabo, *Edward Taylor* [1961] 65–66). Daly (192–93) and Scheick (38–39) discuss how Taylor's view of Christ as the creator gives him permission to use nature as a source of imagery. However, according to Wallerstein (227), the practice of meditation on the creatures took on a negative capacity when treated by Puritans such as Calvin; man's depravity was seen as reducing, if not eliminating, his ability to perceive spiritual meaning in carnal reality. Grabo applies this viewpoint to Taylor (*Edward Taylor* [1961] 89–92, 150), even while asserting that Taylor views converted men as obligated to praise because of creation ([1961] 102, [1988] 67).

Taylor does seem to use the creature of the wasp as a ladder in lines 41–42 of "Upon a Wasp Child with Cold" (*Poems* 407; see Lewalski 176, 212, 393).

For other discussions of meditation on the creatures in the seventeenth century, see Lewalski 162–65; Martz 67, 173–74; Miller 207–35; Wallerstein 181–232.

20. See, for example, the "Chrystall Sky" in line 2 of the "Prologue" to Taylor's *Preparatory Meditations* (*Poems* 1).

21. Gatta refers to Taylor's depiction of the cosmos as a tempering of the *contempus mundi* theme with some whimsical overtones (203). Hammond says the beginning of the poem reverses the Creation in the Book of Genesis, "an uncreating of the world by a pious soul who no longer needs it" (*Sinful Self, Saintly Self* 230).

22. Grabo discusses Taylor's "profuse" use of clothing imagery in his poetry to represent spiritual themes ("Holiness" 84). See also Grabo's *Edward Taylor* (1988) 61–64.

23. Howard cites the emblem tradition as a source for Taylor's usual view of nature as symbolical or analogical of spiritual reality (372). Michael Clark discusses the Puritans'

belief that the book of Nature had been "rendered . . . illegible" by the Fall, but that interpretation of it through the allegorical methods of Scripture could help their understanding (69–70). See also Lewalski 162.

24. Gatta reveals that, in Taylor's "Theological Notes," Taylor records the traditional argument for the existence of God from the firmament and creatures (192). He also parallels Taylor's depiction of the playful activities of the heavenly bodies with the poet's own "expectant singing and jumping in 'heart ravishing joy'" to further support the positive side of Taylor's feelings about nature in the "Valedictory Poems" (204).

25. See Blake, who argues that Taylor's production of metaphor is intrinsically related to "a kind of double vision" that gives him, as well as other Protestant poets, "more [of] an earthly than a heavenly sort of eyesight" (23). Daly argues further that Taylor possessed a typical Puritan dialectical view of the world as God's gift tempered by an acknowledgment of its failure to truly image the glory of the creator (44–45, 56–60, 175). See also Michael Clark 76–77.

26. Schuldiner focuses on Meditations 1.36–40 as the crux of Taylor's regenerate faith-doubt dilemma, which he identifies as the third event in the four-part sequence of attaining assurance which structures Series 1 ("Christian Hero" 115, 119).

27. See Howard about the pervasiveness of this theme in Taylor's poetical canon (373–74).

28. That the "praying Saint" is gone from this verse in the third version and replaced by a "Cooing Dove" and a "griping hawk" (3:77) indicates to me that none of these versions can be considered Taylor's final ones.

29. These negative earthly circuits of air provide an additional contrast to Psalm 19, as the sun-bridegroom makes a positive "circuit" in the sky.

30. See also Meditation 2.114, line 30: "Let Grace sing now, Birds singing time is come" (Edward Taylor, *Poems,* 291). Taylor also uses the image of birdsong in "Upon a Spider Catching a Fly" (lines 46–50) to allude to praise after glorification (*Poems* 465).

Scheick cites the allusion to birdsong in Meditation 2.5 to support his contention that Taylor believed in the use of nature imagery because "it reflects and communicates the Word's Art to man" (140).

31. Hammond parallels the dining chamber here to the banqueting house of Canticles 2.4 (*"Ars Moriendi"* 207).

32. See also Gatta, who discusses the attitude of celebration which characterizes Taylor's "subtle identification with the Canticles bride" (188–89).

33. Fithian has established that Taylor's common use of antithesis in the *Preparatory Meditations* is based on David's similar technique in the Psalms ("'Words'" 94–96). Lewalski also discusses Taylor's use of antithesis, although she doesn't make the connection to the Psalms (402–4).

34. Two possible meanings for the undefined ladder might be the "Golden Ladder into Heaven" in line 28 of "The Return," which the context defines as Christ (*Poems* 10) or "the golden Ladder of thy praise" in line 2 of Meditation 2.145, suggesting that Taylor could ascend on the worth of his song (Edward Taylor, *Poems* 345).

Schuldiner points out the connection between the chamber image and the ladder in Meditation 1.20. He posits that in this meditation the ladder, as in "The Return" stands for the divine nature of Christ ("Problematic" 97). He also notes that Luther discusses faith as a ladder (100 n. 16), which could be another connection Taylor has in mind.

35. Perhaps the first critic to note Taylor's theme of the antithetical languages of earth and heaven is Mignon. He goes beyond the commonplace that Taylor's ability to write poetry is tied to his salvation and declares that, even if Taylor is saved, he cannot write truly good poetry until after he is glorified because "even in the elect there is an irreconcilable war between the flesh and the spirit" (1424). Mignon cites Meditation 1.43 as Taylor's own statement of this belief. See also Daly 171–73, 176–77, 195–97; Gatta 69–70; Lewalski 230–31, 249–50, 391; Rowe 271–76; Scheick 113.

Both Rowe and Lewalski posit that Taylor develops a "new" language with which to praise God, but Rowe claims it is based on "Scripture metaphors and types" (265–67, 269) whereas Lewalski calls it a secular language of nonpraise that defers actual biblical usage until glorification (53, 69, 231, 249, 405, 411–13). Johnson agrees with Rowe that biblical imitation allows Taylor, while on earth, to "approximate a perfected language of praise" and anticipate what will follow in heaven (85, 89–90, 96).

Hammond discusses the prominence of the two-language debate in Taylor's late meditations ("*Ars Moriendi*" 191, 202, 209).

36. Schuldiner states that Taylor actually defeated the fear of presumption in Meditation 1.39 ("Christian Hero" 125).

37. Reed (310–11), Daly (195–96), and North (15–16) all acknowledge the "hypothetical" mode. Gatta calls these hypothetical endings a "stylized exorcising of presumption," indicating they are never sincere (60). Lewalski sees Taylor as abandoning this hypothetical mode ("the conditional") for his glorification in Meditations 2.154–65 (423–24).

38. Rowe adds typology to the Canticles allegory as another model for Taylor's late poetical preparation for glorification (274).

Works Cited

Bercovitch, Sacvan. *The Puritan Origins of the American Self*. New Haven: Yale University Press, 1975.

Bible (King James Version). Edited by the American Revision Committee. New York: Thomas Nelson and Sons, 1901.

Blake, Kathleen. "Edward Taylor's Protestant Poetic: Nontransubstantiating Metaphor." *American Literature* 43 (1971): 1–24.

Boke of Psalmes, wherin Are Contayned Prayers, Meditations, Prayses and Thanksgiving to God for His Benefits toward his Church: Translated Faithfully According to the Ebrewe. With Briefe and Apt Annotations. [Geneva Psalter]. London, 1576.

Boys, John. *An Exposition of the Proper Psalmes Used in Our English Liturgie, Together with a Reason Why the Church Did Chuse the Same.* 2 vols. London, 1616–17.

Bradford, William. *Bradford's History of Plymouth Plantation, 1606–1646*. Edited by William T. Davis. New York: Charles Scribner's Sons, 1908.

Chapman, Richard. *Hallelu-jah; or, King David's Shrill Trumpet*. London, 1635.

Clark, Michael. "The Honeyed Knot of Puritan Aesthetics." In *Puritan Poets and Poetics: Seventeenth-Century American Poetry in Theory and Practice*, edited by Peter White, 67–83. University Park: Pennsylvania State University Press, 1985.

Clark, Thomas. *Plain Reasons Why Neither Dr. Watts' Imitations of the Psalms, Nor His Other Poems, Nor any Other Human Composition, Ought to be Used in the Praises of the Great God Our Saviour*. Albany, 1783.

Cope, Anthony. *A Godly Meditacion upon xx. Select Psalmes of David*. London, 1547.

Cotton, John. *Gospel Conversion: Opened by John Cotton, at a Conference in New England—Together, with Some Reasons Against Stinted Forms of Praising God in Psalmes, &c.* London, 1646.

———. *A Modest and Cleare Answer to Mr. Balls Discourse of Set Formes of Prayer*. London, 1642.

———. *Singing of Psalmes a Gospel Ordinance. Or a Treatise Wherein Are Handled These Foure Particulars. 1. Touching the Duty it Selfe. 2. Touching the Matter to be Sung. 3. Touching the Singers. 4. Touching the Manner of Singing*. London, 1647.

———. *A Treatise of the Covenant of Grace . . . Being the Substance of Divers Sermons Preached upon Act. 7.8*. 1654. Reprint, London, 1671.

———. *The Way of the Churches of Christ in New England*. London, 1645.

Craig, Raymond A. "Singing with Grace: Allusive Strategies in Anne Bradstreet's New Psalms." *Studies in Puritan American Spirituality* 1 (1990): 148–69.

Daly, Robert. *God's Altar: The World and the Flesh in Puritan Poetry*. Berkeley: University of California Press, 1978.

Danforth, Samuel. *A Brief Recognition of New England's Errand into the Wilderness*. Cambridge, 1671.

Davis, Thomas M. "Edward Taylor's Valedictory Poems." *Early American Literature* 7 (1972): 38–63.

———. *A Reading of Edward Taylor*. Newark: University of Delaware Press, 1992.

Davis, Virginia L. "The 1651 Revision of the *Bay Psalm Book*." Thesis, Kent State University, 1976.

Dickson, David. *A Brief Explication of the First Fifty Psalms*. 2 vols. London, 1653.

Fithian, Rosemary. "The Influence of the Psalm Tradition on the Meditative Poetry of Edward Taylor." Diss., Kent State University, 1979.

———. "'Words of My Mouth, Meditations of My Heart': Edward Taylor's *Preparatory Meditations* and the Book of Psalms." *Early American Literature* 20 (1985): 89–119.

Foote, H. W. *Three Centuries of American Hymnody*. Hamden, Conn.: Shoe String Press, 1961.

Gatta, John, Jr. *Gracious Laughter: The Meditative Wit of Edward Taylor*. Columbia: University of Missouri Press, 1989.

Gosselin, Edward. *The King's Progress to Jerusalem: Some Interpretations of David during the Reformation Period and Their Patristic and Medieval Background*. Malibu: Undema Publishers, 1976.

Grabo, Norman S. "Colonial American Theology: Holiness and the Lyric Impulse." In *Essays in Honor of Russel B. Nye*, edited by Joseph Waldmeir, 74–91. East Lansing: Michigan State University Press, 1978.

———. *Edward Taylor*. New York: Twayne, 1961.

———. *Edward Taylor*. Rev. ed., Boston: Twayne, 1988.

Guruswamy, Rosemary Fithian. "The Sweet Defender of New England." *New England Quarterly* 63 (1990): 294–302.

Hall, David D. *Worlds of Wonder, Days of Judgment: Popular Religious Belief in Early New England*. New York: Knopf, 1989.

Hambrick-Stowe, Charles E. *The Practice of Piety: Puritan Devotional Disciplines in Seventeenth-Century New England*. Chapel Hill: University of North Carolina Press, 1982.

Hammond, Jeffrey A. "Approaching the Garden: Edward Taylor's Progress Toward the Song of Songs." *Studies in Puritan American Spirituality* 1 (1990): 65–87.

———. "A Puritan *Ars Moriendi*: Edward Taylor's Late Meditations on the Song of Songs." *Early American Literature* 17 (1982/83): 191–214.

———. *Sinful Self, Saintly Self: The Puritan Experience of Poetry*. Athens: University of Georgia Press, 1993.

Haraszti, Zoltan, ed. *The Bay Psalm Book: A Facsimile Reprint of the First Edition of 1640*. Chicago: University of Chicago Press, 1956.

———. *The Enigma of the "Bay Psalm Book"*. Chicago: University of Chicago Press, 1956.

Hooker, Samuel. *Righteousness Rained from Heaven*. Cambridge, 1677.

Hooker, Thomas. *The Application of Redemption*. 2 vols. 2nd ed. London, 1656.

Howard, Alan B. "The World as Emblem: Language and Vision in the Poetry of Edward Taylor." *American Literature* 44 (1972): 359–84.

Jackson, Thomas. *Davids Pastorall Poeme. Seven Sermons on the 23. Psalme*. London, 1603.

Johnson, Edward. *Johnson's Wonder-Working Providence, 1628–1651*. Edited by J. Franklin Jameson. New York: Charles Scribner's Sons, 1910.

Johnson, Parker H. "Poetry and Praise in Edward Taylor's *Preparatory Meditations*." *American Literature* 52 (1980): 84–96.

Keller, Karl. *The Example of Edward Taylor*. Amherst: University of Massachusetts Press, 1975.

La Roche, Antoine. *Moste Excellent Meditations uppon the xxxii Psalme*. Translated by W. Watkinson. London, 1579.

Lechford, Thomas. *Plain-Dealing: or Newes from New-England*. London, 1642.

Lewalski, Barbara K. *Protestant Poetics and the Seventeenth-Century Religious Lyric*. Princeton, N. J.: Princeton University Press, 1979.

Lowance, Mason I., Jr. *The Language of Canaan: Metaphor and Symbol in New England from the Puritans to the Transcendentalists*. Cambridge: Harvard University Press, 1980.

Luther, Martin. *Works*. 30 vols. Edited by Jaroslav Pelikan. St. Louis: Concordia Publishing House, 1955.

Madden, Etta. "Resurrecting Life Through Rhetorical Ritual: A Buried Value of the Puritan Funeral Sermon." *Early American Literature* 26 (1991): 232–50.

Martz, Louis. *The Poetry of Meditation: A Study in English Religious Literature of the Seventeenth Century*. New Haven: Yale University Press, 1954.

Mather, Cotton. *Magnalia Christi Americana*. 7 vols. London, 1702.

———. *Proposals for Printing by Subscription "Psalterium Americanum."* Boston, 1718.

———. *Psalterium Americanum. The Book of Psalms, in a Translation Exactly Conformed unto the Original; but All in Blank Verse, Fitted unto the Tunes Commonly Used in Our Churches* . . . Boston, 1718.

Mather, Increase. *Some Important Truths Concerning Conversion*. Boston, 1684.

Mather, Samuel. *The Figures or Types of the Old Testament*. 2nd ed. Edited by Mason I. Lowance Jr. 1705. Reprint, New York: Johnson Reprint Co., 1969.

Mignon, Charles W. "Edward Taylor's *Preparatory Meditations*: A Decorum of Imperfection." *PMLA* 83 (1968): 1423–28.

Miller, Perry. *The New England Mind: The Seventeenth Century*. Boston: Beacon Press, 1961.

Murdock, Kenneth B., ed. *Handkerchiefs from Paul*. New York: Garrett Press, Inc., 1970.

North, Michael. "Edward Taylor's Metaphors of Promise." *American Literature* 51 (1979): 1–16.

Owen, John. *Meditations and Discourses of the Glory of Christ, in His Person, Office and Grace*. London, 1696.

Reed, Michael D. "Edward Taylor's Poetry: Puritan Structure and Form." *American Literature* 46.3 (1974): 304–12.

Reid, W. Stanford. "The Battle Hymns of the Lord: Calvinist Psalmody of the Sixteenth Century." In *Sixteenth Century Essays and Studies*, edited by C. S. Meyer, 36–54. St. Louis: Foundation for Reformation Research, 1971.

Roston, Murray. *Prophet and Poet: The Bible and the Growth of Romanticism*. Evanston: Northwestern University Press, 1965.

Rowe, Karen E. *Saint and Singer: Edward Taylor's Typology and the Poetics of Meditation*. New York: Cambridge University Press, 1986.

Scheick, William J. *The Will and the Word: The Poetry of Edward Taylor*. Athens: University of Georgia Press, 1974.

Schuldiner, Michael J. "The Christian Hero and the Classical Journey in Edward Taylor's 'Preparatory Meditations. First Series.'" *Huntington Library Quarterly* 49 (1986): 113–32.

———. "Edward Taylor's Problematic Imagery." *Early American Literature* 13 (1978): 92–101.

Taylor, Edward. *Edward Taylor's Minor Poetry*. Edited and with an introduction by Thomas M. Davis and Virginia L. Davis. Boston: Twayne, 1981.

———. *The Poems of Edward Taylor*. Edited by Donald E. Stanford. New Haven: Yale University Press, 1960.

———. *Treatise Concerning the Lord's Supper*. Edited by Norman S. Grabo. East Lansing: Michigan State University Press, 1966.

Taylor, Thomas. *Davids Learning, or the Way to True Happinesse*. London, 1617.

Wallerstein, Ruth. *Studies in Seventeenth-Century Poetic*. Madison: University of Wisconsin Press, 1950.

Welde, Thomas. *A Briefe Narration of the Practices of the Churches in New-England, in Their Solemne Worship of God*. London, 1647.

Willard, Samuel. *A Compleat Body of Divinity*. Edited by Edward M. Griffin. 1726; rpt. New York: Johnson Reprint Co., 1969.

Contributors

NANCY BIRK is Associate Professor of Libraries and Media Services at Kent State University. After Thomas M. Davis established the Greek Exchange Program at Kent Sate University, she was the first faculty member to participate. She subsequently worked with Tom to develop the program and, upon his retirement, took over the position of Coordinator of the Greek Exchange Programs. She is an assistant editor on the Cambridge University Press edition of Joseph Conrad, has published on Greek libraries and rare books, and is the indexer for *Civil War History*.

RAYMOND CRAIG is Associate Professor of English at Kent State University. He completed his M.A. under the direction of Thomas M. Davis. He has published on Puritan poetics in the work of John Cotton, Anne Bradstreet, and Edward Taylor, and has published *A Concordance to the Minor Poetry of Edward Taylor* (1992). He is now completing a book on Puritan poetics and a concordance to the complete works of Ann Bradstreet.

ROSEMARY FITHIAN GURUSWAMY is Associate Professor of English at Radford University in Virginia. Her Ph.D. was directed by Thomas M. Davis. She is currently serving as president of the Society of Early Americanists and has published on Edward Taylor and other aspects of colonial American literature. Her work in progress involves an exploration of the Renaissance roots of Anne Bradstreet.

JEFFREY HAMMOND is Professor of English at St. Mary's College of Maryland. Thomas M. Davis directed his doctoral work. He has published widely on Taylor, Bradstreet, Wigglesworth, John Cotton, Edward Bellamy, and the New England Puritan funeral elegy. His most recent books are *Sinful Self, Saintly Self: The Puritan Experience of*

Poetry (1993) and *Edward Taylor: Fifty Years of Scholarship and Criticism* (1993).

JEFF JESKE is Associate Professor of English and Director of Writing at Guilford College. Thomas M. Davis directed his dissertation. He has published on several American and British writers, including cotton Mather, Solomon Stoddard, Herman Melville, Henry David Thoreau, and Arthur Hugh Clough. He has also written about collaborative learning, the role of research in writing instruction, and the use of film in teaching composition. He is currently completing a book on etymology.

J. DANIEL PATTERSON is Assistant Professor of English at California State University, San Bernardino. His dissertation was directed by Thomas M. Davis. His published work treats Edward Taylor and early American nature writing. He is coediting with Rochelle Johnson a new edition of *Rural Hours* (1850) by Susan Fenimore Cooper for the University of Georgia Press and also coediting a collection of eco-critical essays. He is completing an edition of Taylor's poetry.

MICHAEL SCHULDINER is Professor of English at the University of Alaska Fairbanks. Thomas M. Davis directed his dissertation. He has published on Edward Taylor, Solomon Stoddard, and Ezra Pound and is author of *Gifts and Works: The Post-Conversion Paradigm and Spiritual Controversy in Seventeenth-Century Massachusetts* (1991). He is currently working on a book about Edward Taylor's poetry and is completing an edition of Mordecai Noah's writings.

Index

Compiled by Nancy Birk